THE LIFE AND DEATH OF PETRA KELLY

Lying to the young is wrong.
Proving to them that lies are true is wrong.
Telling them
            that God's in his heaven
and all's well with the world
                        is wrong.
They know what you mean.
                  They are people
too.
Tell them the difficulties
                  can't be counted,
and let them see
            not only
                  what will be
but see
      with clarity
            these present times.

YEVGENY YEVTUSHENKO (1952)

THE LIFE AND DEATH
-OF-
PETRA KELLY

Sara Parkin

Pandora

An Imprint of HarperCollins*Publishers*

For Colin and Douglas

Pandora
An Imprint of HarperCollins*Publishers*
77-85 Fulham Palace Road,
Hammersmith, London W6 8JB

Published by Pandora 1994

1 3 5 7 9 10 8 6 4 2

© Sara Parkin 1994

Sara Parkin asserts the moral right to
be identified as the author of this work

A catalogue record for this book
is available from the British Library

ISBN 0 04 440896 X

Typeset by Harpers Phototypesetters, Northampton
Printed in Great Britain by
HarperCollinsManufacturing Glasgow

CONTENTS

ACKNOWLEDGEMENTS

It has taken just over a year to research and write this book, something which was only made possible though the help and support of a great number of people. In particular, Mr and Mrs Kelly showed great generosity and patience at a very painful time, and allowed me early access to the Petra Kelly Archive; for all of this I am deeply grateful. I am also endebted to Robert Camp and Susanne Hilbertz at the Archiv Grünes Gedächtnis (where the Petra Kelly Archive is kept) for their kindness while I was working there; and to Heinz Suhr and Agnes Steinbauer who provided me with a warm and friendly home during the weeks I was in Bonn. Together with Lukas Beckmann and Erika Heinz, they all have been especially diligent (and swift) in answering all my last-minute questions, and in searching out missing or overlooked documents and photographs.

For translations and assistance with research my thanks go to Ursula Eyrich, Stanley Forman of ETV Films, Paul Harrison, Horst Lohrer, Christel Maury, Renate Mohr and Brian Zumhagen. While I was conducting interviews, Lester Brown in Washington, Kennedy Fraser in New York, Claire Greenfelder in Berkeley, Máire Mullarney in Dublin, Mary O'Donnel in Cork, and Ian and Laura Parkin in London were generous in their hospitality – much appreciated when on the interview trail. Special thanks go to Charlene Spretnak for the greenest dinner I've ever eaten, and to the Elmwood Institute for extensive use of their administrative facilities.

For their patience during interviews and, in some cases, for letters, documents and follow-up questions, my thanks go to Ingrid Aouane, Stephen Batchelor, Marieluise Beck, Lukas Beckmann, Rene Böll, Bob Brown, Eberhard Bueb, Marianne Birthler, Bärbel Bohley, Dieter Burgmann, Gerlinde Bod, Fritjof Capra, Ramsey Clark, Tony Catterall, Maria Colgan, Anthony Coughlin, Leo Cox, Sidney Crown, the Dalai Lama, Rickard Deasy, Geraldine Dwyer, Ludo Dierix, Freimut Duve, Daniel Ellsburg, Lord David Ennals, Richard Falk, Eddie Feinberg, Uli Fischer, David Fleming, Carol Fox, Bruce French, Susan French, Heidi Hautela, Ed Hedemann, Erika Heinz, Mark Hertsgaard, Christiane Gollwitzer, Monika Griefahn, Gerald Häfner, Brigadier Michael Harbottle, Richard Hendrick, Amy Isaacs, Carlo Jordan, Mary Kaldor, Bruce Kent, Petra Kleins, Martha Kremer, Arnold Kotler, Otto Kuby, Bernhard Köbl, Helmut Lippelt, Joanne Landy, Admiral Gene La Rocque, Patricia McKenna, David McReynolds, Freda Meissner Blau, Vladimir Mijanović, Bogjana Mladenović, Renate Mohr, Dr Albert Mott, Jack Munday, Jo Noonan, Tswang Norbu, Jonathon Porritt, Eva Quistorp, Patricia Redlich, Horst-Eberhard Richter, Jeremy Rifkin, Adi Roache, Professor Abdul Said, Kirkpatrick Sale, Trevor Sergeant, Otto Schily, Michael Schroeren, Achim and Irmgard Schuppert, Andrea Shalal-Esa, Vandana Shiva, Charlene Spretnak, Adam Stolpen, Heinz Suhr, Anna Tomforde, Jonathan Tyler, Jacob von Uexkull, Jo Vallentine, Roland Vogt, Elisabeth Weber, Vera Wollenberger, Cora Weiss, Eric Williams, Frieder Wolf. (I hope that's everyone!)

My agent John Button, I thank for being (as always) helpful and calm at all the right moments. The original idea for the book came from Sara Dunn at Pandora. She wielded her editor's pencil through the thickets of my prose with tremendous skill, and sent non-threatening postcards as deadlines approached. For all that, and for the unswerving confidence and support of Sara, Karen Holden, Belinda Budge and everyone else at Pandora, I am extremely grateful. Finally, to my husband Max, my love and immeasurable gratitude for his cheerful and affectionate encouragement throughout the whole process.

CHRONOLOGY

This chronology is intended for quick reference for the reader. For a larger picture of Petra's travels and activities see the list of speeches at the end of the book.

27 November	1947	PETRA KARIN LEHMANN born in Günzburg, Bavaria, West Germany.
Autumn	1953	Starts school at the Englisches Institut, Günzburg.
March	1956	First operation for kidney stones.
December	1958	Mother remarries Lt. Col. John Edward Kelly, US Army.
May	1959	Half-sister Grace Patricia Kelly (Gracie) born.
June	1959	Moves to elementary school on US base at Nellingen (near Stuttgart).
December	1959	Kelly family moves to Fort Benning, Columbus Georgia, USA.
August	1960	Half-brother John Lee Kelly (Johnny) born.
Autumn	1960	Enrols at Baker Junior High School; Nominated 'top scholar' in final year.
	1961	Berlin wall built.
	1963	US President John F. Kennedy assassinated.

Autumn	1964	John Kelly posted to Fort Munro, Hampton, Virginia, USA. Enrols in Hampton High School.
	1966–9	Kurt Kiesinger (CDU) Chancellor of Federal Republic of Germany in grand coalition with SPD.
Summer	1966	Graduates with honours from Hampton High School. Awarded school Speech Club trophy, nominated Class Poet and to the Most Likely to Succeed Hall of Fame.
Autumn	1966	Enrols in School of International Service at American University, Washington DC.
Spring	1967	Grace's cancer diagnosed.
May	1967	Awarded scholarship and nominated Most Outstanding Foreign Woman Student of 1967.
June	1967	Kelly family move to Würzburg, Bavaria.
April	1968	Martin Luther King Jr assassinated.
June	1968	Grace's audience with the Pope.
November	1968	Hubert Humphrey election campaign.
	1969–74	Willy Brandt (SPD) Chancellor of Federal Republic of Germany.
February	1970	Grace Patricia Kelly dies.
May	1970	Graduates BA cum laude in International Relations (East/West European Studies). Receives Alan M. Bronner Memorial award, Bruce Hughes Award, and Woodrow Wilson Scholarship.
Autumn	1970	Enrols at Europa Institute, University of Amsterdam. Kelly family move to Newport News, Virginia.
Spring	1971	Sponsors Nima Chonzom, Tibetan refugee orphan.
May	1971	Awarded Diploma in European Integration, Europa Institute.
October	1971	Six-month internship in European Commission, Brussels. Awarded one-year

		research grant by the Christian Democrat Press and Information Office.
April	1972	Registers for doctorate with Institute of Political Studies at the University of Heidelburg.
June	1972	Transfers to cabinet of Sicco Mansholt, President European Commission.
November	1972	Appointed administrator to the Health and Social Policy Section of the Economic and Social Committee of the European Commission.
July	1973	Establishes Grace P. Kelly Foundation.
	1974–82	Helmut Schmidt (SPD) Chancellor of Federal Republic of Germany.
Autumn	1977	Elected to board of Bundesverband Bürgerinitiativen Umweltschutz (BBU) umbrella organization for citizens environmental action groups in Germany.
	1978	Jointly edits, with John Carroll, *A Nuclear Ireland?*
March	1979	Sonstige Politische Vereinigung (SPV) – Die Grünen formed in Frankfurt-Sindelfingen. Elected head of list for forthcoming elections to the European Parliament.
June	1979	Election: Europe – Die Grünen poll 3.2 per cent, no seats.
July	1979	Founding Coordination of European Green and Radical Parties.
January	1980	Founding conference of Die Grünen.
January	1980	Major General Gert Bastian resigns from the army.
March	1980	Petra Kelly elected one of three speakers of Die Grünen.
October	1980	Election: Bundestag – 1.5 per cent, no seats. Heads list in Bavaria.
November	1980	Leaves Catholic Church with a letter to John Paul II.

November	1980	Meets Gert Bastian for first time.
November	1981	Krefelder Appell rally and concert, Dortmund.
	1982	Jointly edits, with Jo Leinen, *Ökopax – die neue Kraft* (Eco-peace – The New Force). Jointly edits, with Manfred Coppik, *Wohin denn Wir?* (Where Are We Going?)
October	1982	'Constructive no – confidence vote' in Schmidt SPD government. Helmut Kohl (CDU) becomes Chancellor of Federal Republic of Germany.
October	1982	Election: Bavaria – Die Grünen 4.6 per cent, no seats. Head of list in Kempten, Allgäu district.
November	1982	Two-year term as speaker for Die Grünen ends.
December	1982	Awarded 'Alternative Nobel Prize' by the Right Livelihood Foundation, Stockholm.
	1983	Publishes *Laßt uns die Kraniche suchen* (Let us look for the cranes.)
	1983	Publishes *Um Hoffnung kämpfen* (Fighting for Hope).
February	1983	International War Crimes Tribunal for possession of weapons of mass destruction, Nürnburg.
March	1983	Election: Bundestag – Die Grünen polls 5.4 per cent, 27 seats. Petra heads Bavarian list, is elected. Becomes member of Foreign Relations Committee. Elected one of three speakers of *Fraktion*.
May	1983	Bundestag: maiden speech.
September	1983	Bitburg and Mutlangen blockade.
October	1983	Peace Woman of the Year Award, Philadelphia.
October	1983	Bonn Peace Rally.
October	1983	Meeting with Erich Honecker in East Berlin. First visit to dissidents.
November	1983	Bundestag votes to accept US nuclear missiles.

February	1984	Gert Bastian resigns from *Fraktion*.
February	1984	Resigns from Krefelder Appell with Gert Bastian.
April	1984	End of term as speaker for *Fraktion*.
June	1984	Election: Europe – Die Grünen polls 8.2 per cent, 8 seats.
July	1984	Bavarian party conference insists Petra 'rotate' (hand over her parliamentary seat to her successor) in 1985.
November	1984	Trial of dissidents in Yugoslavia.
September	1985	Occupation of German Embassy, Pretoria.
September	1985	All *Fraktion* rotates, except for Petra. Appointed representative on Western European Union (until 1987).
	1986	Publishes *Hiroshima*.
	1986	Publishes *Viel Liebe gegen Schmerzen: Krebs bei Kindern* (Love can conquer Sorrow: Cancer in Children).
Spring	1986	Bundestag votes DM 2 million for research into facilities for children with cancer.
April	1986	Visits Guernica. Fiftieth anniversary of German bombing. Chernobyl accident.
May	1986	Die Grünen conference abolishes 2-year rotation principle for MPs.
January	1987	Election: Bundestag – Die Grünen polls 8.3 per cent, 42 seats, Petra re-elected. On Committee for Europe.
February	1987	Moscow Peace Forum. Meets Andre Sakharov and Mikhail Gorbachev.
April	1987	Opens campaign against Single European Act in Ireland.
October	1987	Bundestag unanimously supports motion on human rights in Tibet.
November	1987	*Autonomen* shoot 2 policemen in Frankfurt.
November	1987	East German police raid Umweltbibliothek.
December	1987	Closed meeting of Die Grünen calls Bonn leadership 'theatre of monkeys'.

January	1988	Demonstration in East Berlin on anniversary of Rosa Luxemburg's death – dissidents arrested and expelled to West.
June	1988	Publishes, with Gert Bastian, *Tibet – ein vergewaltigtes Land* (Tibet – a violated Country). Dalai Lama present.
March	1988	Becomes Chair of German Association for Social Defence (until 1990).
April	1989	Organizes first International and Non-Partisan Hearing on Tibet and Human Rights, Bonn.
June	1989	Brutal repression of demonstrators, Tiananmen Square, Beijing.
June	1989	Elections: European – Die Grünen polls 8.4 per cent, 8 seats.
November	1989	Berlin Wall breached.
December	1989	Visit of Dalai Lama to East Berlin.
	1990	Publishes, with Gert Bastian and Klemens Ludwig, *Tibet klagt an* (Tibet Accuses).
February	1990	Publishes *Mit dem Herzen denken* (Thinking with the Heart).
February	1990	With Dalai Lama in Prague.
March	1990	Elections: East Germany – Bündnis 90 polls 2.9 per cent, Die Grünen 2 per cent.
October	1990	Reunification of Germany, both parliaments meet in Reichstag, Berlin. German President, Richard von Weizsäcker, receives Dalai Lama.
October	1990	Final speech in Bundestag.
December	1990	Election: Bundestag (all Germany) – 4.9 per cent, Die Grünen (West) no seats, Bündnis 90/Die Grünen (East) 6.1 per cent, 8 seats.
	1991	Publishes, with Gert Bastian and Pat Aiello, *The Anguish of Tibet*.
April	1991	Bündnis 90/Die Grünen (unified West/East parties) conference: Petra obtains only 39 votes in election for party speaker.
August	1991	Profiled as one of the 1000 makers of the

		20th century by *The Sunday Times*, London.
September	1991	Morelia Conference in Mexico.
	1992	Publishes, with Gert Bastian, *Guernica und die Deutschen*.
January	1992	Begins to moderate series of environment programmes for SAT 1 television.
March	1992	Gert Bastian's accident in Munich.
September	1992	Attends World Uranium Hearing, Salzburg, and Global Radiation Victims' Conference, Berlin.
1 October	1992	Petra Karin Kelly shot dead by Gert Bastian who then killed himself.
26 October	1992	Funeral of Petra Kelly, Waldfriedhof cemetery, Würzburg.
31 October	1992	Memorial service for Petra Kelly and Gert Bastian, Bonn.
1 October	1993	Dedication of a new joint memorial to Petra Kelly and her sister Grace.

PERSONALITIES

This is a list of the main personalities mentioned in the book. Several of those making only a single appearance are not included.

PETRA'S FAMILY

Kunigunde Birle (Omi)	grandmother
Margarete-Marianne Kelly	mother
John Edward Kelly	stepfather
Grace Patricia Kelly (Gracie)	half-sister
John Lee Kelly (Johnny)	half-brother
Richard Siegfried Lehmann	father

OTHERS

(AU = American University; DG = Die Grünen; MP = member of parliament; US = United States; for other terms and abbreviations see Glossary, page xxiii.)

Karin Amirany	penfriend
Ingrid Aouane	assistant (1982-3 and 1987)
Major General Gert Bastian	retired NATO officer
Charlotte Bastian (Lotte)	Gert Bastian's wife
Eva and Till Bastian	Gert Bastian's daughter and son

Stephen Batchelor	Buddhist scholar
Marieluise Beck	former DG MP; co-speaker 1983
Lukas Beckmann	co-founder DG; party manager
Philip and Daniel Berrigan	US brothers (former monk and Jesuit priest) admired for non-violent actions
Joseph Beuys	German avant-garde artist
Marianne Birthler	member executive Bündnis 90/DG, former East German dissident
Gerlind Bode	parliamentary assistant (1984–5)
Bärbel Bohley	East German artist and dissident
Günter Bohnsack	STASI disinformation officer
Heinrich Böll	Nobel Peace Prize winning author
Willy Brandt	former SPD Chancellor of Germany
Robert Camp	DG archivist with responsibility for the Petra Kelly archive
John Carroll	President, Irish Transport and General Workers' Union
Vladimir Chernousenko	Ukrainian nuclear physicist
Nima Chonzom	Petra's Tibetan foster daughter
Ramsey Clark	US civil rights lawyer
Jutta Ditfurth	leader of DG *Fundi* faction
Freimut Duve	publisher and SPD MP
Rudi Dutschke (Red Rudi)	radical 1968 student leader
Geraldine Dwyer	Irish peace campaigner
Daniel Ellsburg	US anti-nuclear campaigner; leaked 'Pentagon Papers' on US decision-making in Vietnam
Eddie Feinberg	former AU student; psychologist
Joschka Fischer	former DG MP, leader *Realo* faction
Carol Fox	Irish peace campaigner
Carl J. Friedrich	professor, University of Heidelburg
Bruce French	former AU student; now a lawyer
Susan French	former AU student; close friend
Joachim Gauck	heads the committee managing the archives of the STASI
Hans Dietrich Genscher	former German FDP Foreign Minister
Christiane Gollwitzer	friend
Helmut Gollwitzer	radical theologian, uncle of Christiane

Monika Griefahn	SPD Environment Minister, Lower Saxony
Kelsang Gyaltsen	Dalai Lama's representative in Geneva (previously Bonn)
Gerald Häfner	former DG MP from Bavaria
Erika Heinz	close friend
Richard Hendrick	US TV producer
Erich Honecker	former Head of State, East Germany
Milan Horaćek	former DG MP
Hubert Humphrey	former US Vice President
Raymond Hunthausen	Bishop of Seattle
Amy Isaacs	former AU student; director, Americans for Democratic Action
Jaya Jaitley	Indian journalist and activist
Gerhard Kade	historian and political scientist
Bruce Kent	former Chair, CND
Martin Luther King	US black civil rights activist
Gyorgy Konrad	Hungarian philosopher
Lew Kopelew	Russian author
Arnold Kotler	US publisher, Parallax Press
Martha Kremer	Parliamentary assistant (1983–4)
Heinz Kuby	EC administrator
Otto Kuby	senior administrator, EcoSoc
Oscar Lafontaine	SPD MP
Gene La Rocque	director, Centre for Defense Information, Washington DC
Lyndon LaRouche	US leader of cult-like European Workers' Party
Jo Leinen	SPD MP; former editor of Forum magazine
The Lötters	neighbours who looked after Petra's house when she was away
Rosa Luxemburg	socialist revolutionary, died 1919
Sicco Mansholt	former president, European Commission
Freda Meissner Blau	former Austrian Green MP
Vladimir Mijanović	Yugoslavian student dissident
Renate Mohr	former DG press secretary

Dr Albert Mott	professor, AU
Ralph Nader	US consumer rights activist
Christa Nickels	former DG MP
Anne Nilges	DG press secretary
Tswang Norbu	parliamentary assistant (1989–90)
Hartmut Otto	commissioner, Bonn Murder Squad
Gerd Poppe	Bündnis 90/DG MP
Horst-Eberhard Richter	psychiatrist; peace campaigner
Walt Rostow	former special advisor to US President Lyndon Johnson; his wife Elizabeth befriended Petra
Abdul Aziz Said	professor, AU
Pierre Salinger	US journalist; former press secretary to President John Kennedy
Otto Schily	former DG MP; civil rights lawyer; now SPD MP
Michael Schroeren	former DG press speaker; former editor BBU journal
Achim & Irmgard Schuppert	Petra's doctor and his wife
Andrea Shalal-Esa	parliamentary assistant (1984)
Hannelore Siabold	Petra's *Nachrücker* who couldn't take her seat in 1985
Altiero Spinelli	former European Commissioner
Charlene Spretnak	US author and green activist; wrote book about DG in 1983 (see bibliography)
Adam Stolpen	former AU student; businessman
Franz Josef Strauss	former leader CSU
Heinz Suhr	former DG MP; now press speaker for Bündnis 90/DG *Fraktion*
Palden Tawo	Tibetan doctor
Thich Nhat Hanh	Vietnamese Zen Master
Walter Verheydeen	EC administrator; Petra's supervisor during her *stage*
Roland Vogt	former DG MP; peace researcher
Antje Vollmer	former DG MP; theologian
Ludger Volmer	former DG MP; speaker DG executive
Hartmut Wächtler	Gert Bastian's lawyer

Elisabeth Weber	staff member Bündnis 90/DG *Fraktion*
Cora Weiss	director, Samuel Rubin Foundation (US peace organization); co-ordinated Petra's application for Sakharov Award
Konrad Weiss	Bündnis 90/DG MP
Frieder Wolf	former parliamentary assistant (1984–9); secretary general Heinrich Böll Foundation
Marcus Wolf	former East German 'spy master'
Vera Wollenberger	Bündnis 90/DG MP
Milo Yellow Hair	Oglala-Lakota Indian (South Dakota)
Yevgeny Yevtushenko	Russian poet
Jörg Zink	pastor who conducted Petra's funeral

GLOSSARY

POLITICAL PARTIES

Sonstige Politische Vereinigung (SPV)-Die Grünen	the precursor of Die Grünen, established to contest the 1979 European elections
Die Grünen	the German Greens
Bündnis 90	Alliance 90, an alliance of East German dissident groups
Bündnis 90/Die Grünen	after the 1990 all-Germany elections, Bündnis 90 and the East and West German Green parties united to formed one party
CDU	Christian Democratic Party (W. German)
CSU	Christian Social Union (the Bavarian version of the CDU)
DKP	West German Communist Party
FDP	West German Federal Democratic Party (Liberals)
PDS	reformed SED (q.v.)
SED	East German Communist Party
SPD	Social Democratic Party (W. German)

OTHER TERMS AND ABBREVIATIONS

angst	anxiety; fear of impending disaster. As a psychological disorder, it is the most common of the psychoneuroses – a state of anticipation of something unpleasant about to happen, accompanied by a feeling of inner tension, with physical manifestations

	such as tense muscles, sweating, tremor and tachycardia (palpitations)
AU	American University, Washington DC
Autonomen	violent part of 'independent anarchists'
Anfrage	question to Parliament. *Grosse* (major) *Anfrage* require a reply in the chamber, *kleine* (small) *Anfrage*, a written reply
Bundestag	German federal parliament
Bundeswehr	German army
Bürgerinitiativen	citizens' action groups
BBU	Bundesverband Bürgerinitiativen Umweltschutz. Umbrella organisation for citizens environmental action groups
CIA	Central Intelligence Agency (US)
CND	Campaign for Nuclear Disarmament (UK)
Commission	'Civil Service' of the EC (q.v.)
Doppelselbstmord	double suicide
EC	European Community. Originally the European Economic Community, in 1986 the middle E was dropped, and in 1994 the word Community was replaced by the word Union. To avoid confusion EC is used throughout the book
EcoSoc	Economic and Social Committee, a sub-committee of the EC (q.v.).
Einsatzgruppen	SS mobile security groups during Second World War
END	European Nuclear Disarmament movement.
Fraktion	German parliamentary group
Fundi	faction in Die Grünen preferring fundamental opposition rather than compromise (see also *Realo*)
Grundgesetz	Basic Law (constitution) of Germany
Heimat	homeland
Historikerstreit	historian's debate
ITGWU	Irish Transport and General Workers Union
Jahr Null	year zero, going back to square one
JEF	Young European Federalists
JUSO	Young Social Democrats Organization
Grace P. Kelly Foundation	registered charity established by Petra in 1973 to support research and for children with cancer
innere Führung	inner (moral) leadership
KGB	Soviet secret services
Kofferträger	baggage carrier
Krefelder Appell	petition against stationing of intermediate range nuclear missiles in West Germany
Land/Länder	region(s), state(s)
Landkreis	electoral district

Nachrücker	successors; those waiting to replace sitting Die Grünen MPs (until 1987 party rules required MPs to be in post no more than two years)
NATO	North Atlantic Treaty Organisation
Ostpolitik	policy towards East Europe in general, East Germany in particular
Realo	faction in Die Grünen supporting pragmatism, including coalitions with other parties (see also *Fundi*)
Schadenfreude	pleasure at the misfortune/mistake of others
SIS	School of International Service, American University, Washington DC
stagière	trainee, apprentice
STASI	East German secret police
Staatsbürger in Waffen	citizens in uniform
Sture Böcke	'stubborn rams' (prejorative term for old Nazis)
Szene	the 'Scene', the German alternative movement
TAZ	*Tageszeitung*, newspaper of the *Szene* (q.v.)
Trümmerfrauen	'women of the rubble' who cleaned the streets after wartime bombing raids
Untermenschen	'subhumans'
Wahlkreis	electoral district
Wehrmacht	military forces

INTRODUCTION

At first I didn't want to write this book. Petra was a friend, and the pain of losing her (and the shock at how she died) was great. Then, as I read the newspaper and magazine articles written about her after her death, I changed my mind. There was a general assumption that, because she was a passionate, driven woman, she had, more or less, brought it on herself. Petra burnt her candle at both ends, it was said, therefore she was destined for a short life. This was – and is – nonsense; and it made me angry. Petra at the end of her life was still essentially the same person she was as a teenager. Some of her faults had become more marked with maturity, but then so had some of her virtues. And why should not old women be passionate? Indeed, it could be argued that an influx of mature, passionate women into public life (particularly politics) is exactly what this world needs.

I was also moved by the letters from all over the world which expressed bewilderment about her death. For many Petra was the personification of the European green political movement, so her death was widely interpreted as the end of the movement too. I agree that history will see Petra's death like a punctuation mark in the development of green politics, but it will be as a comma, not as a full stop. Environmental degradation continues unchecked, as does the concomitant human misery, making the ecological approach to solving humankind's predicaments more, not less, relevant. If the 1980s was about setting out the problems, then the 1990s will be about working out how to solve them.

So, out of my sense of loss, my irritation over the assumptions made about the way she died, and my concern that the effect of her death be neither exaggerated nor underestimated, I decided to write this book.

I have used mostly texts in English; many of Petra's early papers were in English, and much of what she wrote, especially her speeches, were either in English or translations from the German exist. She was a true internationalist, and I have endeavoured to keep that inter-national perspective in recounting her story. In one year and in one book, it is impossible to include every detail. I have not, for example, related Petra's encounters with Mikhail Gorbachev and Andre Sakharov at the Moscow Peace Forum in 1987. An impression of the extent of Petra's activities may be had from the list of her speeches and writings. In the bibliography I have listed almost exclusively English texts, but all her papers (and even her famous collection of T-shirts) have been brought together in the Petra Kelly Archive.[1]

When I started, I did not know how the book would turn out. All I knew was that it would have to be, like Petra was herself, an intimate intertwining of her political and her personal life. I spoke to a lot of people, read a lot of documents, books and cuttings, asked a lot of questions. Many people were, of course, still shocked and grieving, and few greens, I discovered, keep diaries. Recollections therefore veered more to the anecdotal than to the objective, and in the acres of print about Petra, I found that myths seem to endure more easily than fact. Through it all I have tried to steer a steady course to tell the story of one of the most influential political personalities of the century.

By the autumn of 1993, I found that what I was writing was as much a murder mystery as a political biography. From the information I had collected I was looking for an explanation not only for Petra's tremen-dous impact on green politics, but also the reason *why* she died. I found that the story of her life revealed a truly extraordinary person. Like many extraordinary people, Petra was not always easy to live and work with, but, in my view, Petra's own personality did not reveal a single plausible motive for her life to end the way it did.

I was pondering on all this when, one year after her death, a group of us was preparing a service of remembrance for Petra in St James's Church, Piccadilly, London. One of my jobs was to bring from Bonn to London a large (over 2 square metres) picture of Petra which had been used for her memorial in Germany. What the airlines had told me would be no problem turned into a serious adventure – from the moment I had to flag down a passing van to get to Bonn railway station because the picture would not go into the largest of Bonn's taxis, until I ran across the tarmac at Frankfurt airport to a specially delayed Air France plane. Was she, asked the cabin steward as we lashed the package to nine collapsed seats, beautiful? I hesitated. Petra had famously refused to complete an interview after the reporter had asked what a pretty women like her was doing in politics. What would she have done if she had been here? All of a sudden, she seemed to be there, laughing and loving the ludicrousness of the situation and quite aware that this was not the moment to open a debate on sexism. Yes, I told the cabin steward, she was very beautiful. He sighed and brought me a glass of champagne. This I raised to Petra in complicity, and in remembrance of the caring, compassionate friend I had lost. At this moment I decided that I would have to look somewhere else – somewhere beyond her own personality – if I wanted to understand why she had died.

Sara Parkin
Lyon, France
March 1994

---

1. Enquiries should be addressed to Robert Camp, Archiv Grünes Gedächtnis, Romerstarsse 71, 53332 Bornheim-Widdig, Germany.

1

OCTOBER 1992

BEETHOVENHALLE

The Beethovenhalle is a modern, unexpectedly squat building in central Bonn which frowns at the passing traffic through a stand of tall, straight-trunked trees. As my taxi sped up the drive towards the main entrance, the yellow and gold branches of the trees were dancing – somewhat inappropriately I felt – in the glorious autumn sun. It was five minutes to noon and I was a little late, but not concerned. Over the years, of all the events I had attended organized by the West German green party Die Grünen, none had started on time.

This time I was wrong. Except for Heinz Suhr, press speaker for the Green parliamentary group, and Frieder Wolf, secretary general of the Heinrich Böll Foundation and one of Petra Kelly's most loyal parliamentary assistants, the rather bleak foyer of the Beethovenhalle was empty. Both men moved anxiously towards me, relieved me of my coat and, after giving me instructions about reading some overseas messages of condolence, they ushered me quickly into the main hall. The memorial service for Petra Kelly and Gert Bastian had started.

Inside the auditorium, around 1,500 people were already seated in front of a podium brilliant with autumn flowers and leaves marshalled here into a more suitable solemn stillness. As I crept to my seat near the front I glimpsed and nodded to a few faces, more familiar when smiling cheerfully from above a comfortable jumper, but today looking strained and pale over a collar and tie. A quartet played some Telemann. Everything had been arranged to perfection. My heart tightened, remembering how often Petra had railed at the inefficiency and disorganization of the party she had helped to establish and how much she would have approved of this. How sad that she should have to die for it to happen.

And there she was, smiling a little wistfully from a huge black and white photograph in the centre of the stage. Beside her was an equally large picture of Gert Bastian, the retired NATO general who, thirty days previously, had shot her at point blank range before turning the gun on himself.

I found myself avoiding his embarrassingly steady and amiable gaze. After what had happened it seemed wrong to keep them side by side in this way. Later, when I talked with friends about my unease, many agreed with me. But the short time (only twelve days) since the bodies had been discovered had not been long enough for anyone to separate psychologically, never mind practically, two people for so long regarded as inseparable. Petra Kelly and Gert Bastian could hardly be more different in character or in background, yet press and friends alike found it hard to speak of them as other than one person – PetrandGert.

Within less than twenty-four hours of being called to the house in Swinemünderstrasse on the evening of 19th October, the police had ruled out the possibility of 'third party involvement' in their deaths. Bastian had pulled the trigger twice. Yet even with nearly a week to digest this information, on 26th October the German weekly magazine *Der Spiegel* could not separate them: 'Two pacifists who have fought for peacefulness . . . two human beings who took care of relatives and friends . . . two politicians who understood that their words and actions were a form of open protest.' PetrandGert.

Later, the Greens told me they had talked very long and very hard about how they should prepare the memorial. In the end they had concluded that how the relationship between Petra and Gert had ended (speculation was still rife), should be less their concern than the relationship they both had to the party. *Ergo*, both must be remembered in the memorial – PetrandGert.

On 31st October 1992 in the Beethovenhalle, any unease caused by the decision to hold a joint memorial was nothing compared to the sense of collective guilt that hung over the proceedings. Somehow we had failed her. 'What might have happened,' Freda Meissner Blau asked in her address, 'if all the love and affection shown here today had enveloped them like a protective cloak while they lived?' Everyone was absorbed in the same question: Petra's family; her closest friends like Erika Heinz the cartographer from Calw, Bärbel Bohley the artist and dissident leader from East Berlin and Lukas Beckmann, a co-founder member of Die Grünen and now general secretary of the parliamentary group in Bonn; her more distant friends like myself and Freda Meissner Blau, former Green member of the Austrian parliament; her colleagues from her earliest political days in Germany like Oscar Lafontaine and Freimut Duve of the Social Democratic Party, or from more recent years like Christa Nickels and Ludger Volmer of Die Grünen; her many other friends and colleagues (so often the same thing for Petra) from her many campaigns like Lew Kopelew the dissident Russian author, Milo Yellow Hair of the Lakota people and Kelsang Gyaltsen from Tibet – everyone was absorbed with the same question. What could we have done to prevent this? Why had none of us been intimate enough, either personally or professionally, to be privy to the couple's everyday movements? Their bodies had lain undiscovered for nearly three weeks; yet missed engagements, unreturned telephone calls and fax messages had not inspired our concern. No one was quite sure where they were.

As we sat with our varying thoughts, disbelief gnawed at the edges of our sorrow and guilt. Petra, the passionate pacifist, had been shot at point blank range by the man she loved and trusted most. Shock at the violence of her death and the grisly delay before their decomposed bodies were found, had locked almost everyone who knew her – from the few hundreds in the Beethovenhalle to the many thousands who Petra had somehow touched during her life – into denial. 'I still cannot believe they are gone,' said Bärbel Bohley. 'I do not know how to commemorate Petra and Gert as I have yet to comprehend they are no longer with us,' said Christa Nickels. 'I have yet to comprehend it rationally, I have yet to comprehend it emotionally. I cannot move so quickly from life to commemoration.' Only Petra's beloved Omi (grandmother), Kunigunde Birle, had moved swiftly and uncomplicatedly into the second phase of grief – anger. Pure anger at the man who did it. She did not attend the memorial.

Some remained unconvinced by the police assertion that no third party was involved, and there was a swirl of rumours and counter-rumours. Lew Kopelew saw the marks of a KGB plot and the Ukrainian nuclear physicist Vladimir Chernousenko, who had received considerable financial support from Petra, circulated letters in which he said he was certain it was the 'nuclear mafia'. A journalist feared a Chinese assassination to put a stop to the couple's championing of Tibet, and friends from the United States wrote with concern about a possible neo-Nazi attack. A few, who knew a little about the forensic evidence, wondered about a *Doppelselbtsmord* (a double suicide) prompted either by depression over the couple's political marginalization, fears of bankruptcy, or even imminent exposure as spies for the STASI (East German secret police).

Anyone who knew Petra well, however, gave no credence to the *Doppelselbtsmord* theory; she had not chosen to die. Because she was often energized even more by adversity than she was by success, they knew suicide to be alien to Petra's character, never mind her principles. Her mission had been a continual affirmation of life. Furthermore, even by the most remote of possibilities that Petra should have wanted to end her life, we knew she would not dream of doing so without sending us all (and the press) a fax. Petra did not just make political statements, she *was* one. Any opportunity to make a point, even this last one, she would not knowingly have missed. Most of the people listening to the speeches and the music in the Beethovenhalle were desperately trying to understand why the quiet, precise and unfailingly courteous Gert Bastian smiling down at them should suddenly be moved to take her life before taking his own. 'Until he did this', remarked Heinz Suhr who had worked with them both since 1983, 'I thought I knew him.'

As I waited for my turn to go up onto the podium, it occurred to me that I hardly knew Gert Bastian at all. Petra I had met for the first time at the end of the 1970s. We had warmed to each other as women do when they find their own passionate engagement mirrored in the other. Since then, we had stayed in touch, writing letters, exchanging information, and meeting from time to time, usually at meetings or conferences. Most often, we spoke by phone. She liked to work late when all was quiet in her office at the Bundestag (German parliament) and she kept her automatic telephone dialling list programmed to all continents. The years had also been peppered by her famous postcards, often from unexpected places but always covered with affection, humour and exclamation marks. The last one she sent to me was posted from Berlin two days before she died.

Even though Gert's name had been at the bottom of most of her letters and postcards for a long time, and he was invariably with her when we met, always charming, always kind, I couldn't say I ever really knew him. He rarely joined our conversation and usually devoted himself to ordering food or drinks, making phone calls or fetching bags, while Petra and I talked. Once, at a meeting in Florence, he distracted my two young sons for hours with spaghetti and ice-cream while Petra and I chatted about the ups and downs of European green politics. Thinking about this, it occurred to me that I had never been curious enough about him to bypass Petra and talk to him directly. When Bastian had hit the headlines in 1980 with his resignation as a NATO officer, giving as his reason his hostility to the stationing of nuclear missiles on German soil, I was, I admit, impressed; military officers usually take care to wait until *after* retirement before adopting radical positions. Three years later, he became, with Petra, one of the 27 members of Die Grünen to enter the West German parliament.

It was around this time, I reflected, that Petra Kelly and Gert Bastian became PetrandGert in a way that went beyond the usual linking of a couple who do everything together; but there could hardly be two people more different, in age, in style, in life experience and in personality. Later I quizzed people about this. 'Why do you say PetrandGert when I ask you about Petra? Why is it so difficult to separate them in your mind?' Initially startled, sometimes upset by the question, the conclusion, inside and outside Germany, was almost always the same. Gert Bastian had been perceived by most people as little more than an inevitable extension of Petra. If you asked Petra to speak, to visit or write, you invariably got him too. Even amongst the circle of close colleagues and friends in Bonn, from about 1985 onwards Bastian had ceased to exist as an individual. He was Petra's personal assistant, doing everything from her shopping to her photocopying – he was her *Kofferträger* (baggage carrier). The general had become a batman.

I listened to the speakers cope with the difficulties of speaking of the murderer in the same breath as the murdered. Some promoted their own favourite conspiracy theory, a few managed to avoid using names at all, but most heroically ignored the implications of the police report and spoke firmly about PetrandGert. The eminent psychiatrist and peace campaigner Horst-Eberhard Richter urged that 'we should now accept with respect what we cannot understand, and remember them as we perceived and experienced them to the last – as two people who, with very different temperaments but with the same courage and the same willingness to fight – gave their all to prevent the irresponsible abuse of political, military and technological power.'[1] It was only when my turn came to go up on to the platform that I realized why the speakers had appeared so discomfited. There, in the middle of the front row, sat Gert Bastian's widow Charlotte and his daughter Eva.

NUMBER 6 SWINEMÜNDERSTRASSE

Petra Kelly and Gert Bastian spent the last ten days of their lives in Berlin. Between 21st and 25th of September 1992 they attended the Second Global Radiation Victims' Conference before staying on to hear the Vietnamese Zen master and peace advocate Thich Nhat Hanh speak at the European Buddhist Union Congress. On Friday 25th Petra met an American television producer, Richard Hendrick, to discuss plans for an interview series. On 4th October Richard Hendrick sent a fax to Petra at her home in Swinemünderstrasse in Bonn; 'I have tried to call you many times since we met in Berlin . . . I think the next step is for me to write these ideas into a more formal treatment . . . Could you give me a list of the six interviewees you feel would be the most interesting . . .?' Nine days later Hendricks sent his fax again. This time he wrote on the bottom 'Petra! have you received the above fax? Where are you? Please let me know what is happening . . .' Silence from Swinemünderstrasse.

On the evening of 18th October Richard Hendrick telephoned Charlotte Bastian at home in Munich, using a number which Gert had given to him in Berlin. Frau Bastian did not know where they were, she had recently returned from a holiday in Rhodes and had heard nothing from Swinemünderstrasse. The following day Charlotte Bastian called Petra's grandmother, but Kunigunde Birle had heard nothing from Petra for nearly three weeks. This was unusual, for Omi was the one person Petra would be certain to tell about all her movements. Now worried, Charlotte Bastian telephoned the home of the Lötters, a couple who looked after the house for Petra when she was away. They promised to pop round that evening.

When Rosemarie Lötters and her two sons unlocked the door, they knew instantly that something was amiss. Yards of fax paper filled the tiny entrance hall and several books were scattered on the curved wood stairway leading to the first floor. From there emanated a strangely sweet smell, an unmistakable signal of death even to those who have never encountered it before.

Alerted at 9.27p.m., the police were quickly on the scene. By early the following morning, the news was all over the world. Forty-four-year-old Petra Kelly, the passionate peace campaigner, and her lover, sixty-nine-year-old former Major General Gert Bastian, were dead. On distant continents, some of the news agencies reported only the death of Petra. They had no idea who Gert Bastian was.

Number 6 Swinemünderstrasse is in the not very fashionable sub-urb of Tannenbusch, to the north-west of Bonn. Petra had moved into the modest terraced house in a quiet cul-de-sac when she was elected to the German parliament in 1983, largely because it had a cellar and room enough to take all her books and the already copious archive she had assembled during ten years as a civil servant in the European Commission in Brussels. To Petra the house quickly came to mean much more than a repository for her books and papers. It was her sanctuary. Very few people knew its phone number, even fewer its address. There Petra felt anonymous and safe. Safe not only from the bitter arguments in the Green Party, but also from the threats and lunatic intrusions that have become the inevitable lot of many public figures. As a attractive woman known for her compassion, Petra drew more than her fair share of attention from unhappy, unhinged or downright malevolent people.

Behind number 6's solid wooden front door with its traditional wreath of wood carved flowers, the hallway opened directly on to a spacious sitting and dining room. To the right of the hall, open-tread stairs curved tightly to the first floor, to the left was a small kitchen. When the police arrived they found all the rooms (even the kitchen) full of papers and books. At first it seemed disordered, and the police suspected an intruder, but after a while it was clear that the piles had a discipline and the books were arranged on and beside the shelves with a logic. In the main room, they saw more shelves filled with souvenirs – including brass figures mainly from northern India and Tibet – and, inside a glass case, mementoes of Petra's half-sister Grace who had died twenty years ago of cancer, at the age of ten. The walls were covered with framed photographs, mostly of Petra, either on some important occasion (meeting the Dalai Lama, Andrei Sakharov or Mikhail Gorbachev) or smiling beside her family or with cherished friends or colleagues. The photographs crowded up the stairs, where, on the narrow landing, the police found the body of Gert Bastian.

The lightly-clothed body filled the landing and was too decomposed for immediate identification. Beside it lay a gun – a short, fat-barrelled .38 Derringer special, the traditional 'personal' gun of a *Wehrmacht* officer. Designed for 'close up work', these guns have only two bullets. The equally traditional protective glove in which such guns are kept had been tossed down the stairs where it lay beside some books from a small bookcase on the landing. This had been toppled by the body of Bastian as it fell into the cramped space.

To the left of the stairs the door of a small narrow study was open. At the far end of the room on a desk underneath the window, an electric typewriter hummed, an unfinished letter still in the carriage. The typist had broken off in the middle of a word. The letters *müs*, from *müssen* (must) waited patiently for their companions.

The last door on the landing opened onto the main bedroom. Like the other rooms, it was not very big, so the double bed seemed to fill the room. On the side of the bed nearest to the door, wearing a black leisure suit patterned with roses, lay the body of Petra Kelly. Beside her were her reading glasses and an open book – *Letters from Goethe to Charlotte von Stein*. The book was brand new, published in East Germany, so probably bought recently in Berlin. On the table beside the bed was a little box with her contact lenses and her rings. 'When Petra did sleep, she really prepared herself and slept very soundly,' her friend Erika Heinz said. Because of the bedcovers, Petra's body was less decomposed than that of Gert Bastian.

The main reason the police concluded so swiftly that Bastian shot first Petra Kelly – possibly in her sleep – then moved out of the room and shot himself, was the mess. The Derringer is a gun designed to kill at pointblank range. Its short fat barrel allows the bullet a generous rotation before it even leaves the gun. This makes the gun useless for aiming over a distance but ensures an explosive effect on a close target. A more conventional handgun would certainly cause damage if used at close range but because its very fast bullet might even pass right through the body, it cannot guarantee death the way the Derringer does. More than anything else, the pattern of the blood stains all over the walls and ceilings of the small bedroom and narrow landing confirmed that no other person could possibly have been anywhere near when the shots had been fired. If they had been, an interruption to the pattern of the stains on the walls would have been evident.

WÜRZBURG WITH GRACIE

Würzburg is a pretty, walled Bavarian town on the banks of the Main, roughly halfway between Frankfurt and Nürnburg. Here, in the beautiful wooded hilltop Waldfriedhof cemetery, Petra's half-sister Grace Patricia Kelly was buried in February 1970, after her three-year struggle to survive a sarcoma in her right eye was lost in the cancer hospital at Heidelburg. On Saturday 26th October 1992, finally separated from the man she described as her closest personal and political companion, Petra Karin Kelly joined the halfsister she described as the source of all her inspiration, energy and courage: 'Whenever things are tough I think of Grace and know I can never suffer as much as she did.'

About four hundred relatives, friends and colleagues accompanied Petra to her grave beneath Gracie's headstone, on which was carved an angel and the English words:

Do not stand at my grave and weep
I am not here, I do not sleep.

Lukas Beckmann, Frieder Wolf and another close friend, Milan Horaćek, helped Petra's stepfather John Kelly and her stepbrother Johnny, to carry the plain wood coffin. There was a bitterly cold wind and press photographers darted between the trees in the search of camouflage for lenses aimed at intimate moments of grief.

Lew Kopelew, every inch a Russian dissident in his flowing grey beard and strong passionate voice, affirmed his belief that 'they did not leave us by their own free will'. One of Petra's closest friends and colleagues, Lukas Beckmann, normally a man of few public words, became unusually poetic as he recalled his first meeting with Petra in 1979, when greens came together to contest the first direct elections to the European parliament. Her voice, he recalled, 'bubbled like a spring and her pen moved across the paper as if in flight'. Knowing that in life Petra's greatest fear was to be alone, Beckmann also quoted from a poem Heinrich Böll had written for his granddaughter shortly before his own death in July 1985. From the first, Böll had been a firm champion of both Die Grünen and Petra.

We come from afar
my dear child
and must go far
have no fear
we are all with you

The ceremony was conducted by Jörg Zink, a pastor from Stuttgart. He recalled his first meeting with Petra: 'We were sitting in a tent opposite Fessenheim nuclear power station in Breisach. It was about twelve years ago. We were celebrating a church service; I was speaking about the part of the Sermon on the Mount which deals with non-violence, and for a long time afterwards we sat together talking about the strange fact that the original impulses which Christianity gave to world history are today in the hands of those who seem, outside the Church and almost without its assistance, to do what Christianity hardly remembers today.'

As he spoke beside the grave and family and friends moved tearfully forward to place their flowers on the coffin to the tune of 'Amazing Grace', the rest of Germany was settling down to read the weekend papers. The shocked news reports of the beginning of the week had already given way to detailed consideration of every possible motive for the deaths.

On the front page of *Der Spiegel* was a picture of Gert Bastian looking grim and Petra looking tragic under the title, 'The mysterious death'. Inside, a new title – 'The Old Man and the Maiden' – took up the story by explaining Petra's predilection for older men as a search for a father figure, which in turn accounted for what the paper described as her increasingly neurotic and suffocating symbiosis with the aging general. A few days later *Stern* magazine adopted a similar theme, not only naming the men, but picturing them too. There were the lovers – former President of the European Commission Sicco Mansholt and President of the Irish Transport and General Workers Union John Carroll; the admired friends – Nobel-Prize-winning author Heinrich Böll and artist Joseph Beuys; and the political heroes – former German Chancellor Willy Brandt (who had died on 8th October) and Russian ex-President Mikhail Gorbachev.

Several newspapers ran pieces on other famous couples who had intentionally died together, including the poet Heinrich von Kleist and Henriette Vogl, and the writer Arthur Koestler and his wife Cynthia. A miscellany of psychiatrists, especially in the tabloid press, confidently revealed the 'classic analysis of the killing of your intimate partner'.

Very few burrowed deeper, but those who did focused on the personality of Petra Kelly. She was known to work incessantly, and to expect those around her to demonstrate the same commitment. Had her demands and her dependency (she frequently said she could not live without him) driven Gert Bastian to kill her, with the unavoidable suffix that he must kill himself too?

Or was he weary, still weakened from his car accident in March? This had required surgery to his left knee and shin and a long period of rehabilitation, quite a blow to a man proud of his physique and his virility. Perhaps he felt Petra's plans for the future – the television series and the European parliament – held no place for him. Although he loved to travel abroad with Petra to conferences and to meetings, he was known to be against any prolonged stay out of Germany. Had he felt death the only way he could keep her with him?

Despite his love of his country Bastian was also known to be dismayed at the rise of the neo-Nazis. This brought back 'evil memories of my youth', as he wrote in an article published in *Die Zeit* in mid-September.[2] He may not have relished leaving Germany for another country, but was his despair at his fellow Germans so great he felt death to be the only answer? Did Gert Bastian therefore kill Petra Kelly because he believed *she* could not manage without *him?*

The fact that Petra and Gert had lain undiscovered and unmissed for nineteen days received much attention. Speakers for Bündnis

90/Die Grünen[3] contradicted themselves. Some were quick to point out that Petra had plans. 'We have recently had several meetings with Kelly and Bastian in the context of the struggle against the extreme-right,' said Anne Nilges, speaking for the party executive. 'Petra was preparing her candidature for the European parliament and we supported that. We saw them in September and they were very happy.'

Others, like Otto Schily, who had been, with Petra and Marieluise Beck, a co-speaker for the first Green parliamentary group in 1983 but who now sat in the Bundestag for the Social Democrat Party, spoke of his sadness at the solitude of the couple who had been so instrumental in putting green politics on the map in Germany. Konrad Weiss, one of the eight East Germans elected to the Bundestag in December 1990 from the Bündnis 90/Die Grünen alliance underlined this: 'The delay in discovering their deaths proved how much we had dropped them'.

For those who preferred more concrete motives, sexual jealousy was promoted. During 1989 and 1990 Petra had had an affair with a Tibetan doctor, Palden Tawo. 'Petra Kelly's last secret' shouted the headlines. Alternatively, there was speculation that Bastian was fearful of being exposed as 'an operationally relevant person' in the many-tentacled operations of the infamous East German secret police – the STASI. The trial of Marcus Wolf, the former spymaster (on whom John le Carré is supposed to have modelled his fictitious character Karla) was due to start in 1993. One of the many probable witnesses, Günter Bohnsack, former head of one of the STASI disinformation departments, claimed to have provided speeches for Bastian while he was a member of parliament for the Greens.

Some papers still pondered the possibility of the involvement of some outside agent in the deaths. As well as the assertion of journalist Peter von Stamm (who had worked with Petra in preparing a hearing on Tibet in Bonn in 1989) that the hand of the Chinese could be seen in the deaths, and of others who saw the fag-end of the KGB at work, still more felt that, in a climate of national concern about the rise of neo-Nazi sentiment since German reunification, threats Petra and Gert Bastian were said to have received from some gangs should be taken seriously.

Arnold Kotler of Parallax Press, Petra's Californian publisher who had been with her in Berlin, joined with some of her closest American friends like Joan Baez, the singer and human rights activist and Charlene Spretnak, a leading writer on the spiritual dimension of green politics, to send a statement to the memorial service in the Beethovenhalle: 'Because the circumstances surrounding their deaths remain so unclear, and in the light of the fact that they had received repeated death threats, we think a thorough investigation is called for.' Writing in *The Indian Express* of 1st November, Jaya Jaitly, who had known Petra for many years, urged the German government to 'institute an enquiry which can examine the possible motives of new Nazis, international gun runners, those who want old NATO secrets kept under wraps'.

Well over a year later all these theories persisted. Even the theory that both were killed by a third party still had echoes. The clumsiness of the official explanations, the deep psychological dislocation caused by thinking of Petra as dead with the 'gentle general' as a murderer, and the awfulness of their bodies lying for so long as to be unrecognizable, conspired to make the conspiracy theory both comfortable and comforting.

Perhaps if the Bonn police had chosen to reveal information about the bloodstains rather than simply cite the presence of powder burns on Bastian's hand as evidence that no third person had been involved, a lot of speculation would have been avoided and friends and colleagues might have been spared a lot of pain and confusion.

In addition, the man in charge of the enquiry, Police Commissioner Hartmut Otto of the Bonn Murder Squad did not always choose his words carefully. Shortly before handing over to the Public Prosecutor he said: 'I don't know what was going on inside his [Bastian's] head. Perhaps it is a good thing.'

Although they are supposed to provide only concrete evidence and not an opinion, through this and other infelicities the police managed to give credence to a conclusion that it was a double suicide they were dealing with. To the irritation of Petra's family, the word *Doppelselbstmord* persisted right through the investigation. Despite the forensic evidence that Petra was asleep when she died and despite family and friends' unanimously asserting that there was no sign she was contemplating suicide and that indeed it would be entirely out of character for her to do so, the final report of the Public Prosecutor's Office, published five months later in March 1993, spoke of 'the sui-

cide of both'. Eventually, and only after the family and close friends of
Petra (who, strangely, were not interviewed at any point during the
enquiry) had protested, the Bonn Public Prosecutor's Office, although
rejecting demands to reopen the enquiry, did write a formal letter to
Mrs Kelly's lawyers which put aside any notion of a double suicide by
stating clearly that Gert Bastian had deliberately killed Petra Kelly
before committing suicide himself.

This new official version received very little press coverage, particularly in Germany; the full report quite intentionally still left the question open. A spokesman for the Public Prosecutor's Office pointed
out that 'all that concerned us was establishing whether anyone else
was involved . . . We concluded that Bastian killed Kelly, but whether
it was with or without her consent was not a matter for us – we can't
conduct investigations against a deceased person.'

The details of what happened may never be known. What we do
know is that Petra and Bastian remained in Berlin after the Radiation
Victims' Conference longer than they originally intended. They had
stayed from 19th to 27th September in Hotel Boulevard, before moving to the Hotel Kempinski at the other end of the famous West
Berlin Kurfürstendamm for two extra, unplanned nights. We don't
know why they did this, nor what they did during this time, apart,
that is, from write postcards. Mine is dated 28th September. It urges
me to get in touch so we may talk about my recent, much publicised
departure from the UK Green Party. 'It is all reminding me of my
own struggle within the Green party! Gert and I are hoping that you
are *inside* (soul and heart) well and that you are not suffering too
much from all the terrible Green hurt and pain . . .' As usual the card
is covered with writing, at every possible angle. The picture on the
front is of the Medicine Buddha and a note points out that this is the
embodiment of all the Buddha's healing qualities. Petra had underlined the words *healing qualities* twice.

We also know that they returned to Bonn by car (not by train as the
papers reported) on Wednesday 30th September, visiting
Sachsenhausen and its memorial to concentration camp victims on
the way, and arrived at Swinemünderstrasse late in the night. This
Gert Bastian wrote in a letter to his wife which was found addressed
but unstamped beside his typewriter in the little study.

Before going to bed, Petra looked through the faxes waiting for her.

One was from an American political scientist who had been commissioned to prepare a short biography of Petra for a book on contemporary west European leaders. Petra corrected the text, marked it 'page ten and one missing. Urgent. Send from the office on Thursday evening.' She also prepared two faxes in the early morning of the 1st October. One to Ken Emerson of *New York Newsday:* 'I would like to mail you per fax a commentary about the present situation in Germany written by my *closest* political + personal ally and friend Gert Bastian (see biogr. sketch enclosed)' and one to Peter Murphy, of *Broadside* magazine in Australia: '. . . enclosed a commentary written by Gert Bastian about the increasing neo-Nazi activities in Germany . . .' The faxes were not sent, but placed ready to be taken to the Bundestag offices the following day. We don't know what time she went to bed. Petra always felt at her best at night, and would often work until 4 or 5 o'clock in the morning.

Gert Bastian, on the other hand, was known to be an early riser. He certainly rose early on the morning of 1st October, because he commented on the hour in his letter to his wife Charlotte. It could not have been a more humdrum letter, describing the trip to Salzburg and Berlin, the detour on the way home, his recently published article in *Die Zeit* ('look out for it!'), and wishing his wife well for her imminent trip to Rhodes with their daughter Eva. 'Unfortunately,' wrote Gert Bastian to his wife a few hours before killing himself, 'I seem to have caught a stupid cold in the last few days.'

The next letter to go into in the typewriter was to his lawyer in Munich, Hartmut Wächtler. Petra's best friend Erika Heinz was having trouble with her boss. Bastian wanted to help out and was going to ask his lawyer to send a letter. He stopped this letter halfway through the word 'must'.

Much emphasis has been given (particularly by those keen to keep the intruder theory going) to the fact that Bastian, a good typist, broke off in the middle of a word. What interruption other than the sudden sound of an intruder could have been abrupt enough, demanding such instantaneous response? Many people affirmed that when typing they would always finish the word, if not the sentence, even if called most urgently. Some wondered if the the word *müssen* brought to the surface of Bastian's mind some inner purpose, a plan either already well formed or perhaps still muddled? If this is so, what could have caused Gert Bastian to formulate a plan which involved such an extreme action? Jealousy? An escape from the frantic Kelly *ménage*? Unhappiness about his political impotence in the new, and to his mind, ugly Germany? All possible, yet still, whatever the problem, whatever Bastian's dilemma might have been, surely reaching for his gun would be his last, not his first, resort?

Bastian's son Till, a doctor, believes his father may have had some sort of physical attack. Some years ago, during a long airplane journey, Bastian had suffered a blood clot in one of the deep veins of his leg, and occasionally he took pills for mild pain from angina. Perhaps, suggests Till, his father experienced a heart attack, or a blood clot affected his brain (a stroke). Fearing Petra would not manage without him (or unable to bear the thought that she should go on without him) he might have decided to end both their lives there and then.

Or maybe he stopped typing because he sneezed. After all, he had a cold, and what could be more urgent than an impending sneeze with no handkerchiefs within reach? Running through most speculations about what happened inside 6 Swinemünderstrasse that day is the assumption that the break in the typing, the shooting of Petra Kelly, and then the shooting of himself occurred smoothly, easily, seamlessly. There was no anguish, there were no doubts, no delays.

But there is no reason why many minutes, or even hours, should not have passed between the break in the typing and the firing of the bullets. The search for handkerchiefs may have extended to the preparing of another cup of coffee (he drank at least one that day), to becoming distracted by some papers and faxes in the kitchen. The kitchen table was usually covered with the most urgent jobs to be done and Petra had been at work that night.

We also know for sure that Bastian spoke to Lukas Beckmann in the Bundestag offices at around noon that day. Two days earlier Beckmann had sent a fax to Swinemünderstrasse asking Gert to call him as soon as he could. Beckmann, in a hurry to leave for a meeting when Bastian called, quickly explained that it concerned the applications of the Green parliamentarians to see their STASI files. The normally meticulous Bastian had already omitted to include photocopies of the necessary personal identification with the forms for himself and Petra, but this time Beckmann was seeking a signature from Bastian and Petra for a letter to go the the Gauck office (which dealt with the applications) to try to speed the process up a bit.[4] Without time to explain in detail, Beckmann asked Bastian to phone the *Fraktion* (parliamentary group) staff member dealing with the matter straight away. Bastian never made that call.

Unlike other famous couples who have died intentionally together, there were no explanatory notes, no messages to family, no political explanations to the corrupt world. And, counter to the 'classic analysis of the killing of your intimate partner', Gert Bastian did not die lying close to the woman to whom he had bound himself so completely in life. When he placed the gun to his forehead, he was standing outside the open door of the bedroom where the body of Petra lay.

Perhaps killing Petra had not been easy. Perhaps the effort to steel himself to do it had been so great, that the shock of the act (and the mess) had made him recoil, move away from the bed and out of the room. The police found the doors of the french windows leading from the sitting room to the garden unlocked, the security alarms off and the keys lying inside the unlocked front door. Perhaps Gert Bastian had roamed the house for a while and even had the presence of mind to make it easy for people to get in. But in order to summon sufficient strength to complete what he had started, to end his own life, he had to return to the upstairs landing. The horror of what he had already done kept him away from the bed, but in order to pull the trigger of the gun he held to his own head he had to keep that horror in his sight.

Notes

1   Beckmann and Kopelew, (eds) (1993).
2   'Der Lack ist Ab' (The varnish is off) *Die Zeit*, 10 September 1992.
3   After the 1990 all-Germany elections, Bündnis 90, an alliance of East German dissident groups united with the East and West German green parties to form a single party – Bündnis 90/Die Grünen.
4   This committee, named for Joachim Gauck its chairman, manages the STASI archives, and processes applications for people wishing to see their own file.

2

NOVEMBER 1947
-TO-
JUNE 1966

GÜNZBURG IN BAVARIA

It is impossible to separate the story of Petra Kelly's life from the story of the country into which she was born. Although Petra left Germany for the United States at the age of 11, and did not re-establish residence until after she was elected to parliament in 1983, she was profoundly influenced, both personally and politically, by what had happened to Germany – and by what Germany had done to others.

The year Petra was born, Germany was still trying to come to terms with its second *Jahr Null* (Year Zero) – a time when everything was so bad that starting anew was the only option. During the Second World War over two million German homes had been destroyed, there were ten million refugees, the economy barely functioned outside a flourishing black market (mainly based on American cigarettes), and the rest of the world felt the Germans might never be trusted to run their own affairs again.

In his book *The Germans*, Alan Watson describes the first *Jahr Null* as the catastrophic destruction of Germany during the Thirty Years War (1618-48) when ordinary German people 'were perhaps the first European people to discover the full horrors of the uniformed mob'. Few settlements escaped the raping and plundering soldiers and around a third of the population are thought to have died. Out of this devastation the 'existential catastrophe of modern Germany' was born, as Michael Stürmer, a conservative historian and advisor to Chancellor Kohl, succinctly puts it. The source of the German nation's *angst* – an anxiety born of insecurity and fear of impending disaster – could well be traced back to the Thirty Years War. It explains, as Stürmer says, why 'Germans yearn for the calculable. We need to know, to be able to measure. To be, as far as it is humanly possible, certain of the direction that events will take.'

This first Year Zero was, of course, very different from the second, but there are comparisons to be drawn. In each case, the German people were morally down and out, physically and emotionally numbed by events, but in 1648 the rebuilding remained a strictly local affair. Germany focused on itself, not as a growing nation state in an expanding and adventurous Europe, but as a mixed bag of very loosely federated principalities. Prosperity, culture and civic pride were all homegrown and they proved satisfying enough to keep the interest and concern of the citizenry happily concentrated on their own back yards right through much of the nineteenth century, until, that is, the Prussian Otto von Bismark set about forging a German State on his famous anvil of 'blood and iron'.

Many historians view 1945 as marking the end of another thirty years war. In the aftermath, the same strong sense of local place was important for the rebuilding of Germany, only this time it was accompanied by the creation of a European Community in which Germany's power could be made eternally benign:

> *In German history the First World War appears more and more clearly as the opening act in a cataclysmic drama rather than as the play itself. Without the First World War, the Nazi movement could hardly have happened. Without the First World War, the Second becomes inconceivable. Without the First World War, the eruption of the superpowers into the centre of Europe could not have occurred. Without the First World War, would Germany have ever been divided between East and West?*[1]

It was therefore with an eye to the past as much as to the future, that Germany's post-World War Two *Grundgesetz* or Basic Law (constitution) recognized the importance of giving local government considerable power. This constitutional arrangement made it possible for each German to combine in their personal idea of *Heimat* (homeland) the 'particularness' of their own community with its distinctive customs and traditions, and a common sense of nationhood. Part of modern Germany's *angst* is a dread of the slightest echo of the Nazi Party's notion of nationalism. By keeping the bulk of economic and emotional patriotism firmly attached to the *Länder* (regions), Germans could keep their national sentiments 'modest'. Modesty was Petra's favourite term when she described how she felt Germans should comport themselves at all times, everywhere. As the process to reunify West and East Germany gathered momentum in 1990, she deplored the fact that 'many of our politicians, including those in the Social Democratic Party (SPD), reverted very quickly back to German nationalist rhetoric . . . "Being German" suddenly took on a new, a special meaning.'[2]

Bavaria, the *Land* into which Petra was born, is renowned for its strong sense of regional identity. Bavarians, in the same manner as the Scots, Welsh or Irish, are especially proud of the 'particularness' of their part of Germany, and will enthuse about its mountains, its forests, its cuisine and its dialect. Petra's Germanness came from Bavaria. When she looked at Germany or spoke about Germany, it was her *Heimat* Bavaria which was in her mind, and like many who have moved much during their life, her sense of and affection for her roots was highly developed. She loved to return there for family occasions and was proud that, even after all her years in America, her Bavarian accent was easily discernable.

Mostly, though, it was Bavaria's people, its politics and its history she thought of. For Petra, home was always more about people than place. Bavaria was the place she had been born, but it also meant 'Omi' her beloved grandmother, around whom the family reunions which meant so much to her took place; and the two *Landkreis* (electoral districts) from which she had been elected to the Bundestag in 1983 (Kempten) and again in 1987 (Freising). Bavaria was also the birthplace of Gert Bastian, who came from Munich.

Bavaria has always been strongly conservative in its politics and Catholic in its religion. Bavarian politics were dominated by the leader of the ultra-conservative Christian Social Union, the bulldog-like Franz-Josef Strauss, one of Petra's political *bêtes noires* who would incense her by describing Die Grünen as 'the Trojan horse of the Soviet Cavalry'.[3] Bavaria was the second most populous region in Germany, and Strauss and the votes he commanded (10 per cent in 1983) were essential to the right-wing Christian Democratic Union (Helmut Kohl's party) obtaining power.

Petra's family were devout Catholics and the conservative catholicism of modern Bavaria was obviously important in shaping her early life. It was only later she became aware of the many connections Bavaria had with the Nazis, something she studied with particular attention during her time at university in the United States. Two of Hitler's best-known henchmen, Hermann Göring (Minister of Propaganda and Public Enlightenment) and Heinrich Himmler (head of the *Schutzstaffen* (SS) protection squad) were Bavarians. So too was the macabre 'Angel of Death', Josef Mengele, Chief Doctor at Auschwitz. He had actually been born in Günzburg, a fact that Petra repeatedly mentioned in speeches and interviews.

The Nazi Party itself had even been founded in Munich, capital of Bavaria. Still in the army after the First World War, Adolf Hitler had been sent to Munich where one of his tasks was to monitor the activities of small political groups. In September 1919 he attended a meeting of the German Workers' Party to discuss the separation of Catholic Bavaria from the rest of Germany, which was largely run by socialists at the time. For Hitler, bitterly deceived by the end of the First World War, the political brew of popular socialist demands, anti-Semitism and intense nationalism was irresistible. Within six months he had left the army and become a full-time political activist.[4] Bavaria became the Austrian Hitler's adopted *Land* and later, when the Nazi Party was at the height of its power, Hitler held huge rallies in Nürnburg, attended by thousands of enthusiastic supporters.

THREE STRONG WOMEN

Petra Kelly's family originally came from Nürnburg. As the Allies had focused their bombing raids on towns and cities with a population of over 50,000 people, Nürnburg had been badly affected. When her own home was destroyed, Petra's grandmother, Kunigunde Birle, had been forced to seek security for herself and her sixteen-year-old daughter, Margarete-Marianne, in Günzburg, a small market-town on the banks of the River Danube, 140 kilometres from Nürnburg. There she stayed in a house which her husband had inherited in a little street just behind Günzburg's marketplace.

Kunigunde Birle, her daughter Marianne and her granddaughter Petra are very alike, though not so much in their larger physical features – even in old age Omi is quite tall and elegant, while Marianne is short and comfortably round. Petra was small like her mother and, though prone to putting on a good deal of weight from time to time, it was her frailness which struck people most. This made her seem smaller than she really was. Tiny, fragile, intensely energetic, were the usual adjectives applied to Petra Kelly. But all three women shared a clear facial resemblance, elegant and expressive hands, a bustling energy – and a tendency to carry several shopping bags wherever they went. Much of Petra's energy, stamina and mannerisms, she obviously owed to her mother and grandmother. And as she grew up in Günzburg, they also influenced her personality.

Like many of their neighbours, most members of the Birle family were taken in by Hitler. But not Kunigunde Birle. She remained resolutely against the Nazi party and everything it stood for. Once, on hearing that her daughter had become entangled with a Nazi organization for young girls, she went straight along to the meeting and yanked Marianne out. Her husband Franz, Petra's grandfather, had been in a protected war job, working with a transport company in Nürnburg and Kunigunde Birle stayed with him, sending the young Marianne to boarding school at Eichstätt, deep in the Bavarian countryside – and so relatively safe. Towards the end of the war Franz Birle was drafted by a now desperate German army and in March 1945, a matter of weeks before the war ended, Frau Birle was widowed. Still only forty, Kunigunde Birle set about looking after herself and her daughter with an energetic independence. She never remarried. In the comfortable house in Günzburg, with its wicket fence and pretty garden, Petra loved to hear Kunigunde Birle tell stories about how she had worked as one of the *Trümmerfrauen* (women of the rubble) painstakingly clearing the streets of Nürnburg after the bombing. 'She took care of my mother and me during the hardest of times.'[5]

When the Allies took over the German prisoner of war camps in Bavaria, the prisoners were required to produce evidence that they had some sort of accommodation to return to before they could be released. After the partition of Germany, many were anxious to establish their residence in the Western sector. One young man in this situation was a Pole from Dresden, Richard Siegfried Lehmann. He had come to know Marianne through a correspondence that had started up between the prisoners and girls from local schools. He wrote to Marianne to ask for her help. Without hesitation, Marianne and her mother welcomed Lehmann to number 6 Hofgartenweg. Although young, he had been well educated, and he quickly found work, first as a journalist with the local paper, the *Günzburger Zeitung*, and then for the Americans at the base in nearby Ulm, where he learnt to speak excellent English. As Marianne Kelly remembers, at that time the best money was to be had working for the Americans.

Within a short period of time, the handsome Lehmann and the pretty Marianne fell in love. In May 1947 when he was twenty-two and she just eighteen, they married. On 29th November that same year Petra Karin Lehmann was born.

The marriage was difficult from the start. Lehmann was war-scarred and rootless. Dresden had been badly bombed and his family scattered. He was also, as Petra remembers, a bit of a dreamer. A romantic and not very dependable, the responsibility of fatherhood and marriage did not suit him. He felt ill at ease in the ordered female household at Hofgartenweg, and his relationship with his wife deteriorated. A Protestant, he also had to bow to the will of the household that Petra be brought up a Catholic. When Petra was six he left and played no further role in supporting his wife and child, and in 1954 he and Marianne were divorced. Putting his relationship with herself aside, Marianne Kelly insists that 'when he was there he was a good father,' and Petra herself remembered only good times. Lehmann played the piano and wrote poetry; he was kind and gentle with her.[6]

Like many daughters of departed fathers, Petra was curious about him, and on several occasions wanted to try to find him. Once when she was working in Brussels she told her mother she was thinking of employing a private detective, but Marianne was against this, fearful her daughter would be hurt. Then, in 1985, out of the blue, Petra received a letter from her father. There was no indication of where it had come from.

As Petra had become more famous, the press had run several articles, even a television documentary, on the lifestory of the passionate 'green goddess'. As usual, accuracy had sometimes been sacrificed, and this prompted Siegfried Lehmann to write to Petra because he was alarmed that, in the reports of her early days, he was getting a bad press. Anyone who has been the subject of this sort of scrutiny of their lives knows very well that even the interviewee can fall into the habit of 'rounding up the truth', if only to shorten the process and get back to work. In one film, searching for the right word to describe the spirit rather than the occupation of her father, Petra had described him as a 'street entertainer'. This at once went down in legend as his profession, and would be repeated at regular intervals for the rest of her life.

Siegfried Lehmann was anxious to set the record straight, with his daughter at least. 'Dear Petra,' he wrote. 'Some of the press are writing the wrong things about me . . . if you don't know the truth, talk to Omi . . . I'm not cross . . . I'm just an ordinary citizen . . . I don't know if you want to see me, but if you do, put an advertisement in the *Frankfurter Rundschau*.' Lehmann then gave very precise instructions as to the day, the wording and the place of the advertisement to be placed in a Frankfurt daily paper. Petra knew it was her father because he included a photograph that only he could have possessed.

Petra placed the advertisement, but for some reason it was not published in the correct section of the classified advertisements. To this day, no one knows if Lehmann saw the advertisement or not, because nothing further was heard from him. When Petra died, the one letter she had received from her father was found near the top of the pile of papers beside her bed.

After her husband left in 1953, Marianne had to support herself and her daughter alone. She too started to work for the Americans, not in Ulm but in the Post Exchange in Leipheim, a brisk five kilometres cycle-ride along the banks of the river Danube. There she was in charge of the sales department.

The bicycle rides at either end of a long working day meant that Marianne had to leave much of the day-to-day raising of her daughter to Omi, and the relationship that developed between Petra and her grandmother became a very special one. With her father gone, and her mother at work all day, Petra understandably fixed on the one unwaveringly present person. When she was young, it was Omi who soothed away the anxieties and who comforted her when she was afflicted by the painful and debilitating bouts of urinary infections and kidney stones which were to trouble her all her life. Much later, as she mourned her younger stepsister Grace, it was to Nürnburg and Omi that Petra would turn for solace and support. Omi's small flat even became Petra's Bavarian office for her various election campaigns and, by 1983, Kunigunde Birle had become widely famous in her own right as the 'Green Granny' who accompanied Petra wherever she went. Secretary, companion, confidante and unswervingly loyal friend, Omi's patience with the energetic Petra never faltered once. The word I heard most frequently in description of her was saintly. So close did their relationship become that when she was invited in 1988 to contribute a chapter to a book of well-known people writing about their mothers, Petra wrote instead about her grandmother.[7] Marianne Kelly remains remarkably evenly disposed to this situation, to the point of being able to laugh, albeit somewhat wryly, about an encounter she had with an insurance company after Petra's death. Having arranged a meeting to settle some of Petra's affairs, she introduced herself to the official who replied: 'I had no idea Petra had a mother.'

Despite the inevitable hardships of the times, and the departure of her father, Petra's childhood was more comfortable than many. The two women were devoted to her, and Omi showed endless patience, always ready to answer the questions of the curious child. By the time she started school in 1954, Petra could not only read and write, but, thanks to Omi, already associated learning with pleasure. School was at the nearby Englisches Institut, a boarding school for Catholic girls run by nuns, which Petra attended as a day girl. From the first, Petra was marked out as a special pupil. Despite missing a lot of days through illness caused by her increasingly troublesome kidneys, her first half-year report reads: 'A steady, well-behaved, ambitious but anxious pupil, she has completed her school work conscientiously and enthusiastically.' By the end of Petra's third year, her class teacher was noting: 'A good, well behaved and extremely hard-working pupil, deserving of special success.'

After the school day, which ended at noon, Petra would return home to lunch and Omi. In the afternoon Omi liked nothing better than to sit at the table in her cosy house, or, if it was warm enough, on the verandah overlooking her garden, and read about the news of the day. She was particularly fond of current affairs magazines – *Der Spiegel* and *Quick* being her favourites. While Petra did her homework on the other side of the table, Omi would read aloud bits of news that were especially interesting. Petra would respond with questions and Kunigunde Birle would explain everything to her inquisitive granddaughter 'in a way that was simple yet most precise', Petra remembered.[8] The intimacy and trust between them was complete. 'There was no censorship' recalled Marianne Kelly. 'Omi explained everything to the fullest – pictures, headlines, absolutely everything.' Petra remembers her grandmother telling her about the 'Göttinger Appell', an appeal from a group of well-known scientists, including Nobel Peace Prize-winner Albert Schweitzer, against giving the Bundeswehr (German army) nuclear arms. This was in 1957, the year West Germany re-established her own armed forces.[9]

The young Petra also loved to read. Mrs Kelly still has all of Petra's books from that time. 'There must be hundreds of them. She was always reading, and when she got older, when you asked her "What do you like?" She always said "Books." ' After Petra's death when her books and papers were being prepared for removal from Swinemünderstrasse to the green archive in nearby Bornheim Widdig, archivist Robert Camp recorded well over three thousand volumes.

Petra's own memories of her early years are of a very happy time. She recalls being rather an anxious, timid child, but also that there was always someone there to soothe her worries away. It was a very disciplined life, and Petra said it was from the Englisches Institute that she learnt the importance of working hard and forcing herself to complete the task in hand. The security of the caring and disciplined life was so agreeable that Petra could only imagine it continuing for ever. She would become a nun when she grew up she decided, then she could go on living and working in Günzburg for the rest of her life.

Meanwhile, the reconstruction of Germany was continuing apace.

Living in the American zone meant that Petra was amongst the first of the post-war generation of German children to experience the miracles of Coca Cola, jeans and comics. One of her favourite comics at this time was *Mickey Mouse*, and when she was nine she took from one issue the address of a young German girl advertising for a pen-pal. Karin Amirany was five years older than Petra, but their friendship became a close one that endured until Petra's death. It was to Karin that Petra wrote about the pain she felt at the departure of her father and about her firm intention to become a Dominican nun when she grew up.

At the end of 1957, Marianne Lehmann fell in love again. It was with an American lieutenant-colonel in the Engineering Corps, John Edward Kelly, and this time it was for keeps. A tall, gentle bear of a man, as quietly spoken as his wife is talkative, he and the nine-year-old Petra quickly became firm friends. In December 1958 John Kelly married Marianne Lehmann, and the following spring the family was transferred to another base, at Nellingen, near Stuttgart, where Petra entered grade 6 at the American Dependent Elementary School. As her stepfather was to be posted back to the United States in December that year, it was important that Petra should 'get her English up' before they left.

Six months before the family left for the United States, on 25th May 1959, Grace Patricia Kelly was born. It is difficult to know exactly how Petra felt at this time. A lot of things had happened to her very quickly. She was at first very fearful at being uprooted from the routine of Günzburg and moved to the school at Nellingen, but Mrs Kelly remembers she adapted very quickly. And the birth of her sister? Later, Petra would speak only of the great pleasure and excitement she felt at the time her sister was born, though in truth it would have been pretty strange if she had not had mixed feelings. She was eleven when Grace Patricia was born, and very used to being the main focus of attention in the household. Suddenly, within months, everything had changed. Not only did Petra have to adjust to competition for attention at home, a difficult period for any child, but the outside world was turning upside down at the same time.

From an early age Petra had suffered from stones in her kidneys and the infections that frequently accompany this condition. Often the stones passed from the kidney to the bladder, where they were reabsorbed without surgical intervention, but anyone who has experienced it knows that the pain caused by the descending stone can sometimes be unbearably intense. In March 1956, Petra had her first operation to remove stones that failed to descend. She was to have three operations in all, two on the right side and one on the left, before the final operation in Washington in 1967 in which one third of the right kidney was removed. Without a doubt, like any child in pain or fear of pain, Petra will have demanded, and received, a lot of attention.

John Kelly went out of his way to win over his new stepdaughter, something that his warm personality made easy. He was also delighted with her; she was charming and mature beyond her years so he had no trouble in taking Petra as well as her mother into his heart. When I talked with him about his stepdaughter after her death, I found him full of affectionate anecdotes as well as encyclopaedic about her operations and the speeches and election campaigns he and his wife had attended. Marianne Kelly, like Petra, was hopeless with dates.

But John Kelly was also delighted at the birth of his own daughter. In his thirties, deeply in love with his wife, he had waited a long time for this moment, so however carefully the family tried to prevent it, it was perhaps inevitable that Petra should feel a little left out. Furthermore the impending move to the United States, while exciting, was a huge dislocation for the sensitive, anxious Petra. Nellingen Elementary School had already proved to be a very different place from the Englisches Institute in Günzburg and, worst of all, her beloved Omi would be staying behind.

THE CHEER LEADER

Kunigunde Birle watched the departure of the Kellys with a heavy heart. Although she would visit her daughter and her family in the United States, it would be another six years before Petra came back to Germany. As a parting gift, the ever-generous Omi gave the Kellys the proceeds from the sale of the house in Hofgartenweg before returning to Nürnburg and a small apartment.

In anticipation of the move to the United States, much thought was given to whether John Kelly should adopt Petra formally. Petra herself was keen to keep her German nationality. To the twelve year old, surrounded by the commotion of change, cutting all the links with Germany and Omi did not appeal at all. Marianne Kelly thinks it was probably at this time that Petra's sorrow and anxiety about leaving Germany shaped itself into a deeply stored nugget of ambition to return. But Petra was happy to take the name of her new father. She loved him and accepted it would make it easier for her if she carried his name into her new life in America.

The Kellys were stationed at Fort Benning near Columbus, Georgia – one of the largest military bases in the United States – and Petra completed her sixth grade there before enrolling in Baker Junior High School in autumn 1960. With a facility which impressed everyone around her, she managed to pick up English extremely fast and was soon achieving average marks of A and B in everything except maths where an enduring disaffection kept her grades down at C and D. It was while she was at Baker that her parents were called to see the director of the school. He said he knew military families moved around a great deal but he wanted them to know they had a very gifted daughter and hoped they would give her the best opportunities they possibly could.

Petra also threw herself with relish into the social side of American high school life. As well as being 'top scholar' during her final year, she flexed her political talents on the student and junior class councils and her organizational skills on the prom (final year dance) council. She wrote and drew cartoons for the school newspaper and, despite her blind spot for figures, was treasurer of the Beta Tri Hi Y, a social club. But Petra did not restrict her activities only to those which would give her 'points' towards her membership of the National Honor Society – a club for students who have excelled themselves both academically and in extracurricular activities. While at Baker Junior High, Petra Karin Kelly was a cheer leader for the school football team. Her parents have a photograph (sadly too misty to be reproduced) of the woman who in 1991 *The Sunday Times* would list amongst the '1000 Makers of the 20th Century' surrounded by the tools of the cheer leader's trade – the plump paper pom-poms which she waved in synchrony with her girlfriends to encourage the home-team crowd to ever more frenzied support.

In November 1963, John Kelly was posted to Korea. Petra was not happy about this. She did not like the thought of her stepfather going away, of being separated from him. He was very solicitous of everything she did, following her school work carefully and making a point of correcting any error the school made with her grades. Petra had also been reading his military journals and would often discuss his job with him at length. As an engineer, he had not been a frontline fighter, but in September 1945, one month after the atomic bombs had fallen on Hiroshima and Nagasaki, Lt. Col. Kelly had been among the first troops to land in Kyushu, the southernmost island of Japan. From there the convoy moved to the main island where Lt. Col. Kelly and his unit were responsible for setting up the billets for the unit. Petra had quizzed him about his experiences, and worried about the radioactivity he might have picked up. Even though the war in Korea was over in 1955, Petra's growing interest in American politics and the developing war in Vietnam made her anxious for her stepfather. Her anxieties were allayed, however, when John Kelly was transferred to Fort Monroe, near Hampton on the east coast of Virginia a year later.

Despite another operation to remove a stone from her kidney (the size of a fifty-cent piece, her parents recall) Petra continued to do well at her new school – Hampton High. In 1966, the year Petra graduated, a local newspaper in Hampton reported on her selection as class poet and summed up her other achievements like this:

Hampton's Petra Kelly is a native of Germany but came to America six years ago. She spoke no English then; now she is a prize-winner in both the Voice of Democracy and Merigan Legion oratorical contests and as a junior won a district first place and state second place in girls' public speaking, as well as the HHS [Hampton High School] Speech Club trophy given to the best girl speaker each year.

Petra is on the staff of all three school publications – serving the yearbook as copy editor after being faculty editor in 1964 and art editor in '65; she is on the staff of the literary magazine Seafarer and last year she was cartoonist for Krabba Highlight. She also appears on the radio show, Krabba Karavan.

Last year she was president of Future Nurses and this year heads Keyettes [a club which did community service]. She is also secretary of the National Honor Society, vice president of the Speech Club, in the Debate, German and French Clubs and was named Most Likely to

Succeed in the Hall of Fame. She has received the City of Hampton award, a Lions' Club achievement award as a junior and a world history honor as a sophomore...

Petra is also active as a Teen Democrat and in Junior Army Daughters of America. She writes a newspaper column for her former hometown in Germany explaining teen life in America, and is anticipating an interview soon with Sen. Robert F. Kennedy to add to her column...

The highly articulate young lady is a familiar name in the Letters to the Editor column of the Daily Press & Times-Herald *as she has taken time to express her appreciation of her new country where she plans to become a citizen soon. . . . [she has] an eye toward a career in foreign service.*[10]

The impression given by Petra's school record is of a young woman of great natural talent with all the characteristics already in evidence – the powerful speeches and the prolific letter-writing included – which would later make her famous. But behind her natural abilities and the wideranging interests fostered so carefully by Omi in Günzburg lay an enormous amount of study. However talented she might have been, to become sufficiently proficient in a second language to top the academic lists and carry off prizes for speaking and poetry in competition with native speakers, requires a lot of very hard work.

And Petra did work very hard. She also worked long hours. Her stepfather recalls that she would often work late at school in the library, and at home in Nassau Place he would often wake in the early hours of the morning to hear Petra 'peck, peck, pecking away' on the typewriter in her bedroom. 'I'd tell her to sleep, but she wouldn't . . . she said, "I have to work hard at night, that way I'm ahead." '

In Hampton, Petra applied the discipline of her Bavarian convent to set working patterns which she would retain all her life. She discovered she was 'better at night', finding an inspiration and concentration in the solitude and peacefulness of the hours of darkness that was impossible during the day, with all its interruptions and distractions. During the day she did things, during the night she thought, read and wrote. Moreover, by throwing herself into work – learning English and how to become an all-American girl who not only belonged to the crowd, but was ahead of it – Petra managed to bury her homesickness for Omi and Günzburg. From her earliest days Petra lacked self-confidence, partly due to her natural shyness and her childhood illnesses, but certainly consolidated by the departure of her father and the move to America. In Günzburg the nuns had commented on this timidity more than once, but then there had been Omi to wrap around Petra a protective shawl of unquestioning love and support.

After they moved to America, the Kelly household, which now included another baby, Johnny, born in August 1960, was a busy one. Mrs Kelly had her hands full coping with her two youngsters as well as adapting to a new country, a new language and, above all, a new culture. As was her fashion, she set about it with a great deal of energy and verve. Inevitably, she could not provide her elder daughter with the undivided attention and constant reassurance she had grown accustomed to. Petra, therefore, had to learn to become a lot more self-sufficient - both emotionally and practically. Her anxieties, self-doubts and shyness had somehow to be camouflaged – America was for winners, not for losers. Striving for eternal self-improvement became for Petra a survival strategy and, remembering her convent teachers, she set herself the highest of standards in everything she did. The problem was that Petra's lack of self-confidence meant she found it difficult to judge her own progress. She started therefore to use external indicators to prove to her family, to others, and most of all to herself, that she was doing well. Petra learnt to control her inner fears and anxieties by gradually replacing the always reassuring Omi and her loving but often uncomprehending family with a collection of awards, commendations, newspaper clippings and photographs.

When Petra and her family arrived in 1960s America they had found a very self-conscious country in the process of waking from the deep sleep of the post-war 1950s. John F. Kennedy had been elected president in 1960, and his youth and his religion (he was the first Roman Catholic to be elected to the presidency) made him the first of a new generation of world leaders. Very quickly, Kennedy shook America out of its dozing complacency. The economy was slowing, he said, and the American way of life was in trouble; the old and young were neglected, cities and schools were decaying, greed had replaced the traditional American values of generosity and justice. In October 1963 Kennedy said: 'I look forward to an America which commands respect throughout the world, not only for its strength but for its civilization as well.' One month later he was dead.

Petra, a devout Catholic, was, like many of her contemporaries, greatly inspired by Kennedy, his charisma and the principles he stood for. His death upset her so greatly that she sent a letter of condolence to his family. The state of Georgia, where Petra lived for the first four years of the 1960s, was one of the southern states which had most stubbornly resisted the desegregation laws, so black civil rights was a hot topic of debate. Early in 1963, Martin Luther King began to campaign in Birmingham, in the neighbouring state of Alabama, and some marchers were badly harassed by police, some armed with electric cattle prods. Petra followed current affairs with the attention she had learnt from Omi, and she became one of King's greatest admirers. As political and intellectual debate began to stir the sleepy campuses of schools and universities, Petra joined in. One of her orating prizes was for a speech entitled 'I speak for Democracy' (she thought Germany would benefit from a Declaration of Independence) and one of her high school social club projects was with black children in deprived areas.

The new student political engagement divided itself into two main camps – the 'drop outs' or 'flower power' hippies, and the self-styled revolutionaries. Although Petra would often quote Bob Dylan, she was definitely not interested in dropping out, only in getting more involved. She was very attracted to a clear, uncomplicated opposition to all that was 'bad' – racial discrimination, the Vietnam war, heartless bureaucracy. The idea of a revolution against all that was unjust with 'Power to the People' and 'Make Love not War' as the rallying cries also appealed to Petra's evangelical nature. Though it had become less clear how she might achieve it – she no longer thought she would be a nun – her childhood desire to dedicate herself to a higher cause was still burning bright. It was with great enthusiasm and a lot of expectation in her heart that the cheer leader of Baker High set off to university in Washington.

Notes

1   Watson (1992), p. 39.
2   Speech: Beverley Hills (11 November 1990).

3 Hülsberg (1987), p. 14.
4 Stone (1982), p. 25.
5 Chapters and Articles: in Berman (ed.) (1985), p. 113.
6 Sperr (1983), p. 42.
7 Petra Kelly, 'An meine Omi – eine öffentliche Liebeserklärung' (To my Granny – a public declaration of love), in Werner Filmer and Heribert Schwan (eds), *Meine Mutter: Ein deutsches Lesebuch* (Econ, Düsseldorf, 1989).
8 Chapters and Articles: in Berman (ed.) (1985), p. 113.
9 Sperr (1983), p. 48.
10 Hampton VA local paper (no date, 1966).

3

AUTUMN 1966
-TO-
MAY 1970

SCHOOL OF INTERNATIONAL SERVICE

Petra was never in any doubt that she wanted to continue her studies in Washington DC. The seat of the most powerful government in the world, Washington was rich and elegant. It positively oozed power and she was drawn to it like a moth to a flame: 'It's the capital, I can just walk down the street and see everyone.' And, of course, it had the added advantage of being near to home. Petra's plans included going home to Hampton regularly and having her parents visit her in Washington. She was anxious to share her experiences with her family – to involve them in what she was doing and remain closely connected with their lives. They too were proud of her success and visited her at every opportunity. John and Marianne Kelly, often accompanied by little Grace and Johnny, would even turn up when Petra did a presentation in class. It was most unusual that a student's family should be so frequently on campus, but one of Petra's university friends, Bruce French, remembers that after a while everyone became so used to seeing the Kelly family around that 'they simply became part of the crowd'.

Keeping the ties of family tightly knotted and being close to home in every way mattered all the more to Petra when, early in 1967, Grace, aged seven, was diagnosed as having cancer. The tumour was in the tissues around her right eye, a rare and highly malignant sarcoma. By the time it was diagnosed, the possibility of successful treatment was thought to be unlikely. The news devastated Petra. She had developed a very close and loving relationship with both Grace and Johnny.

Deep inside, however, she knew (as her Catholic God knew) that she had not always harboured the sweetest sentiments towards her half-sister; and now Grace was to die. The rational Petra knew that the two facts were not connected. Later, when she was working for the European Commission, Petra would collaborate on a report concerning children with cancer. In it was written: 'Opportunities should not be missed to allow siblings to voice their fears, guilt feelings, anger and thoughts. Siblings with feelings of rivalry should be assured that hostile or angry thoughts do not produce illnesses.'[1] But the anxious, self-doubting twenty-year-old Petra suffered dreadfully; she had sinned and must be punished. When Gracie eventually died in February 1970, after four operations and three years of painful disfiguring treatment, Petra's grief was so intense she even thought of suicide. It was only when sorting out Petra's papers after her death, and coming across some poems written around the time of Gracie's death, that her mother realized the extent of her elder daughter's torment.

Marianne Kelly remembers Petra made her choice of university very carefully, visiting several before finally selecting the School of International Service at the American University. 'I'm sure it was because she always intended going back to Germany, and this was a good place to prepare for it.' But, like Mrs Kelly's feeling that a determination to return to Germany lay behind Petra's decision not to be formally adopted by her stepfather and to only take his name, perhaps her sense about Petra's choice of university came either from hindsight or from an instinct that her daughter had not yet recognized in herself. While she was at Hampton High, and for the first couple of years at American University, Petra spoke frequently of her preparations to apply for American citizenship.

American University (AU) sits elegantly on Massachusetts and Nebraska Avenue, just north of the famous 'Embassy Row' where many of Washington's foreign missions are situated. AU was founded by Methodists in 1898 but subsequently 'secularized', with the old chapel replaced by the Kay Spiritual Centre. The School of International Service (SIS) with its strong European flavour in its International Politics programme was especially attractive to Petra. Although the university itself had 13,500 students, the SIS took only 100, and this made it a cosy, homely place to be. She was also keen on the way American University drew on the government agencies for a rich array of visiting speakers and part-time faculty. Government advisors and important political figures regularly drove through the gates of the university.

When Petra arrived in Washington in 1966, the number of students entering US universities had never been greater, having doubled in the previous decade. Although the touchpaper of dissatisfaction with American society had already been lit by John F. Kennedy, on the whole in 1966 campus politics were still fairly quiet. Protest over the escalation of the Vietnam war was mounting, and Martin Luther King and others were steadily building up the civil rights movement, but the influence of what has been called the 'silent generation' was still manifest. By the mid-1960s, with around 60 per cent employed either in 'white collar' or service jobs, the concerns of most American people were located firmly in mundane, but pleasurable, reality - their suburbs, their pensions, the school gala, the fortunes of the local football team. Outside a few of America's bleakest inner cities and the occasional intellectual hotspot, there was little interest in larger questions such as human rights or the legitimacy of war.

Dr Albert Mott, one of Petra's favourite professors at American University, caricatured American University's campus in 1966 when he was introducing Petra at a class reunion she addressed there in 1990:

> *Girls still wore tartan skirts with big safety pins in them. Young men wore neck ties . . . It was a time when we knew we were the best. When Alan Dulles [head of CIA] came up to the school in a huge stretch limousine there was nobody protesting. We knew the CIA was a most trustworthy institution, and that we were producing young aspirants to it. We knew our Dean was close to God, and that the school served two masters - our country and the divine. When the Methodist Bishops came to our school there was a scurrying about to pick up ashtrays . . . In those days we were short-haired and resolute.*[2]

Petra arrived from Hampton short-haired and resolute all right, but was quite definitely not one of the silent generation. She, like many others entering university at that time, had already been influenced by the vision of John F. Kennedy, been impressed by the courage (and results) of the civil rights movement, and, what's more, felt responsible for things that were happening outside their own backyard.

In a very long poem Petra wrote earlier that year (the one which had won her the coveted title of class poet) she described the new spirit infusing many young Americans. The poem was definitely not written for 'drop outs'. It is the engaged, if not yet the revolutionary, voice of American youth speaking; it is the voice of someone with a more acute sense of her place in history than the average young American. The poem tingles with the anxieties and the ambitions of Petra Kelly as she prepared to leave Hampton for Washington.

IN DEFENSE OF MY GENERATION

This poem itself will soon leave your mind,
Like most modern rhyme you will let it die;
But yet I utter in hope to seek and find
Someone to ascend with me in search of the sky.

Oh, those who are my probing generation,
We are more than a preface or a step
Into hopes, anxieties, and hesitations.
We are a threshold and a payer of debts . . .

We foresee no final peace nor Utopia can we make
The masters of war despite us will be born.
If only some pessimism we can forsake,
Hope can ripen and chagrin be forlorn.

Now we seek with arms outspread
To embrace the world for which we yearn.
To ferret virtues from the vices we met
And merge soul and mind in order to learn. . .

Already our minds reflect on the true and the false.
We fight maturely beside the mature on the front lines.
Upheavals of mankind and the challenge of living calls
For us to constantly illuminate what no longer shines.

Will we as adults be caught in a web of apathy
Thinking of each tomorrow as a new today
Rising like robots, controlled by conformity -
The daily fibre of living in pattern-obsessed ways? . . .

And how much will it be worth to win
To reach the moon, the top, letting success call,
To fill the bucket of materialism to the brim
And discover you can't take it with you after all? . . .

The firmament watches as the sphere speedily turns.
You and I must improve whatever we are and see
And confess in harmony to an inquiry of utmost concern,
'What would this world be like if all were like me?'

Shun mediocrity!
We all can be great.
Potential of greatness lies untapped
In all of us.
We all can reach OUR unreachable start.
Explore our reasons for being a midget, a giant
But dare not compare and compete in size.
We have our 'self' and there alone
Lies greatness . . .

With all the forces in the century,
There is one we cannot equate
And that is the power of love. It can generate
to change this human clan of 1966, and leave it glorified.

Petra loved the life at American University. In June 1967 she gave an enthusiastic interview with a local Virginia newspaper, about the wonderful opportunities available to foreign students in Washington.[3]

She had been able to get into a reading by her favourite poet, the Russian, Yevgeny Yevtushenko; she had met Robert Kennedy at a foreign student reception at the State Department; and with her friend Susan French started a regular exchange of letters with Vice President Hubert Humphrey. Petra had invited Humphrey to attend International Week, an event she had organized in the spring of her first year. He was unable to attend but, instead of leaving it at that, Petra had continued to write often long letters to him about politics and other matters. Humphrey had been struck by the directness and openness of the young student, so he kept up the correspondence (if somewhat more briefly on his side). His secretary recalled that a lot of people wrote to Humphrey, but that Petra wrote more letters than most. 'She [was] a good writer and a very prolific one.'⁴ When Petra told Humphrey about Grace, he was particularly understanding, as his son, Robert, and a brother were both suffering from cancer at that time. There was an exchange of poems, and a bracelet even, and when Petra asked him to send his autographed photo directly to Gracie so she might give it to Johnny for his 'kiss and tell' period at school, Humphrey willingly did so.

In Petra's memories of her time at American University, two of her teachers stand head and shoulders above the others – Professor Abdul Aziz Said and Dr Albert Mott. Two very different personalities, their teaching and their counsel was to have an enormous effect on Petra. The ideas and the writers they introduced to her, and encouraged her to explore, were to provide the intellectual ground from which she launched her political career. And as individuals, because they were nearby at a time when there were so many storms in her private and her public life, Professor Said and Dr Mott did a lot to help her shape her thinking, her worries and her experiences into a personal creed.

Abdul Said is an immensely charismatic man who seems to prompt either adoration or dislike. I met no one with an indifference to his striking good looks and languid manner. Petra immediately fell into the adoration camp. Interestingly, I found Said had very few precise memories of her, even though, in 1970 he wrote:

Miss Kelly is one of the most outstanding students I have ever worked with in my thirteen years of teaching experience, and she possesses the

highest qualities of sensitivity, intellectual commitment, compassion and
warmth. Her contribution to the university community is staggering
and her regard by her fellow students is of the highest calibre.[5]

Some of Petra's close friends suggested there might have been a sexual
tension between them, but others felt that Said inspired Petra, as he
did many others, more by his energy and his genuine brilliance than
his personal magnetism. Either way, he was a highly influential figure,
and was certainly not a run-of-the-mill university professor. Although
unit one of his introduction to politics cracked through all the biggies
of western thought, it started off by contrasting the western view of
the world with some eastern ones, including the Confucian Code and
Taoism. Buddha and the Bible were at the top of the reading list.

When I met Professor Said, he was kind and helpful as he struggled
to trawl up memories of Petra. He remembered long discussions
about spirituality. 'We would talk about Thomas Merton, the Trappist
Monk who became an early critic of the Vietnam war in his book
Conjectures of a Guilty Bystander.'[6] Said has a picture of this monk on
the wall of his study, and Petra, who was learning at the time about
how many Germans claimed to have been unaware of the Nazi
atrocities, was deeply impressed by the extension of guilt from the
perpetrator of any crime or injustice to the knowing, but non-
intervening, observer. 'She was always totally present' recalled Said,
'never reticent, you always knew what she thought.' He had obviously
been affected by her death: 'She was always a walking affirmation of
life, so I do not believe she killed herself.'

Professor Said poured information into Petra, with her well-honed
curiosity and apparently infinite capacity for absorbing facts. 'She was
intuitive and sensitive,' he remembers. 'She caught things very
quickly. It was probably a combination of that and the rich choice
available at SIS – she really took full advantage of that . . . she herself
was interdisciplinary, the cross-fertilization of everything. For her,
learning was a journey, it wasn't a destination and she enjoyed the
journey.'

Dr Albert Mott is also charismatic but in a very different sense from
Professor Said. Where Said was consciously intense, Mott was droll in
an avuncular way, kindly and listening. Everyone loved him. It was to
Dr Mott that Petra would turn most when calamity struck. 'Oh Dr

Mott, you will never guess what has happened!' And, more often than not sitting on the bench under the trees outside the main entrance to the SIS, she would regale him with the latest drama in her life – which could be anything from a lost reference to problems with her grant. Years later, when she had an abortion, she again turned to Dr Mott. Recognizing that Petra needed his support, especially after Grace's illness had been diagnosed, Dr Mott gave it unstintingly. 'I became one of her fathers,' he reflected.

With Dr Mott, Petra studied western politics and history more closely. He remembers very clearly the first time she made a distinct, individual impression on him. 'Where, Dr Mott, is my paper on Oswald Spengler?' she demanded, starting a mystery which was never to be resolved and which remained a standing joke between them.[7] Petra had written, as she often did, an A grade paper. Dr Mott placed it with other papers awaiting collection by his students on the table outside his room. For some reason someone had stolen Petra's.

Dr Mott taught Petra about the history of her own country for the first time. It was a revelation. As a child in Günzburg, for all the close reading she and Omi did of the newspapers, the Germans had applied a considerable degree of self-censorship to the recent past. After the superficially cathartic 1945–6 International Military Tribunal set up by the Americans in Nürnburg, in which 22 top Nazis were put on trial, the emphasis in the news had been mainly on the practicalities of reconstruction.

Petra also attended Dr Mott's courses on the history of ideas from 1840:

> In those courses I remember her very well; so attentive, so engaged in the subject, particularly when we got onto the subject of national socialism and the phenomenon of fascism. Here she was really hooked up – she was born in Günzburg which was the residence of Mengele. I think this was the monkey on Petra's back – the humiliation of being identified with something so horrendous and something which she was so repelled by.

Petra's first year at university ended well. So well that she was awarded a scholarship by the university to pay her tuition fees for the next three years. She also received an award for the Most Outstanding

Foreign Woman Student of the year – the prize being a book of photographs entitled *The Family of Man*.

But the rest of her life was not going so well. Gracie had been given only months to live. American army doctors and specialists saw no hope for her recovery. Despite the removal of her eye, the cancer was already too advanced. After the prognosis, Mrs Kelly returned with her younger daughter to Germany, to a specialist unit at Heidelburg University where more surgery and radiation treatment could be done. Soon after, John Kelly obtained a posting to Würzburg. The whole family decamped for Germany in June. When Petra returned to American University in the autumn of 1967, she was alone.

FROM POP STARS TO POLITICIANS

In celebration of her graduation from Baker Junior High in 1966, John and Marianne Kelly had taken Petra to New Orleans for the weekend. On the Saturday night they went to a concert by the pop-singer Dion held, as was the fashion, in the banqueting suite of a large hotel. It was billed as 'A Night to Remember' and the teenage Petra had her photograph taken arm-in-arm with Dion. Readers of a certain age will remember that Dion achieved the pinnacle of his short-lived fame around 1960 with the songs 'I'm a Wanderer' and 'Teenager in love'. Petra kept this photograph in its presentation frame. She also kept a picture of Perry Como, a popular 1950s crooner, much sellotaped and drawing-pinned from repeated relocating on different walls. Next to Perry Como in the big trunk in which she kept her memorabilia from AU, was a photograph of Robert Kennedy. He too was much sellotaped. Having empathized with the lyrics of 'Teenager in love' at a particularly tender moment of my own teens, I could understand the cheer leader's *faiblesse* for Dion. But my first reaction on finding Perry Como was to think how much I would give to have her near me so I could tease her about it. Later, I discovered that Petra had met Como at a fundraising meeting for Robert Kennedy but the facial resemblance of Como and Kennedy had already made me view Como as a symbol of Petra's transition from a pop-loving teenager to an apprentice politician.

It would be wrong to imply that Petra left her sense of fun behind when she packed Dion and Perry into the trunk. During her university years she did develop the reputation as a serious, committed student and many were in awe at her energy and capacity for work, though only a few say they thought she was driven by some internal force. Eddie Feinburg, who was one of Petra's closest friends, remembers being caught up in International Week. 'She went about things amazingly, people were so struck by the way she engaged them.' He admits to having a crush on her. 'But she didn't have time, and it was hard to take things as seriously as she did. After a march or something, the rest of us would go out drinking, but she wouldn't. She became disgusted at people's lack of commitment.'

But there are also plenty of tales of a more frivolous Petra. Another of her close friends at AU, and who would remain a friend throughout her life, was Adam Stolpen. He remembers a party at which she turned up wearing an 'outrageous' pair of yellow hot pants and thigh-high white boots. He also recounted his first meeting with Petra, when, with a group of students celebrating the birthday of another friend, Bruce French, he had sneaked into the Walter Reid hospital a few days after Petra had had her kidney operation. She had shrieked, they had tried to hide and everyone had got into trouble. Bruce French's sister Susan was Petra's best friend and she recalls many nights in Anderson dorm where studying was leavened by midnight feasts.

When Petra arrived in the United States the star of John F. Kennedy was shining brightly and rising fast. He rose even higher in Petra's personal firmament when, two years after the East German government had built a wall to stop the stream of defectors from East to West, he gave his famous 'Ich bin ein Berliner' speech on the balcony of Berlin Town Hall. In that moment the sixteen-year-old Petra felt her two worlds to be united. In June of that same fateful year, Kennedy gave the graduation address at American University. In it he pursued his quest for a treaty to ban the testing of nuclear weapons and urged Americans:

> not to fall into the same trap as the Soviets, not to see only a distorted and desperate view of the other side, not to see conflict as inevitable . . . [both the USA and the USSR] have a mutually deep interest in a just and genuine peace and in halting the arms race . . . If we cannot end now all our differences, at least we can help make the world safe for diversity.[8]

We know that the Russian leader, Khrushchev, considered this address to be 'the greatest speech by any American President since Roosevelt', but we do not know Petra's reaction at the time. It is certain, however, that when she came to select her university, the association of American University with Kennedy played a significant role in her decision. Like all Americans she had been deeply shocked by his assassination, and she continued to be fascinated by the whole Kennedy clan.

Consequently, when Petra discovered that the scholarship she had been awarded after her first year at AU was to be withdrawn because she was not an American citizen (an essential requirement for any student receiving state or Federal funding) she wrote to Robert Kennedy (then senator for the state of New York) explaining her difficulty. He replied, inviting her to come to his office and discuss the matter. Before she could do this, she met him at a reception for foreign students given by the State Department, and immediately confided her fears that she might have to give up her studies as her parents had little money to spare. 'He told me to calm down and not to worry. Then he gave me some advice about other scholarships, private funds,' Petra explained to the *Washington Post* the following year.[9]

But Petra did more than ask Kennedy for advice. Presidential elections were due. President Lyndon Johnson was deeply unpopular and his escalation of the Vietnam war had mobilized massive opposition. Even the silent generation, as they watched their sons being fed into the meatgrinder of 'the most unpopular war in American history' had become vociferous. Petra, who approved of Robert Kennedy's condemnation of the extending of the war, offered to help with his campaign for the Democrat nomination.

Thus the beginning of 1968 found Petra coordinating the Students for Kennedy group with Susan French and other students from AU and other Washington colleges. An office was opened at 1404 M Street, and a rallying speech by a Kennedy aide brought cheers from the students who had spent the night washing down and decorating the campaign headquarters. 'Kennedy, Kennedy, We Want Bobby' they chanted. The cheer leader was in business again.

In April 1968 Robert Kennedy brought his campaign for nomination into Washington. There was a rally, a meeting and a photo session with his devoted AU supporters.[10] Two months later, in

Los Angeles on the 6th June, Robert Kennedy was shot dead. Distraught, Petra wrote to her by now regular correspondent, Vice President Humphrey, who had himself joined the race for the Democratic nomination in April. He told her Kennedy's death was not the end, and invited her to join his campaign. She did, throwing herself into all the work and excitement with relish. Humphrey found her genuinely useful, which Bruce French believes was because she was totally honest and direct with him, a rare commodity in his usual entourage.[11] Not only could she give him more of a European view of the United States, but she also acted as a sounding board for his appeals to young Americans - who on the whole were not wildly enthusiastic about Lyndon Johnson's Vice President. Humphrey would phone her up at Anderson Hall to seek her opinion, or to ask her to do something for him. Unsurprisingly, this brought her a certain celebrity status amongst her fellow students.[12]

Once he had won the nomination, Humphrey's presidential campaign started in earnest in the autumn of 1968. For the average American, indeed for any observer, this election was possibly one of the most tedious in America's history. Richard Nixon and his running-mate Spiro Agnew were anxious to play safe, so they avoided public debate as much as possible. This made it difficult for Hubert Humphrey to disassociate himself from Lyndon Johnson's policy in Vietnam. The result was a narrow win for Nixon.

For Petra this was a disaster. As any electoral campaigner knows, no one ever campaigns to lose. However long the odds, the central effort is to win, and a belief that this is possible is the only possible fuel. She gave herself to the campaign, body and soul, working as a volunteer in the Washington campaign offices every minute she could spare from her studies. She would even make a point of meeting Humphrey at the airport to put letters in his hand rather than send them by post. The excitement, the tight bonds that develop between people working for a special cause and the heady closeness to power politics sustained Petra's energy despite the tiredness.

In November, for the night of the election itself, Petra was one of the student volunteers invited to join the candidate at his headquarters in the Leamington Hotel, Minneapolis. So convinced was she that Humphrey would win that she took along her application form for American citizenship to obtain a nomination from the new

President. 'But now I won't do it,' she told Humphrey when he passed her after the results. 'You have to have cheer,' he responded. Petra took her pain and disappointment for a walk in the dark cold night of Minneapolis before rejoining the dwindling group of dispirited supporters in the hotel lobby. She waited for two hours for the lift to bring Humphrey back down from his lair on the 14th floor. When he eventually came, she pushed through the crowd and told him: 'I am going to make my citizenship.' 'Now that's good,' he replied, 'thank you darling. I'll see you back in Washington.'[13]

This fruitless campaign taught Petra a lot about the art of political campaigning; the massive organization needed, the sometimes ruthless exploitation of people's energy, time and goodwill; there was no room for passengers. It taught her about the drudgery, the grind and the minutiæ which dominate politics; it taught her that the sparkling moments are few and far between and even then very hard-earned. She learnt about herself. She had stretched herself mentally and physically to the limits, and survived. She had experienced the ecstasy of expectation as she mounted the airplane to Minneapolis, and looked into the well of misery when the results were known. She had given herself to a cause completely. When the cause was lost, she had managed to pick herself up and carry on.

WASHINGTON RIOTS, THE POPE, AND PRAGUE IN SUMMER

Humphrey's attempt at the presidency was part of a milestone year in Petra's life. As if the experience of the campaign and the murder of Robert Kennedy were not sufficient, three other dramatic events punctuated that year: the assassination of Martin Luther King and the campus riots which followed; an audience, along with Gracie, with Pope Paul VI; and a summer holiday in Prague with Omi - at the very moment the Soviet tanks rolled in to crush the brief flowering of reform (the Prague Spring) in Czechoslovakia.

On 4th April, shortly before the assassination of Robert Kennedy, the Revd Martin Luther King was killed in Memphis, Tennessee. Washington burned as the black suburbs erupted into the city centre that night. Fearing for her safety, Petra went to stay with Walt and Elizabeth Rostow. Rostow was special security advisor to president

Johnson, and his wife had befriended Petra. The house being full, a spare bed was made up for Petra in the library. During the night the president called Rostow from the White House on a direct line which rang in the library and Petra listened as the two men discussed new bombing targets in Vietnam. Coolly, clinically, they made decisions which would affect thousands of lives, yet at no time did either of them acknowledge this. There was no hesitation, no agonizing over the number of lives which would be lost. Earlier in the evening, with equal dispassion, Rostow had discussed the war with his guests over a chicken dinner. Petra never forgot that night.

Nor did she forget the killing of Martin Luther King. Yet another of her political heroes was dead. Petra had been introduced to the theories of non-violent disobedience and the power this could give to otherwise powerless individuals through a writer on Professor Abdul Said's reading list - Henry David Thoreau, in particular through *On the Duty of Civil Disobedience*. For Petra, King was 'Thoreau in practice' and she was also deeply impressed by the way King acknowledged Gandhi, as well as Thoreau and Christianity, to be the inspirational forces which guided him. Physical force, King said, should be confronted by 'an even stronger force, namely, soul force'. To the Black Power Movement, impatient at the speed of change, he said: 'In advocating violence it is imitating the worst, the most brutal, and the most uncivilized value of American life. . . There is no salvation for the Negro through isolation.'[14]

The violent demonstrations which followed the death of King shocked Petra. How could the death of the man who had incarnated non-violence inspire, not an emulation, but a rejection of his tactics? And when the students in America began to emulate their *confreres* in Germany and France and take their campus grievances onto the streets, she observed but did not participate. How was it that, of all sections of society, students should fail to come up with more imaginative ways of making their protest felt than hurling bricks and stones? Bruce French does not recall Petra participating in any of the demonstrations: 'She absorbed and synthesized what was going on, but she was a not an activist in the strict sense of the term.'

With his usual sense of humour, Dr Mott recalls the campus unrest which followed the killing of King as it melded into rage against the Vietnam war and dissatisfaction at the narrowness of university life:

*The place was boiling. The campus was loaded with rhetoric. Daily,
professors were standing on soap boxes unloading all their grievances
and the kids were boiling with fury. One day our revolutionaries were
carrying baskets of rocks, they were going to radicalize the front row of
protesters outside on Ward Circle [the crossroads outside American
University]. They were throwing the rocks over the heads of these
innocents at the visored police. The police moved in; the chaplains were
removing the baskets of rocks; the rabbis were running around helping
them - it was a kind of interfaith activity - and then, suddenly, the tear
gas - on campus. And then in the middle of it all, a man in a laboratory
coat ran out screaming. They had just destroyed his three-year study on
obesity by releasing all his rats!*[15]

These incidents are memorable for their tragi-comedy, but it was in
this context that Petra Kelly came to political adulthood, and the
violence had a great impact on her. To understand Petra, Mott insists,
means understanding her 'absolute rectitude about non-violent
protest. . . She insisted on it, and had a steely capacity to stick with it
which was thoroughly admirable. Martin Luther King really was her
fundamental model.'

That summer, Petra sent Dr Mott two postcards from Europe. In
the first she recounted Gracie's meeting with the Pope. At Grace's
request, Petra had written to Pope Paul VI in May, requesting an
audience for the suffering child and her family. The Vatican
responded with a letter from the office for papal audiences, reserving
five seats for the Kellys on 19th June. Printed on the envelope was the
advice that all should wear black, except children under the age of
twelve who should wear white. The family (minus Omi) made the
long journey from Würzburg to Rome by car, and Grace held Petra's
hand tightly as she moved forward to receive the benediction. 'Our
meeting with the Pope was most precious and meaningful,' Petra told
a local newspaper in Virginia a few weeks later.[16] To Dr Mott she
wrote: 'The Pope spoke with us, blessed us, and put his hand upon
the surgical side of Gracie's [head] and said "I shall pray for you". He
was with us too long - I still can't understand it all.'

The second postcard was dated 21st August but posted in Germany
a week later. It read:

Arrived in my 'golden city' yesterday afternoon and was proud of its progress and peoples. Last night I danced with proud and happy Czech peoples - this morning I am terrified. My idealism has dwindled to 0. Russian tanks now pass my window, people cry silent tears. The freedom they now slowly had gained is drowned out by tanks, planes and shooting. I don't know when I'm able to leave. Now I'm in my hotel - waiting. No food is available. TV, Radio + phone stations have all been taken over, the armies were flown in secretly last night w/out Czech knowing. Will mail this at the border - if . . . Petra.

Written at the top of the card is a postscript which reads: 'I am sooo unhappy - why must might always try to prove right. Oh GOD - all these people crying.'

Petra and her grandmother, intending to holiday in Czechoslovakia, had found themselves embroiled in the Soviet suppression of the Prague Spring. For five days they were under house arrest in their hotel near Wenceslas Square, and Petra witnessed not only the tanks crunching down the narrow streets, but many incidents of resistance: an old woman daring a tank to run her down; boys who removed or moved street signs; Czech soldiers drinking openly to Dubcek; a woman trampling on a soldier's dropped hat. In April 1990, she recalled her feelings in a speech at Bradford School of Peace Studies:

What I saw in those five days in 1968 was the beginning of social or non-violent defence . . . Czechoslovakia and its leaders remained steadfast in passive resistance, storing up the kind of positive patriotism through sacrifice and suffering which the country had had never before and will profit from greatly in the future - as we have witnessed those special days this past November and December [1989] in Prague.[17]

Petra and Omi were among the first tourists to leave Czechoslovakia, after a slow and arduous journey over bumpy forest roads in a bus which was frequently stopped and searched by Russian soldiers. As soon as she got back to university, Petra began to write and speak about her experiences. In a paper she wrote in January 1969 she reviewed an entire century of Soviet foreign policy through the prism of her personal encounter with it.[18]

And so a pattern had begun to emerge, in which Petra would make the directest of connections between her personal experiences and her public politics, and vice versa. Despite her post election anguish in the Leamington Hotel, Minneapolis, she gave an interview to the press about it the same day. The public experience of the death of Martin Luther King and the private experiences of Rostow's cold calculation over his chicken dinner both, in different ways, shaped her personal creed. While she disapproved of the violence of the student rioting she had seen, she wondered in an address made the following year if 'this unrest and cacophony' was the coming of a new age.[19] And despite her fear (and she was *very* frightened) during her experience in Prague, she turned it into a subject for seminars and dissertations. The dividing line between the personal and the political was beginning to dissolve.

When Petra enrolled at AU in 1966, she had found herself among a fair number of foreign students who, while they derived some advantages from their foreignness (such as invitations to meet visiting foreign poets and Robert Kennedy), nonetheless experienced difficulties in being non-American. No representation on the student union board, for example, and no public scholarships. The first problem she dealt with by getting elected as secretary to the union board. Once there she collaborated with the president Bruce French to democratize the whole system of student representation and transform the board into a directly-elected senate. The second, she had resolved in her own case by seeking help from Robert Kennedy, then for others by setting up the Robert F. Kennedy Foreign Student Scholarship in 1969. The proceeds of International Week would be given to the AU's foreign student advisor to create a fund from which an annual scholarship could be awarded. 'This will go to students in the same fix I was, 'she told the *Washington Post*. 'I went through it and I don't want anybody else to have to.'[20]

Having enjoyed the advantages and sorted out some of the disadvantages of being a foreign student, Petra then noticed that there was a rich resource which wasn't being tapped. American University did have good relationships with many parts of the government administration, and outings were made to other Washington institutions like the World Bank, but here, on the doorstep of AU was a vast amount of knowledge about the rest of the world which was not being exploited. Not only were there all the embassies just down the road, but inside the university itself were large number of students from all corners of the world. A lot of information in the mouths of a lot of horses which were never herded together so they could talk to each other. How much better it would be, thought Petra, to learn about other countries and their cultures 'live' instead of only reading about them in books. Bringing people together to good effect was to prove to be one of Petra's talents.

So with the munificent budget of US$250 Petra organized her first International Week in 1967. She did it largely by herself but managed to rope in a few organizations in and outside the university on the way. A photocopied one-page programme announced the theme of the first Week to be 'Toward World Understanding' and besides films, an international buffet and a foreign student song and dance festival, Petra organized talks from the Ambassador of Kuwait, the Chief of Protocol from the White House James Symington (widely regarded as a real coup), and the Acting Secretary of Commerce, Alexander Trowbridge. Vice President Hubert Humphrey telegrammed his apologies. Despite her efforts, the week was a limited success. As Petra herself wrote in a brisk critique: 'Participation and talent in the fashion show was limited; so were the audiences for the [three visiting speakers].'

The events of spring 1968 meant that it was November of that year before she gathered together interested people in order to start planning another event for the following March, but Petra moved straight from her disappointment over Humphrey's failure in the presidential elections to preparing a second International Week.

This time she had a committee, but she was still the driving force behind it. 'I don't think she slept more than four hours a night for weeks,' recalls Eddie Feinburg. Petra seemed to involve half Washington. The programme was expanded and made more varied. As well as the usual formal talks, it included everything from a film about Yeats (who, along with Yevtushenko, was another of Petra's favourite poets) to international student-faculty soccer games. Five hundred colleges in the area were notified and embassies and businesses were contacted. Many contributed in some way, with even the Russian Embassy being persuaded to donate some caviar, which it sent along with a big map publicizing the New York to Moscow flight route. In remembrance of 21st August 1968 Petra drew another route on the map, between Prague and New York. When the Russians saw the second line they washed it off as best they could; but kept the caviar coming.

Three hundred and fifty people turned up to the international buffet at $2 a head, and Petra found herself the subject of a full-page profile in the *Washington Post*.[21] The key to her triumphant International Week, it said, was Petra's indefatigable letter-writing. She wrote to everyone. Not simple formal letters either, but long ones, the sort that impose the obligation of a reply on the recipient. She was, everyone agreed, a brilliant communicator.

VOTE FOR A STRONG WOMAN

The Hubert Humphrey presidential campaign was not, strictly speaking, Petra Kelly's first election campaign. In the middle of a turbulent April in 1968 she stood for election to the student senate of AU. In her election address she said she would not be a 'Friday Senator' and promised to make her role in the Senate, if elected, a 'daily task of communication' and putting 'realistic' ideas into action.[22] Demonstrating the pragmatism of a seasoned political campaigner, Petra cited her creation and organization of International Week, and her success in obtaining voting rights for foreign students on the student union board as evidence of her abilities. She proposed a nationwide university conference on social problems and the liberalizing of present drinking and curfew regulations as evidence of her future plans. Her campaign, run under the slogan of 'Vote for a strong woman' included posing for photographs with a motorbike. She was elected overwhelmingly and remained on the senate for the rest of her stay at American University.

From her teens onwards, Petra had been attracted to the writing of extraordinary women. Not necessarily overtly feminist women, but women who had either done something out of the ordinary or had had something special happen to them. Often there was tragedy in their stories. One of her earliest and most enduring favourites was Anne Morrow Lindbergh. She was the wife of Charles Lindbergh, the dashing aviator who became the first to fly the Atlantic non-stop between New York and Paris in 1927. The tragedy in her life was the much publicized kidnapping and murder of their first child.

Lindbergh wrote a hugely popular book in 1955 called *Gift from the*

Sea. Based on her own feelings and experiences, it examined the different phases of a marriage, comparing each to a shell found on her favourite beach. Petra particularly appreciated Lindbergh's attitudes to love:

> *We all wish to be loved alone. 'Don't sit under the apple-tree with anyone else but me,' runs the old popular song. Perhaps, as Auden says in his poem, 'this is a fundamental error in mankind.'*
>
> *For the error bred in the bone*
> *Of each woman and each man*
> *Craves what it cannot have,*
> *Not universal love*
> *But to be loved alone.*
>
> *Is it such a sin? In discussing this verse with an Indian philosopher, I had an illuminating answer. 'It is all right to wish to be loved alone' he said; 'mutuality is the essence of love. There cannot be others in mutuality. It is only in the time-sense that it is wrong. It is when we desire continuity of being loved alone that we go wrong. For not only do we insist on believing romantically in the "one-and-only" . . . we wish the "one-and-only" to be permanent, ever-present and continuous. For there is no "one-and-only". . . there are just one-and-only moments.'* [23]

Writing to Dr Mott at the beginning of one of her first, most anguished love affairs a few years later, Petra was to reshape the last line ('I have discovered there are not one and only persons . . . but one and only moments - makes life worth living and loving!'). She remained an incurable romantic in her dealings with men, easily bowled over by the most conventional and transparent masculine overtures, but always quite genuine in her search for the essence of love. It was the problem of continuity she was never able to resolve.

Petra was rather more successful in her friendships with women. She remained in touch with her childhood penfriend Karin Amirany, and AU friends Susan French and Amy Isaacs all her life, and friends of later years, like Erika Heinz and Christiane Gollwitzer, were devoted to her. Through her international work, Petra also made many longlasting working and personal relationships with women. It was always easier to work with women, she would say, and she used the network she built up when she needed trustworthy information quickly. Petra was generous in her friendship too: she never forgot birthdays; enjoyed offering gifts out of the blue; would organize a party (or buy a cake) at the slightest excuse; and her regular letters and postcards confirmed to even her most widely-scattered friends that they were often in her thoughts. Susan French remembers bringing her children to visit Petra in Europe: 'On each occasion Petra had organized the whole trip; she knew all the places children love to go. She was a wonderful friend.'

Not all Petra's female role models were as equally concerned with the essence of love as was Anne Morrow Lindbergh. In 1986 Petra wrote that her teenage fascination with strong women was born of anger:

> *about the way in which women had been obliterated in the pages of history or in the pages of the Bible or other religious documents. Most women were subordinated, always dependent upon men for their own realization and value, always needing to seek men as their only path to fulfilment. I became enraged at this and began reading Rosa Luxemburg's writing, particularly her diaries in prison. I began searching through biographies of Aleksandra Kollontai, George Sand, Emma Goldman, and Helen Keller and other women who have put a very special stamp on history, yet have been up to now ignored by male historians and male scholars. I set out to rediscover these brave women. I never had much respect for the Karl Marxes and Friedrich Engelses and all those other dogmatic macho men, theorizing and philosophizing about the working classes and capital and yet at the same time discriminating against their wives and children and leading the lives of 'academic pashas', and always being rejuvenated by their wives and mistresses! They could not cook or clean or sew or take care of themselves. They always needed women for their most basic needs.*[24]

On the door of her office in the German parliament Petra kept a big picture of one of the women who inspired her most - the Polish Marxist revolutionary Rosa Luxemburg (killed in 1919 at the age of forty-eight). Immediately below was a poster of Martin Luther King. Among the books beside Petra's bed when she died were an auto-biography of Aleksandra Kollontai, Lenin's education minister; the diary of Franziska Gräfin zu Reventlow (1895-1910), an orientalist; a book by Yelena Bonner, the widow of Andrei Sakharov; and the letters and travel-writing of Alexandra David Néel, a Tibetan scholar. None had any inscription, so they were probably all bought by Petra herself. With these books by women were two other books, both by men and both given to her by men. One, by the Chilean writer Pablo Neruda was dedicated affectionately to Petra in 1972 by Sicco Mansholt, the European Commissioner with whom she had a passionate affair, and the other was Willy Brandt's autobiography, which Gert Bastian had given her on her forty-second birthday.

'. . . IF THERE WHEN GRACE DANCES, I SHOULD DANCE' (W. H. AUDEN)

When Petra went to Germany to join her family for Christmas in 1969, she found Gracie's condition considerably worsened. She wrote to Hubert Humphrey:

> *Radiation has brought about considerable skin damage and though this will heal, the suffering becomes greater. More malignant swellings have set in - some in critical areas preventing air to reach the nasal passage [sic]. The sarcoma cancer has always been successfully burned and dried out by radiation, yet the complications that have set in through swellings, breathing difficulties and much loss of weight, have complicated all.[25]*

During the holiday the family took a trip to Berchtesgaden, where Hitler had had his rural retreat. 'I wish I could record all my emotions when I am here,' Petra wrote on a postcard to Dr Mott. 'It is sooo beautiful and peaceful in these mountains. Am most happy to be with my sister. Will need a long talk w/you - always - PETRA.' By now the ten-year-old Grace weighed only 41 pounds and her resistance to colds and flu had been reduced by the repeated radiation treatments. She was suffering from flu during the holiday. Nine days before Grace died Petra wrote:

> *We have never given up hope because of the faith Gracie has always provided for us with her eternal willpower and love for life. She dries*

*our tears – and comforts us and when she creates, as through her very
sensitive and beautiful poems or artwork that amazes many, she displays
how bravely and with how much love and self-understanding she accepts
her suffering and such handicap as the loss of her right eye three years
ago. It is so inexplicable how a child never is angry at life – but accepts
all with an inner faith and sense of love unknown to adults.*[26]

After the holidays Petra did not want to return to Washington but, as
her close friend Amy Isaacs (now national director of Americans for
Democratic Action) recalls, her family insisted. Isaacs had been in the
same German class as Petra at AU and they had developed a
friendship based, says Isaacs, 'more on family and shopping than
politics'. When Omi came to Washington to visit Petra, she would
stay on the sofabed at Amy's flat – a convenient two blocks from the
university. In 1968, when the Kelly family returned to Würzburg with
Gracie, Isaacs graduated and went to Germany to continue her
studies. She became a frequent visitor to the base, even when Petra
was not home for the holidays, so she got to know the family well.
'Whether there was any jealousy before the tumour or not, I can't say,
but afterwards there was no sign of it. It eradicated all sorts of sibling
feelings to have that sort of crisis. These were adorable children, and
Petra clearly adored them.'

On 17th February 1970, Grace Patricia Kelly died in her mother's
arms, and Eddie Feinburg drove an intensely grieving Petra to New
York so she could return to Germany. He had been supposed to spend
Christmas with her and her family, but at the last minute it had been
felt that Gracie was too ill. 'I was impressed by her conviction that
God had called Gracie to heaven. I have actually never met anyone as
ritualistically religious as she was.' When Petra returned to AU to go
through, as she put it, 'the mechanics' of completing her work in
order to graduate in May, Feinburg remembers she went to Mass a
great deal. 'She could not be bothered with earthly considerations.'

Grace's death, and her courage in the final years, touched Petra
profoundly. Part of the reason may well have been compensation for
early bouts of jealousy, but this is not an adequate explanation for
Petra's conviction that her sister Grace 'always pushed me in the right
direction - during her life, and also since her departure from this
world'. Much later, Petra was to write:

There is a strange, whole, and wholly mysterious interconnectedness between me and my sister in the other sphere of existence; I have felt completely attuned and committed and connected to her during my past life and feel this even more so now. I feel intuitively there is proof of life after death. . . . When times are rough and my soul and body are tired from all the battling and struggling for green politics and all the trouble from the triple lives I must lead, at such time I always feel rejuvenated and strengthened by my sister Grace. I know she is watching me, guiding me somewhere all around me from transcendent spheres.[27]

That was written in 1986, at a time when Petra was feeling pretty low and disillusioned with green politics, but it probably reflects quite well her state of mind when Grace died. Petra's mother and stepfather were understandably immersed in their own misery at the time, and admit that they were not fully aware of the depth of Petra's pain. In addition, despite the intensification of her religious rituals during the agony of Grace, it seems that Petra was already losing her faith in catholicism.

However much Petra tried to grow a worldly carapace in order to protect herself from the knocks of life she never succeeded. Petra's emotions were like a flayed skin, instantly over-responsive to stimuli. Kindness and friendship acted as an instant balm and were received with warmth and pleasure. People meeting Petra for the first time, even at the height of her fame, were struck by the natural and genuine warmth with which she greeted them. The down side of this sensitivity was that even small hurts and slights caused pain, and sometimes (especially if she was tired) they would prompt a reaction which seemed exaggerated. This was baffling to those who did not know her very well. Petra could cause offence as easily as she could be offended.

For the hyper-sensitive and anxious Petra the whole of the 1960s had been very difficult. She had achieved a lot, but she had also suffered a lot, so it was not surprising that the death of Grace put her on the deck for a while. But Petra had already learnt that to grit her teeth and carry on could reduce the pain. When she returned to Washington to complete her studies this time she was not alone - Gracie was with her. In his letter of recommendation for Petra's applications to postgraduate schools, Dr Mott wrote that Petra had been crushed by the death of her younger sister. 'Before she had ambience, now she has maturity from this terrible loss.' What Dr Mott meant was that the spirit of Grace had provided Petra, if not with a carapace, then at least a cloak to protect her from some of the harder knocks of life.

Petra graduated BA cum laude in International Relations (West/East European Studies) in May 1970. She was also awarded the Alan M. Bronner Memorial Award for 1969–70, and the Bruce Hughes Award for intellectual maturity. Shortly before Grace died, Petra also learnt she had been awarded a coveted Woodrow Wilson fellowship after a final interview at Princeton, the only student from AU to do so that year. This scholarship was worth US$10,000 and a very welcome boost to her funds as she prepared to return to Europe. Initially Petra had considered postgraduate colleges in Bruges (no scholarship) and the Johns Hopkins University in Bologna (a scholarship but too far from Würzburg). Finally she decided to go to the Europa Institute in Amsterdam to study European Integration, after obtaining a supplementary scholarship from the Netherlands University Foundation for International Cooperation.

As she crossed the Atlantic to settle once again in Europe, her mother, stepfather and brother Johnny, now aged ten, were moving in the opposite direction. John Kelly had had his orders to Vietnam postponed on several occasions on compassionate grounds, with both his superior in Frankfurt and Petra in Washington lobbying the Pentagon on his behalf. 'With both of them rooting for me, how could I fail?' he recalls with a smile. But by 1970 his term of service was up. Aged forty-five, John Kelly decided to take up the chance to return to civilian life, and eventually took a job as an administrator in Riverside Hospital in Newport News, near to Hampton. Petra would never again be domiciled in the same continent as her parents.

Notes

1   Chapters and Articles: in Steffen (1980).
2   Dr Albert Mott, Introduction to Petra Kelly speech at School of International Service Alumni Dinner, (19 November 1990).
3   *Daily Press*, Newport News VA (25 June 1967).
4   *Washington Post* (30 March 1969).
5   Letters of recommendation from Professor Said, Dr Mott, Hubert H.

  Humphrey, Prof Trowbridge (UNA of the USA), (March/April 1970).
6 Thomas Merton, *Conjectures of a Guilty Bystander*, (Doubleday Press, Garden City NY, 1966).
7 Oswald Spengler was a controversial German philosopher. During the First World War he wrote *The Decline of the West*. In some notes made for her famous paper on him, Petra had written that this book had a powerful influence on the 'process of intellectual softening up by which Hitler profited'.
8 Blum *et al.* (eds) (1968) p. 819.
9 *Washington Post* (30 March 1969).
10 *The Eagle* (5 April 1968).
11 'Men at the top listen to Petra Kelly', *Stars and Stripes* (14 May 1968).
12 'HHH phones girl in dorm; Students join VP on TV', *The Eagle* (22 October 1968).
13 *Minneapolis Tribune* (7 November 1968).
14 Blum *et al.* (eds) (1968) p. 832.
15 Dr Albert Mott, Introduction to Petra Kelly speech at School of International Service Alumni Dinner (19 November 1990).
16 'Pope grants wish', *The Stars and Stripes* (2 August 1968).
17 Speech: Bradford (4 April 1990).
18 Essay: (January 1969).
19 Speech: Washington DC (1 November 1969).
20 *Washington Post* (30 March 1969).
21 *Washington Post* (30 March 1969).
22 *The Eagle* (23 April 1968).
23 Lindbergh (1992) p. 64.
24 Chapters and Articles: in Berman (ed.) (1985) p. 115.
25 Letter to Hubert Humphrey (8 February 1970).
26 Letter to Hubert Humphrey (8 February 1970).
27 Chapters and Articles: in Berman (ed.) (1985) p. 114.

4

AUTUMN 1970
-TO-
JANUARY 1980

EIN KLEINES ROTES HAUS IN THE
EASTERN SUBURBS

While it may be tempting to see the hand of destiny drawing a straight line between Petra's university years and green politics – a sort of foreordained trajectory between Hubert Humphrey and the Bundestag – chance was as much at work as fate during the twelve years she spent in Amsterdam and then at the European Commission in Brussels. Certainly, Petra herself did not feel any sense of destiny when she arrived back in Europe. She was still grieving deeply for Grace as she settled into Amsterdam for her postgraduate year, and when she went on from there to take up an apprenticeship in the European Community (EC) in Brussels it was simply because this was a normal progression for someone with her qualifications.

There are few papers in Petra's metal trunks from the time she spent in Amsterdam, and even fewer friends with memories of her time there, but she was certainly busy. To start off, it had been difficult to find somewhere to live. Not only were flats near the city centre and the Institute where she was studying expensive, but she also met with a hurtful reluctance on the part of local people to rent their property to a German. For many Dutch people the memories of the war were still too fresh to see any difference between the young woman on their doorstep and the sins of her nation. Eventually she

found a flat, one room with toilet, shower and sink, on the ground
floor of a tiny red-painted house at 37 Hogenweg, but it was stuck out
in the eastern suburbs of Amsterdam, a long tramride from the
Europa Institute.

Between September 1970 and the May of the following year Petra
followed courses and took exams in every aspect of European
integration, ranging from the EC decision-making process to a review
of non-Community organizations. She also began a research project
entitled 'The development and influence of private European
organizations which have promoted European integration and unity'.
Somewhat prophetically in the light of recent events in the EC, she
quoted from Machiavelli's *The Discourses* on the front page of the
outline she prepared:

> *Therefore, as the organization of anything cannot be made by many,
> because the divergence of their opinions hinders them from agreeing as
> to what is best, yet once they do understand it, they will not readily agree
> to abandon it.*[1]

On 13th May 1971, Petra was awarded a Diploma in European
Integration by the Europa Institute of the University of Amsterdam,
and given a letter which pointed out that this diploma was equivalent
to an American Masters Degree. In many ways the Amsterdam year
was a year of transition for Petra – between her student and her adult
years. She was twenty-three and living alone for the first time, and
after a while, she began to enjoy it. With the addition of plenty of
books, a huge yellow beanbag and a bunch of dried edelweiss in a
frame, her flat began to feel like a home, and (despite the initial
rebuffs when she was flat-hunting) she loved Amsterdam. The small
friendly streets were in great contrast to the heroic marble
architecture of administrative Washington. Even her favourite
Washington neighbourhood of Georgetown, with its old, prettily-
painted wooden and brick buildings, could not match the rich
atmosphere which centuries of human history and culture had
produced in Amsterdam.

The city of Rembrandt was also a great inspiration to the artist in
Petra. She had become a keen painter, though her output of vivid 'oil-
photo montages' as she called them perhaps did not owe much to the

old Dutch masters. She described her new technique to Dr Mott: 'children with balloons painted onto raving yellow and then Brandt kneeling at the Warsaw ghetto with Hitler taking a child into the gardens . . . [a] combination of my painting and a photo from an archive that speaks many words'. Petra had started to paint while still in Washington and had even taken some classes in figurative painting. This had led to a memorable evening when Professor Said was entertaining some students to dinner at his home and Petra had turned up with her latest painting as a gift. It was a large female nude. In the strictly non-*avante garde* surroundings, accompanied by his wife and children, Eddie Feinburg remembers Professor Said gave a rare demonstration of discomfiture: 'Oh, I thought you might do fruit.' Fruit, of course, did not feature strongly in Petra's repertoire, and she soon abandoned figurative painting altogether to deploy the full palette of colours and unstructured forms as a way of pouring out her feelings.

One of the messages the canvases clearly sent was her mourning for Gracie. As often as she could Petra took the train to Omi in Nürnburg so they could visit the Würzburg cemetery where Grace was buried. Petra had made a pledge to her mother to keep a place for Gracie in her home, wherever that might be, and in the tiny red house in Amsterdam Petra began a collection of relics. Adam Stolpen, her close friend from American University, visited Petra frequently in Amsterdam and recalls the photos she carried with her and kept about her. In his second year of law school, Stolpen was on study-leave in France so he often went to Amsterdam for the weekend, or joined Petra for a trip to Omi in Nürnburg. Once, on the way back to Amsterdam from Omi's, Adam decided to stay on in Amsterdam for a few weeks. He established himself in a hotel near to Hogenweg, and he and Petra ate together once, if not twice, every day. She was interested in the bookshops and music, and he was keen on the art galleries and antiques. Together they explored every corner of Amsterdam and much of the surrounding countryside, and went to parties with fellow students. No politics, remembers Stolpen, just study and pleasure.

Adam Stolpen tells a tale, dismissed by others as fantasy, but which he insists is true. One day, while visiting the Keukenhog Gardens near Haarlem, he took a photograph of Petra standing on a slight hill

beside a little girl in a red coat. When he approached Petra the girl
had disappeared and Petra denied seeing her. However, the developed
picture showed the little girl and Petra was convinced it was Gracie.
After this, says Adam, she became calmer about Gracie's death.

Although the whereabouts of the picture are no longer known, the
incident was certainly part and parcel of Petra's separation from the
Catholic Church which had once been so central to her life. Petra's
first indication that the Church might be fallible had come on the day
of her first communion in Günzburg. Because her mother was
divorced, she had not been allowed to participate. The limits to the
compassion of the Church were thus revealed to the devout little girl
in a way which was quite incomprehensible. Why should Petra and
her mother be punished because her father had left? It simply did not
make sense in the light of the Church's teachings on forgiveness and
compassion.

In Günzburg, Petra had been immersed in a Catholic tradition. Her
school was a convent school, her family and many of the families
around them were practising and believing Catholics. However, like
many Catholic children in those days, Petra learnt her religion
through the Catechism, not the Bible. It was as if the Bible was
considered to be too difficult or too subversive a book to be given to
young impressionable minds, so the Church had to interpret it for
them – at least until the young souls were firmly signed up. Petra did
not see a Bible until she moved to America. Paradoxically, it was in
the non-denominational schools of Georgia and Virginia where she
first had a chance to analyse and question her faith. In 1968, she
recalled how she felt at that time:

> Since I no longer had the security of Catholic teachings and was
> detached from a Catholic environment . . . Conflicts and contradictions
> were discovered and I saw life on this earth as, perhaps, a brief period of
> light between two unknowns. The past is still unclear, despite the skulls
> and spines that have been found, and the future seems meaningless as
> well, when one thinks that one finger pushing a button can trigger a
> world back to a cooled-off globe of stone, air, water, and carbon
> compounds. I asked then: what does it mean that all exists and grows?

When she was at university, Petra wrote excitedly and approvingly of the pronunciations of Vatican II, and the call for the faithful to:

> *live in very close union with the men of their time. . . . Let them blend*
> *modern science and its theories and the understanding of the most recent*
> *discoveries with Christian morality and doctrine. Thus their religious*
> *practice and morality can keep pace with their scientific knowledge and*
> *with an ever-advancing technology.*

She went through what she called a 'phase of confusion, of existen-
tialism, asking along with Sartre and Camus why the past, present,
and the future are made up of pain and anxiety and love and joy and
why a seemingly meaningless death can cast a shadow over all of it'.
She placed a lot of hope in the 'great and magnificent reawakening' of
the Catholic Church promised by Vatican II, and returned more
intimately to her own catholicism, by 'looking at it from many critical
viewpoints'.[2]

But it was always clear that however progressive the announcements
from Rome might be, the Church itself, as Petra was fond of pointing
out, was in much the same situation as the Communist Party of the
USSR; it was a huge, massively bureaucratic institution, incapable of
change in anything but glacial timescales: 'The Church is still
surrounded by the medieval mist. Paul VI in his fourth-floor
apartment has had to calculate the effect of his every word and
gesture on the group of those 2,300 Bishops in the basilica below.'
Later, her insights into the theological and organizational dilemmas
of the Catholic Church would greatly colour her opinion of the
European Community institutions.

Petra became interested in the teachings of the liberation
theologists while she was still at American University. They had
interpreted Pope Paul VI's 1967 encyclical *Populorum progressio* as a
signal that they could speak freely, and were even challenging the
Church's continued hard line on birth control. 'It does no good,'
Petra quoted one of them as saying, 'to make criminals and sinners of
those who cannot for social and personal reasons achieve the ideal.'[3]
She herself agreed with the part of the Old Testament which warned
people that as long as there was 'a beggar at their gate who is not
cared for', the act of worship was a waste of time.[4]

At the time of Grace's death, Petra did seem to worship with increased intensity, but her spiritual comfort came more from the ritual of devotion than from the creed of the Church. At a time when what she needed most of all was an affirmation that life was sacred and worth living, she found Roman Catholic teachings to be more about a denial of the world than an affirmation of it. The more ardently she tried to find hope for herself and for all people on earth in her religion, the more it escaped her.

Whether the incident with Adam and the girl in red was true or not, it symbolized the time when Petra shifted her focus of inspiration from the passion and pain of the Virgin Mary and her Son, to the passion and pain of her halfsister Grace. (Petra did not formally leave the Catholic Church until 1980, writing a characteristically detailed letter to the Pope explaining why.) On the first anniversary of Grace's death Petra visited Würzburg. That same year, through an organization called SOS Kinderdorf, she started to sponsor an orphaned Tibetan girl living in a refugee centre in north India. Life had become worth living again, its positive purpose was restored, and nine-year-old Nima Chonzom was the evidence.

Despite her disappointment with the Catholic Church, Petra never lost interest in questions of faith. She actively sought out radical theologians of all kinds, such as Pastor Jörg Zink, the priest who would bury her, and the theologian Helmut Gollwitzer (another Bavarian whose niece Christiane became one of Petra's friends). Petra was attracted to Gollwitzer through his bestselling book *Unwilling Journey*, which told the story of his years in prison in Stalin's Soviet Union, and the struggle he had as a socialist Christian in coming to terms with what was happening there. Arrested in the last month of the Second World War, Gollwitzer had established a formidable reputation as an anti-Nazi preacher and activist. Later, working in Berlin during the turbulent late-1960s, Gollwitzer also proved a solid ally of the protesting students, taking into his home the badly-wounded radical student leader Rudi Dutschke.

Whenever she could, and especially in the regular letters she wrote to the Pope, Petra would extol the virtues of religious leaders who openly dissented from the official Church position on issues of peace and justice. One of her favourites was Raymond Hunthausen, Bishop of Seattle, who in the early 1980s began to withhold some of his income tax in protest against nuclear arms build up. The brothers

Philip and Daniel Berrigan (a former monk and a Jesuit priest respectively) also rated highly on Petra's list. In 1968, in protest against the Vietnam war, they broke into a US Draft Office, singing hymns and reciting psalms while they poured their own blood, and napalm, over 400 sets of draft papers. Petra appreciated their meticulously prepared and ritualistic actions very much.

Petra thought hard about her faltering Catholic faith during her year in Amsterdam, and, as she came to terms with the death of Grace, she also began to rediscover her zest for life. According to Adam Stolpen, who was never amorously engaged with Petra but to whom she would frequently confide her romantic adventures, it was in Amsterdam that Petra had her first significant love affair. He was a lecturer at the Institute, aged forty-five and married. Stolpen remembers it being a gentle and romantic relationship carried out most furtively for fear that the lecturer's wife would find out. How it ended is not known. Petra certainly did not talk about her first lover as openly she did of her later ones. At American University Petra enjoyed a reputation for not being interested in romantic attachments. She liked parties, and was great fun to have around, but had no serious relationship.

Petra's youthful timidity with men was partly rooted in her upbringing. She found the 'free sex' environment of the 1960s unattractive, but not just because she was a good Catholic girl. It was also because she could not imagine a sexually intimate relationship with anyone with whom she had no wider and deeper affinity.

Around the time of this first love affair in Amsterdam, one of Petra's all-time favourite books: *Jonathan Livingston Seagull* was published. Many protagonists of the 1960s student movement – whether they had searched for the truth through drugs or political engagement – liked to see themselves in Jonathan, the seagull quite unlike the rest. Jonathan's aim was to fly faster than any gull had ever flown before.

> *He was alive, trembling ever so slightly with delight, proud that his fear was under control. Then without ceremony he hugged in his forewings, extended his short, angled wing-tips, and plunged directly towards the sea. . . . He was flying now straight down, at two hundred fourteen miles per hour. He swallowed, knowing that if his wings unfolded at that speed he'd be blown into a million tiny shreds of seagull. But the speed was power, and the speed was joy, and the speed was pure beauty."*

Jonathan's thrill at power, joy and beauty struck a chord with Petra as she slowly recovered her faith in life. The seagull became her favourite bird.

After her exams, Petra signed a contract with the University of Amsterdam to work as a research assistant for a further four months. Still connected to the Europa Institute she worked officially with one of the professors there, Irving Horowitz, and unofficially with Dr Mott, both of whom were preparing books on European politics at the time.

THERE IS NO REAL SUN OVER BRUXELLES

On 1st October 1971 Petra started a six-month contract as a *stagière* (trainee) in the General Secretariat of the European Commission. As long as she had no clearly formulated idea of what she wanted to do with her life, consolidating all that she had learnt in Amsterdam by a stint at the EC in Brussels seemed to be the most logical thing to do next. By chance she was allocated to the cabinet of Altiero Spinelli, who at that time was commissioner with responsibility for industrial, technological and scientific policy. He was also a devoted European federalist who had been writing on the topic since before the end of the Second World War. Petra became friendly with Spinelli and his German wife Ursula, and travelled with them to meetings about the future of Europe, including the Young European Federalist (JEF) organization, which she joined.

Petra was at once excited and horrified by the EC world she found herself in. As a commissioner, Spinelli's office was at the heart of the European Community administration and Petra found that heart all aflutter. The six founding member states (Belgium, France, the Federal Republic of Germany, Italy, Luxembourg, Netherlands) were in the process of negotiating the membership of Denmark, Ireland, Norway and the United Kingdom. As the Treaty of Accession was to be signed on 22nd January 1972, Petra became involved in the tedious aspects of this procedure, including a study on the Rome Treaties for the British. She wrote to Dr Mott in early November about an impending visit to Britain:

But on my twenty-fourth birthday one does not exactly like to sit in seminars and lectures about whether or not the English are Europeans. They are in (thank heavens) but the question remains as to whom they send here – many good people are already here – but not as Eurocrats. Will second rate people fill their shoes and are they only here to help Pompidou in his psychological fear of Germany? Or do they really feel that this is the only feasible answer for Europe – instead of only swimming about their own isles?

Of her time as a trainee, her supervisor Walter Verheydeen wrote, 'A *stagière* remarkable by her ardour at work. She has acquitted her duties promptly and efficiently all the tasks given to her, and has worked prodigiously to perfect her own knowledge. The *stage* seems to have been profitable both for the institution and for the *stagière*.'

Before leaving Amsterdam, Petra had applied for a scholarship to continue the research project she had started in the Europa Institute. This had been elaborated into the snappily-titled: 'A comparative study of the development of the political strategy within various private European organizations which have since 1945 attempted to promote European unity.' Shortly before Christmas 1971 she received a letter to say that the Christian Democrat Press and Information Office would fund her research with a *bourse* (grant) of 100,000 Belgian Francs for one year (to be paid in two halves) on condition that she be attached to a university. In April of 1972 Petra registered her thesis at the Institute of Political Studies at the University of Heidelburg for a doctorate under the renowned Professor Carl J. Friedrich. She had discussed with him her reluctance to continue her formal studies, and he had advised her to stick with it. 'If you have it [the doctorate] no one asks you, if not, they may.' He promised to sort out the harmonization of degrees between Washington and Amsterdam, and arranged that Petra should attend classes in Heidelburg four times a month. The study would be presented first to the Commission in English and then turned into a doctoral thesis in German.

Gradually, Petra settled into the life and politics of Brussels, though she never warmed to the city. Although it was *de facto* the capital of Europe, after Washington and Amsterdam Brussels seemed grey, and provincial – and, she said, it seemed always to be raining. Petra rented a flat at 134 Ave de Cortenberg, to the east of the huge Berlaymont building, seat of the Commission, where she she was based. Before long the excitement of being in the thick of the Commission was tempered with frustration at its ponderous nature. The same dispassion Petra had witnessed in Walt Rostow as he organized the next bombing raids in Vietnam was at work in the EC institutions. Decisions would be taken that would ultimately affect millions of people, but with as much emotional engagement as a twice-smoked kipper. And Petra found the atmosphere alienatingly masculine. 'At times, I should like to inscribe into the flags blowing so gently in the wind outside the Berlaymont that "Europe is Strictly for Males" ' she wrote in the staff journal in 1973.[6]

And she was indeed in a very manly world. Of the 1,625 posts for senior administrators in the Commission, only 99 were filled by women, and only four of those were in the top three grades. Many women did work in the EC, but most were in service jobs, as secretaries and translators with no direct route to promotion as administrators. 'Europe is one big male supremacy bastion – the Church, the political parties, the trade unions, the national bureau-cracies, the European Institutions,' Petra said in a speech in 1975. She set statistics against a story from her local post office: before her in the queue one day had been an elderly lady, there to collect a registered letter addressed to herself and her husband. On producing her identity card, however, she was refused the letter, only her husband could collect it.[7]

By the time Petra took up a new post as administrator to the Economic and Social Committee (EcoSoc) in 1972, she was beginning to adopt a strong feminist position, not only in her work, but in her increasing activity with the federalist and socialist movements in Brussels. They, like the EC institutions, were predominantly male-dominated organizations. This irritated her immensely, just as later on, she would be irritated by her male green colleagues who would insist that 'women's issues' should be dealt with by women, not by men and women together. In 1973 she wrote:

One must in all cases avoid falling into the trap of creating additional barriers between men and women – therefore, the warm parlours of European Women's Lib-move™ᵒnts, women's clubs and feminist political parties may serve the temporary cause of gathering wood – but they are not the place to start a longlasting fire. The aim is ultimately to confront and meet men on their own ground, namely politics, and to build an equal partnership with them . . . It must be remembered that there are no 'female questions' which at the same time are not also of importance to the society as a whole . . . the creation of a new woman of necessity demands the creation of a new man! *(original emphasis)*[8]

Thus one of Petra's earliest crusades was to make women's rights one of the priorities of the European institutions. As part of the preparations for International Women's Year in 1975, she had been asked by EcoSoc to produce background documents on the situation of women in the European Community countries, and she used the hard facts and figures she unearthed to give passionate speeches, mostly in Germany and in Ireland.[9]

Many rights, she pointed out, were *theoretically* enshrined in various directives, not least the Treaty of Rome itself (the founding document of the European Community which came into force in 1957) where Article 119 clearly commits member states to guarantee men and women equal pay for equal work. In exploring why this seemed so difficult to enforce, Petra found herself returning again and again to the violence and oppression inherent in any system dominated by men. Throughout the 1970s her speeches increasingly examined the connections between sexual discrimination, poverty, environmental degradation and nuclear policy (both civil and military). By 1977 she was writing of the frustration of being merely the 'token' or 'fig-leaf' woman: 'No matter how successful a woman becomes or is, there is still a man looking over her shoulders putting his paw marks on something . . . we are still stuck with a set of attitudes that are like a brick wall.'[10]

It was with speeches such as this that Petra really began to hit her stride. Her audiences loved her passion and gift for using 'ordinary' images to make her point: 'It will be a great day when our schools get all the money they need and the airforce has to hold a bake sale to buy a bomber.' [11]

'ME – A CIVIL SERVANT!'

While she was carrying out her research for her doctorate, Petra
stumbled on a pretty large wrinkle in the Euro-carpet. She had been
examining how various European organizations had been promoting
European unity. Pretty quickly she fell upon what she saw as a 'special
relationship' between the more conservative organizations of industry
and finance and the European Community. Petra described what she
found to Dr Mott:

> An unpublished financial . . . 'naiveness' as the EC gives aid to all
> groups without making any concrete prerequisites . . . only as long as
> they seem to be European-minded. In the foreground there are many
> conservative Bavarian-type European groups, while the true action-
> minded more left-oriented groups are largely ignored. The EC cannot
> make any policy [on this] as then they would be defining the kind of
> political Europe they desire.

Not surprisingly, this sort of talk got her into trouble with the source
of her funding, the Christian Democrat Press and Information Office,
who decided not to allocate the second half of her bourse.

Her EC 'bosses', particularly the cabinet of Altiero Spinelli, were
placed in a difficult position over this. In 1927, Spinelli had been tried,
imprisoned and banished from Italy for 'conspiracy against the
authority of the state' – he had organized against the fascists. In 1943
he had founded the European Federalist Movement in Milan, and he
worked in the resistance. He therefore had considerable political
sympathy with Petra's plight, but little power to help. Petra got some
translation work to tide her over until she could find another salaried
post. Unfortunately, because of the accession of Ireland, United
Kingdom and Denmark a 'freeze' on EC jobs was in place until
December 1972, when a reorganized and expanded bureaucracy would
be able to offer jobs to applicants from all nine member countries.

Petra wrote to Dr Mott at this time, aflame with indignation that
her discoveries had run into the sands of the Commission bureaucracy
and bursting with frustration about the time the translations took
from her research and her political activities. She also bewailed her
lack of funding, and spoke of hardship, but her salary as an EC *stagière*

plus half the bourse, while not exactly riches, were not exactly poverty either. Throughout her life, no matter what her income, or the balance in her bank account, Petra remained chronically insecure about money; her own poverty was never relative to any externally established criteria.

Despite her mini-crises, Petra continued to work hard:

My schedule in Bruxelles has become a 'strict 10 am to 5 am' . . . I find that I must hear dawn coming! then my fingers are sore from typing or painting and the eyes hurt . . . and I lay to rest restlessly . . . either because there is yet so much to be done or because there is nothing worth living for. I am never in between . . . only on top or on bottom.

Petra battled on with her research and with her studies in Heidelburg, visited Würzburg and Nürnburg and took Omi to Rome to visit the Vatican 'where Gracie walked'. She also attended a series of meetings on federalism, the Young European Federalists in Luxembourg, the Europa Union in Bonn, the Pan Europa Anniversary in Vienna, and the Movement for a Federal Europe in Nancy. As part of her research, Petra had been travelling all over Europe to talk to organizations concerned with the building of Europe, but she found little connection between them and ordinary people. In 1972, she challenged all federalists to come up with a 'strategy for engaging the European housewife, student, worker, businessman, teacher in the Europeanization process . . . in which the action-program is clearly outlined'. She had many plans for the United States of Europe on her desk, she said, but no idea of how ordinary people could be made to feel engaged in any of them. 'Can we build the human Europe of which Jean Monnet spoke: "We are not making coalition between states, but a union of people"?' [12]

Heinz Kuby, a former journalist who worked in the Secretariat of the European Parliament, was also concerned about building a new Europe. He belonged, as Petra now did, to the German Social Democratic Party, but while she had joined out of what she called 'utopian hope' in the new leader Willy Brandt, Kuby said he remained a member in order to temper Brandt's efforts to distance the party from the Marxist roots it had severed at its famous conference in Bad Godesburg in 1959.

Kuby, whom Petra described as a 'mentor and friend' discussed poetry and music with her and also encouraged her to read more pure Marxist doctrine – which she did. But Petra complained that, combined with her worries about her job and money, reading Marx made it difficult for her to write about anything, which worried her even more. To confuse matters further, she was being drawn to Kuby emotionally as well as intellectually – and he was forty-eight and married:

> *I will spend some time with him in Rome next month . . . but I fear for cups overflowing. [He] drives me to Aachen's dom (cathedral) with Bach's Oratorium playing in the car tape recorder in February and we speak no word till reaching Bruxelles – yet though – really we have been speaking – via Bach and the setting sun . . . then he can make me fight and argue and lose my outward self-assurance when it comes to the topic of Marx and force and change . . . also I am more and more discovering the Menschlichkeit (humanity) implied in pure Marxist thoughts.*

However, Petra had more difficulty with the practical proposals Kuby had for the revolution:

> *I cannot yet share the hopes within this present anti-consumer consuming New Left youth as being the locomotive that brings the proper revolution . . . Heinz Kuby finds that hope emerging via Italian Fiat workers and . . . in JUSO (Young Socialists) etc. I have been perhaps too much reminded of the past sad AU rebellions which have no ideological meat . . .*[13]

As 1972 progressed, Petra's practical problems began to dissolve. By June she was writing warmly not only of Heinz Kuby, but of Sicco Mansholt, President of the Commission. Through Kuby, he had heard of Petra's plight, and was sympathetic. He too was interested in transnational political formations, but was thinking more of the established parties than of revolutionary youth groups. He promised to try to sort out Petra's impasse with the Commission bureaucracy by finding her a temporary post. In the meantime, she should move from Spinelli's cabinet to his own. From the moment he met her, Mansholt was obviously enchanted by Petra, and she seemed just as delighted with him: 'I shall trail along as I think as I have discovered one of the most sensitive and gentle and yet radically revolutionary men in Sicco Mansholt!'

Sicco Mansholt was born in 1908, to a Dutch farming family of active socialists. He had spent twelve years as minister of agriculture in the Netherlands before becoming one of the first vice-presidents of the new European Community in 1958. A big, charismatic man, Mansholt was also a powerful politician. He was the architect of the Common Agricultural Policy, with a decision-making and financial machinery designed to survive the attempts of the French President Charles de Gaulle to destroy it.

Taking over the presidency in 1972, Mansholt was determined to end his political career on a high public note. 1972 was the year of the UN Conference on Environment and Human Development. The debate about the limits of the earth's powers to support the apparently unlimited demands of the human economy was raging, and the seriousness of what Mansholt called 'the crisis', had been underlined by mounting deaths from famine in Africa.[14] As far as Mansholt was concerned it may not be a catastrophe for the rich but it was already one for those who have died during the last famines. All the remedies were known, but the west was deaf to them.[15] Mansholt queried the notion that economic growth was sustainable. He was keen to leave a 'testament' of thought along these ideological lines for the future Commission, when the Community became a group of ten instead of six countries.[16] 'Where is Europe going and why?' was the question Mansholt felt they should address: 'Will the EEC become a powerful agent for improving living standards and opportunity in solidarity with less fortunate countries? Or will it remain a select inward-looking club of some of the world's richest nations? Will it continue to produce "bigger, faster and more" for "some" to the detriment of the global environment and the welfare of the "rest"?'[17]

In the autumn of 1972 Mansholt told Petra that there might be a post, temporary to begin with, with the Economic and Social Committee (EcoSoc) which was being enlarged in numbers and powers ready for the new community of ten nations. She would work with the health and social policy section and her superior would be Otto Kuby, brother of Heinz. 'Me – a civil servant – a bit unreal!' wrote Petra excitedly.

Although the Commission was obliged to consult EcoSoc, its role was purely advisory; the committee had no power to block or instigate legislation. Members were nominated by each state from different sectors of society – trade unions, industry, consumer associations and so on. This meant EcoSoc was probably the nearest the EC got to anything resembling representation for ordinary European citizens. When Petra arrived, nobody was aware that her temporary appointment came directly from 'the cabinet of Mansholt', and when the job freeze ended she participated in the normal open competition for posts and her excellent languages ensured she had no trouble in winning a permanent A7 grade civil service post.

So began in earnest the always fraught, sometimes unhappy, relationship between Petra and the European Community. It is difficult to imagine anyone more unsuited to the disciplined role of a civil servant. Her duties on behalf of the subgroup on health and social policy included preparing agendas, meetings, minutes and documentation. It was very much low-level brokering politics, and Petra's soaring mind and passionara approach made this difficult.

Amazingly, Petra was to stay in this job until she took up her seat in the Bundestag in 1983. Towards the end of the 1970s, when she was spending most of her weekends (and even some weekday nights) in Germany, she would sometimes work beyond the point of exhaustion, but by and large, she found some superhuman strength and, when she was there, did her EC job. Her colleagues agree that there were almost permanent tensions around her erratic timekeeping and that she sometimes had difficulty separating her developing political life from her professional duties, but she was not the only extraordinary or difficult personality around, and her dynamism and apparently endless energy made up for much. Before she finally left, EcoSoc had to respond to questions in the European Parliament about the time Petra took off work to campaign in Germany, and although Petra often painted Otto Kuby as an ogre of repression, in reality he gave her an enormous amount of freedom. He well remembers the pleasures and the tensions of working with Petra. 'It is wonderful what you do,' he would tell her, 'but the essence of being a professional is that you have to be there!'

FOR THE LOVE OF A STRONG MAN

When they met in the spring of 1972, Petra was twenty-five and Mansholt was sixty-four, but he had the physique, vigour and looks of a much younger man. He had been married for nearly forty years and preparations for retirement with his wife were well advanced. At the very moment he was due to bow-off the world political stage, he became overwhelmingly attracted to an intense, fragile, beautiful and intelligent young woman preparing to step on to it.

Mansholt quickly became infatuated with Petra and would talk about her to friends – and even to virtual strangers – on every occasion. Freimut Duve, publisher and member of parliament for the Social Democrats in Germany, remembers visiting Mansholt's farm in 1973, supposedly to discuss a publishing venture. Mansholt insisted they go for a walk – so he could talk about Petra and advise Duve to look out for this immensely talented young woman. 'This is the girl I have been looking for all my life,' he told anyone who would listen.

As their relationship developed Petra experienced

> *a kind of communion which I never believed could happen – to me – for I lead, as you know, a very isolated unfeminine life – that is to say, the world of men and love and romantic relationships. I seemed always cynical toward them and though I had my deep 'rencontres' as in Amsterdam and in Rome . . . I never felt that I could be tied in this way to any one man . . . so I would take off and roam alone again, no encounter lasted long although I am a comrade to all now. And there was so little time always . . . I had and have so many open questions and tasks to complete before I die . . . so I run.*

During the summer of 1973, Sicco Mansholt phoned Petra at her parents' home in the United States where she was on holiday. He was to arrive in New York for a meeting at the United Nations. Would Petra meet him at the airport on the afternoon of 3rd September? She did. He declared his passion, and his desire that they should live together. She kept the theatre tickets and all the restaurant and hotel bills in the trunk, alongside Robert Kennedy and Perry Como. 'It was THE ultimate explosion that had no time for growth and ripening . . . it was ripe, and is ripe and was in itself complete,' Petra wrote of that weekend in New York. 'As if he had with his now sixty-six years (birthday on 13.9) waited all these bitter alone years for me – as if I had in my twenty-six restless cynical years saved all the love in me for him . . . a kind of predestination.'

Back in Brussels a flat was rented at 13 Square Marguerite, and Petra insisted she would pay for her own share. He travelled a lot, so did she, but they found time to visit both Dr Mott and Petra's family in the United States, and to spend some weekends in Mansholt's Sardinian house. When they were apart, Mansholt wrote passionate notes: 'No words are necessary to verify our love – you do not take my hand without realizing that it is offered as a promise from me to you . . . This means my love is eternal.' Petra kept them all.

Less than a year later, Mansholt told his wife about Petra. His plan was to leave, after thirty-eight years of marriage. Her plan was to celebrate his retirement in the seventeenth-century farmhouse which they had recently renovated. All hell broke loose. Mansholt's wife was prostrated, his four grown-up children (with families of their own) and his friends rounded on him as a madman.

Petra was shocked. The ties of thirty-eight years' common experience proved powerful; the war and their work together in the resistance, and their four children and grandchildren were not to be erased so easily. Furthermore, the romance of Sicco and Petra 'planning new lives together' ran into difficulty sustaining itself in the face of reality:

> Our short flight, of a freed 'Jonathan' [is] already again in agony . . . [it is] incredibly complex, as I must always stay independent – also in every way financially. It is engrained in me deeply . . . and I must have the freedom to be Petra Kelly and not a second Mrs M. So this alone caused adjustment . . . would I give up my post now, for we certainly do not want Bruxelles as a common base . . . and where do we go and what happens to the farm and the woods and his political circles in Holland and his duties there . . . what happens to his wife?

Then in July, Mansholt had a blood pressure crisis which could have been fatal. His wife's distress deepened. Petra departed with her brother Johnny for a holiday in Kusadasi in Turkey. When she returned to Brussels, Heinz Kuby was dying of cancer. She wrote a long letter to Dr Mott:

*I was there up to the last 48 hours, and now I have the isolation of this
damned city Bruxelles . . . alone with my piles of books and
sentimentalities in this tiny flat .. a Sunday night .. and I had some
coffee in a decadent cafe in the area of the Bourse . . . I bought a book of
Rodin sculptures just now and decided to return home to write to you. . .
The little old ladies in Bruxelles lace drink their beer and the war
veterans wear all the Sunday medals . . . and there is no real sun over
Bruxelles.*

After a tryst at Christmas in the house in Sardinia, Petra's affair with
Mansholt spluttered to an end, with a sad inevitability that was almost
as romantic and enjoyable as the explosive passion of its beginning.
'Lover lets beloved be free,' she noted. The following year Petra left
Square Marguarite and moved into a two-bedroom flat in Avenue
Lebon near the Free University of Brussels.

It seems that Petra's doctoral thesis in Heidelburg also fizzled out
during this time. She was listed in the European Directory of Political
Scientists for 1974, but her student card was not renewed for the
1974/75 academic year and she was known to have had a difference of
opinion with Professor Friedrich over the direction of her research.
Among her papers there is only a list of the people she interviewed for
the project, plus letters she wrote in search of a publisher for all the
material. She told several people that her research documents had
been stolen. After that she lost heart. But she had lost interest anyway;
through Heinz Kuby and then Mansholt Petra had become interested
in the notion of transnational political parties in the future. She was
much less concerned with producing an academic description of what
had occurred in the past.

The pressures on her time were also mounting. Not only was her
job with the Economic and Social Committee time-consuming, but
her involvement in politics was increasing, with the German Social
Democrats (JUSO), the Young European Federalists (JEF), and as a
follower of the developing citizen's action movements in Germany, in
particular the anti-nuclear movement. Three months after the death
of Grace in 1970, Petra had attended a meeting in Washington held
by Ralph Nader, a well-known consumers' rights activist, where the
links between radiation and cancer had been the main topic of debate.
This Petra remembers as the starting-point of her anti-nuclear

politics. In 1973 she set up a foundation in the name of her sister to research these links and help provide more sympathetic care for children suffering with cancer. She also began to follow the activities of the US anti-nuclear movement, which was at that time more active than its European counterpart.

By chance, in April 1974, while she was in Washington receiving treatment for a kidney infection, Petra also attended Nader's first major national anti-nuclear meeting – Critical Mass '74. Petra was keen to interview as many of the experts as she could. She wanted Jo Leinen, then editor of *FORUM E*, the journal of the Young European Federalists, to publish an article based on the interviews. He was reluctant as he did not see what nuclear power had to do with federalism. Petra persisted, and eventually it was published in March 1975, much to the appreciation of the rapidly growing number of citizens' action movements demonstrating against the proposed construction of nuclear plants at various sites in Germany.

One of the most famous of these proposed sites was near the village of Whyl in the *Land* of Baden-Württemberg near the German border with Switzerland and France. Petra first visited Whyl in 1975 when she had taken Sicco Mansholt's place at an Easter rally. Roland Vogt, a peace researcher from Berlin who was studying non-violent change, was also there, with his wife and three small children. He had already been in contact with Petra as part of his research, but when he saw her and heard her speak – she spoke of Grace and drew on the material she had brought from America to make the connections between radiation and health – he fell immediately in love. He remembers it was all slightly ludicrous because he was trying to tell Petra how much he enjoyed her speech while simultaneously changing the nappy of one of his children. Nonetheless Petra felt she had found a kindred spirit in the bearded peace researcher. Although he came from a very different background from her (he had studied in Berlin) he had come to the same conclusions as she had about the links between non-violence, ecology, feminism and the need for a new sort of European federalism. At this time Petra felt most other people were still only groping their way towards it. Also, Roland Vogt was not afraid of the language of spirituality.

But Vogt was not the only candidate for the post-Mansholt void in Petra's heart. At the height of the drama surrounding Sicco

Mansholt's blood pressure attack, Petra told Dr Mott about 'some Irish trade unionist' with whom she was working. The accession of Ireland, United Kingdom and Denmark to the European Community had brought with it a new contingent of Eurocrats. EcoSoc had been enlarged appropriately, and nine of its 144 seats were allocated to Ireland. One of the nine Irishmen who turned up in Brussels was John Carroll, a leader of the Irish Transport and General Workers' Union (ITGWU). A dark-haired, blue-eyed man with a crumpled friendly face, he turned up in Petra's life at exactly the right moment. He was a good-going socialist, an ardent anti-nuclear campaigner and, like herself, full of apparently boundless energy. A very different character to the spritual Roland Vogt, Carroll was to play his counterpoint for several years.

The passage of Carroll's relationship with Petra throughout the rest of the 1970s was marked by the large numbers of speeches and visits Petra made to Ireland. These supplemented the visits he made to Brussels for the eight or nine annual plenary sessions of the committee and the various working group meetings. Often, he would stay with Petra in her flat.

They also travelled together to Australia in 1977 at the invitation of the Australian Railways Union. They attended a Hiroshima Day Rally in Sydney; visited Maralinga, a heavily contaminated nuclear testing site; visited several Aboriginal groups who had been affected; and spoke at meetings organized by the Movement against Uranium in Australia. This was Petra's first visit to Australia and she caused a sensation. The extent of her Australian knowledge and understanding impressed all those she met, and she did not hesitate to attack the 'opportunistic and nebulous pro-uranium statements' of Australian Labour Party leader Bob Hawke. [18]

Carroll and Petra also produced a book together – the edited proceedings of an energy symposium organized by the ITGWU in Dublin in May 1978.[19] Despite its title, the conference was entirely devoted to the case against nuclear energy, with Petra helping to rally contributions from Britain and the USA. Petra would also turn up in all weathers to campaign with the Irish anti-nuclear movement at Carnsore Point, and particularly remembers the festival she and John Carroll attended in August 1978 in torrential rain. In Ireland, as in Australia, people were struck by the combination of prodigious knowledge, intense energy and fragile beauty she possessed.

Patricia Redlich, an Irish journalist with whom Petra sometimes stayed, remembers her as terribly sophisticated, carrying in her briefcase, alongside her papers, herbal tea for her kidneys and a beautifully wrapped gift for her hostess' son. Carol Fox and Geraldine Dwyer of Irish CND both remember how much Petra's presence meant to anti-nuclear activists at that time. Even before she was elected to parliament, Petra exuded both confidence, hope and power. This was just what activists needed to lift them out of the grind of everyday campaigning – and her passionate speeches and unabridged opinions about other politicians guaranteed the press would turn up. The reputation Petra gained in Ireland during the anti-nuclear campaigns of the 1970s stood her in good stead ten years later, when she returned to support the Irish campaign against the Single European Act.

Another event punctuated Petra's relationship with John Carroll. During the trip to Australia she became pregnant. A proponent of natural birth control methods, something had gone awry. Later, Petra said she would have liked to keep the baby, but circumstances made this impossible. John Carroll was married and a Catholic. Indeed, babies and changes of life plans were not on the agenda of either of them. Petra, as at all times of crisis in her life, needed desperately to talk about it; but with whom? To talk of such matters was not easy with either the devoutly Catholic Omi (who was very upset about it), or her mother across the Atlantic (also Catholic and never at ease with the way Petra conducted her private life). One journalist recalls that Petra's need to 'sort things out' caused her to turn up on John Carroll's doorstep one day; 'She never recognized the boundaries that other people did.'

But just as the affair with Mansholt could never have been more than an affair, so the relationship with Carroll was not destined to be for keeps. In the autumn of 1977, Petra went to the United States to have the pregnancy terminated, a hugely painful decision, but a realistic one in the light of her personality and priorities. The experience obviously affected her greatly.

She expressed great concern that the baby might be abnormal because of the many X-rays she had had when she was younger, but the risk of this does not make as much medical sense as the risk associated with the fragile state of her kidneys. Nevertheless, in a typical melding of her personal experience with her policics, when Petra wrote for *FORUM E* about her abortion and the disquiet she felt, she set it firmly in the context of nuclear issues:

> *For six weeks, the question remained with me – could all the X-rays I had to have over the past few years be an acceptable risk? And what about the additional exposure to radiation as a result of the frequent visits to my sister Grace, in the radiology department of a hospital in Heidelberg? Also, could my visits to various nuclear power plants while they were on stream have had further negative effects on my body? How high is the level of radiation in Belgium where I am living at present? What is the concentration of radioactive particles in the fish, cereals and beef that I eat? Are there any experts in radiation protection who can tell me the truth about my embryo?*[20]

After her abortion, John Carroll sent Petra a huge bunch of carnations. She did not like carnations, a detail she would always refer to later when speaking about her feelings of that time. The wrongness of the flowers became very much a symbol of the wrongness of the whole situation. By concentrating on the minutiæ Petra somehow managed to cope with the greater emotional trauma. Her friend Adam Stolpen summed it up neatly, using Petra's fondness for painting as a metaphor. 'Petra,' he said, 'was very good at painting a landscape in broad brush strokes, leaving others to fill in their own details. But the other side of her could be found down in one corner, painting the legs on every ant.'

Despite the trauma of the termination of her pregnancy, Petra continued to work closely with John Carroll. He continued to share her flat in Brussels when he was there, and worried jealously about her, by now, blossoming relationship with Roland Vogt. Unconcerned, Petra and Vogt continued to campaign together, and sometimes invited Carroll to speak at meetings they organized around Germany to help them get the anti-nuclear message over to the more reluctant German trades unions. Vogt, more at ease with the situation than Carroll, remembers the first time their paths actually crossed; as he reached to shake Carroll's hand, Carroll raised his fists and adopted the mock defensive pose of a boxer. It was not until 1982 and the advent of Gert Bastian that Petra's affairs with both Roland Vogt and John Carroll finally came to an end. Though she and Vogt remained close colleagues – they were both elected to the Bundestag in 1983 – she did not meet Carroll again for several years. During one of Petra's visits to Dublin in the late 1980s (with Bastian in tow) Carroll turned up at the back of the hall where she was speaking. She waved, pleased to see him – 'Oh, its an old friend of mine' – but by the time meeting was over, he had gone.

CITIZENS' ACTION GROUPS AND DIE GRÜNEN

Towards the end of the 1970s, Petra began to live not so much a double life as two parallel full-time lives. She made ends meet, more or less, through her work for EcoSoc, but spent more and more time on trains to and from Germany. From 1978 onwards the list of her meetings and speeches become almost exclusively focused on her political campaigning activities in Germany. Through her anti-nuclear campaigning, she had become very excited by the developments, not in the traditional political parties (they seemed to be more boring than ever), but in the growing number of citizens' action groups. She could see great parallels with the civil rights movements in the United States.

In Germany, the post-war generation of German students were said to be 'blessed by late birth' – born after the war so therefore not responsible in any way for what happened. By the late 1960s these students were going through an existential experience as they tried to come to terms with the history of their country and the values which had prevailed since the war. 'The new generation,' Petra said, 'knows the brownshirts and catastrophes only from history books.' However, unlike Petra, who read the books in distant Washington DC, most German students were in Germany, using German philosophers to try to make sense of the ruthless industrialization of their country through which the past was supposedly to be put aside for good. Respect for the Deutschmark would replace revulsion at the extermination camps. The student revolutionaries began to try 'to solve the dilemma on an ideological basis,' Petra noted in 1969, 'with 'the three 'M's – Mao, Marcuse and Marx'. An intense obsession with theory, verging on the theological, had developed in the ideological space vacated by the German Social Democratic Party's move away from Marxism.

This approach to ideology did not interest Petra one jot. After her university studies and her journeys into 'pure' Marxism with Heinz Kuby, she saw these German students as completely misguided in their attempts to force their analysis of German society into the straightjacket of elderly political theories. 'It seems as if they are almost totally oblivious to the fact that they are no more tolerant than their elders . . . all look upon the proletariat as a mass that needs to be directed from the top – from above.' [21]

She was far more curious about the growing number of people who were 'opting out' of the values of a now opulently consuming Germany to live according to their own principles of frugal living and personal involvement in matters which concerned them. Communes, squats and alternative lifestyles of all sorts were attracting huge numbers of people. A newspaper, the *Tageszeitung*, or *Taz* as it was popularly called, began to cover what was known as the *Szene* (scene) in 1978. By the beginning of the 1980s nearly half a million people were thought to be actively engaged in self-help groups and alternative projects of some sort. [22]

Petra was particularly attracted to the *Bürgerinitiativen* (citizens' action groups) which were mushrooming all over the country. These were mainly concerned with 'backyard' issues, and dismissed disdainfully by the more politically ambitious left-wing groups as of 'secondary' interest. By 1972, however, over a thousand of these 'second-class' initiatives, representing over 300,000 people, came together and formed a national umbrella organization called the Bundesverband Bürgerinitiativen Umweltschutz (BBU). Some 'backyard' issues – such as protests against nuclear installations, pollution, especially acid rain and the *Waldsterben* (forest death) it caused, and road building – now had a vehicle for expression on a federal scale, and the machinery to plan large scale actions and demonstrations.

Petra became involved with the BBU when it was co-ordinating the opposition to the proposed nuclear power plant at Whyl. There was a mass occupation of the site in 1975, which was sustained even after the police intervened; it included citizens' groups from West Germany, Switzerland and France and had been meticulously pre-pared over several years. It became famous as an example of the 'perfect' demonstration. Consensus, non-violence and a strict no-political-party rule were the guiding principles. The conservative winegrowers worked hand-in-hand with housewives and the whole rag-bag of left-wing anti-nuclear campaigners. Petra was delighted. The spirit of Martin Luther King had come to Europe. Her involvement with the BBU deepened, and she was elected to the board, with Roland Vogt, in 1977. In a pamphlet written in 1980, the BBU laid out its stance:

> *Protection of the environment today means more than eliminating or moderating some of the worst effects of the industrial system. This would be dealing with the symptoms only . . . We are beginning to understand that destruction of the environment, economic inequality, social injustice and the growing dependence of the individual on the powers of the state are not avoidable side-effects of the system, but are essential features of it. Our interest is not merely in the correction of errors and the elimination of unpleasant side-effects. Rather our goal is a more just, a freer and a more human social order.* [23]

The movement was on a roll – more and more demonstrations attracted ever greater numbers: in 1977, 70,000 demonstrated at Kalkar; a few years later 100,000 marched to Brockdorf. The 1977 Anti-nuclear Contact Book contained 1,500 addresses.[24] In the citizens' movement Petra had found a home in which her personal and her political concerns and principles could be happily united. In a speech in London in 1979 she explained the work of the BBU:

> *We have tried to unite various movements, including the women's, the environmental, the peace and the anti-military groups, and have attempted to be present everywhere – on the nuclear sites, at the drilling holes in Gorleben, in the courtrooms, inside the city councils and regional parliaments -[taking] the image of the 'flea in the fur' as a multi-strategy.*[25]

Before long, however, far-left groups were bringing violence to the demonstrations by provoking clashes with the police. Overstretched and overreacting, the police helped to turn pleasant weekend outings with a non-violent political purpose into bloody confrontations.

Although it was eventually proved that *agents provocateurs* were also at work, the predominantly right-wing popular press was quick to tar the whole peace and ecology movement with the brush of violence.

Violence at the demonstrations led some to look to the mainstream political process as a new arena in which to campaign. As Martin Luther King had warned, violence, even by a few, could threaten the cause of many. In Whyl, the concern of local farmers about the effect of radiation on their crops had been added to by the shock of discovering that both the state president and the economics minister of Baden Württemburg were on the boards of companies applying for the contract to build the power plant. This political complicity was another signal that the impact of demonstrations would be weakened if they were not part of a broader action strategy. [26]

In several *Länder*, anti-nuclear and environmental groups had begun to forge themselves into 'political associations' and were beginning to contest local elections, with modest, but locally significant, results. They were encouraged by the ecologists in France who, in 1976, polled over 10 per cent in some local elections in Alsace. In a joint article in *FORUM E* in 1977 Petra and Roland Vogt combined their concerns about civil and military nuclear power and the future shape of the European Community. They saw the first direct elections to the European Parliament, anticipated in June 1979, as an opportunity for ecological and peace issues to obtain a campaigning platform throughout Germany. [27]

From this point onwards, the pressure for a new national political party began to build from several other directions. The local political associations were also beginning to think about the European elections, as were some of the more politically aware members of the *Szene*. Although many in the independent peace groups remained sceptical, even the non-party principle of the BBU was beginning to crumble. Their president had threatened to turn the BBU into a new party if the government did not take more heed of its demands. In June 1978 the BBU organized a West German Environment Conference, with 100 delegates (and 1000 observers!), who agreed, after some blistering arguments, to set up a committee (including Roland Vogt and Petra) to prepare for the elections. [28]

Among those arguing against a new political formation were BBU members already involved in the Social Democratic Party (including

Jo Leinen) who demanded Petra and Vogt be 'suspended from their duties' on the BBU board during the European election campaign. Others distrusted party politics altogether. A debate raged about how any party could be different from all the others. Michael Schroeren, former die Grünen press speaker who was editor of the BBU journal at that time, remembers Petra arguing long and hard about how useful the new party would be and how it did not have to get caught up in the bad ways of power politics. The image of a two-legged movement was born, with the 'kicking leg' in parliament and local government, while the other provided stability by being firmly anchored in the movement. A constitution would be drawn up which would ensure the primacy of the movement's role in guiding and controlling the party leg. Rotation of mandates (so no one held power for too long), grass-roots democratic procedures, redistribution of salaries and other organizational techniques would be used to this end. Many felt that it was Petra's failure to keep the promises she made so passionately at this time which, in later years, did more than anything else to harm her position in green politics.

Meanwhile, one of the people dismayed at the left's disarray, and concerned at the conservative nature of some of the local political associations was Lukas Beckmann. A graduate in agriculture, Beckmann was at this time working at Joseph Beuys' Free University in Dusseldorf. He discussed with Beuys, Heinrich Boll and others the possibility of setting up a new political party. Beuys (one of the best-known post-war European artists whose *leitmotiv* was action-art: 'everything under the sun is art') was enthusiastic. Eventually, Herbert Gruhl, leader of one of the political associations, organized a meeting with the power to create a national organization with the express purpose of contesting the European elections. The question of a new political party would be put off until later. On 18th March 1979, delegates from various regional political associations which had tried (with mixed results) to win seats in local elections, and a group from Beuys' Free University, came together in Frankfurt-Singelfingen to create the Sonstige Politische Vereinigung-Die Grünen (Alternative Political Alliance (SPV)-the Greens). Petra and Roland Vogt, there as representatives of the BBU, were elected by the meeting to take first and second place on the list of candidates for the election. Beckmann remembers this first meeting with Petra well. Her vivacity, her knowledge and her commitment impressed everyone. It was clear that any strategy for a new party would have to have Petra at its heart. 'My dream since 1976 has come true', said Petra:

> *We have no option but to take a plunge into greater democracy. This does not mean relieving the established parties, parliament and the law courts of their responsibilities, nor forcing them out of office. Information reaches society via the political parties; and the reverse process is important too: the parties and the trade unions also act as sounding-boards for ideas which first arise within society. But the formation of political opinion within the parliamentary system is undoubtedly a process that needs extending further. It needs to be revitalized by a non-violent and creative ecology and peace movement and an uncompromising anti-party party – the Greens.* [29]

Beuys, Brigitte and Helmut Gollwitzer, student leader Rudi Dutschke, Heinrich Böll and his wife Annemarie joined other German celebrities to act as patrons of this new electoral initiative. This pleased Petra immensely. Not only did she enjoy the company of artists and writers but she felt that politically the support of well-known public figures and intellectuals was extremely important. The authority and gravitas they provided made it possible to carry out lively actions and demonstrations without being dismissed as cranks. When, in the 1980s, the anti-intellectual tide within Die Grünen was running high, Petra was scathing, and cited the party's inability to see how important it was to have support from intellectuals as a major contributing factor to their decline. (Shortly before he died in 1986, Joseph Beuys commented that the party had become *'stinklangweilig'* – stinkingly boring.)

Following the founding meeting, ten people agreed to invest DM5000 each to rent an office in Bonn, and each group was invited to sponsor a volunteer to work on the campaign from there. Herbert Gruhl offered a small two-room office with a cellar at 120 Friedrich Ebert Allee and the campaign was launched.

Contesting the European elections for the green political association meant Petra had to resign from the Social Democratic Party. This was difficult for her. She had joined in 1972, inspired by its then leader and Federal Chancellor, Willy Brandt. As a brave and active resister of the Nazi regime and Nobel Peace Prize winner in 1971 for his *Ostpolitik* (policy of establishing relationships with Eastern bloc countries), he was an inevitable candidate for Petra's hall of heroes. She had been particularly moved when he spontaneously knelt at a Warsaw memorial to Jewish war victims. Later, Petra was to develop her own *Ostpolitik*, often at odds with that of her party, with Willy Brandt's example foremost in her mind. But Petra always insisted that the tears she shed at the time were because she was leaving the party of one of her heroines – Rosa Luxemburg.

Carrying one of Rosa's slogans before her – 'Freedom means freedom for those who think differently' – Petra and SPV-Die Grünen joined the campaign for the 1979 European elections. They found themselves in the company of ecological parties from several countries – Les Verts in France, the Ecology Party in the United Kingdom, Ecolo and Agalev in the French and Flemish speaking regions of Belgium. During the campaign, links were also made with radical parties in both the Netherlands and Italy. The transnational political force was ready to be born. 'All this is *part* of the strategy,' she informed the British peace and ecology movements as they too struggled to combine forces in 1979, 'the strategy of elections not as an *end*, but as *one* of many, many *means* to fight FOR LIFE, for the survival of the human species.'[30] Like Thoreau, Petra could not be convinced that voting was evidence enough of individual change. There was always a danger that, once having voted, personal responsibility would be shrugged off.

Four days after the Frankfurt meeting Petra sent a letter to everybody she could think of:

> *Having being elected to the number one candidate on the ecological ticket (but followed by a number of men, of course, including Roland Vogt for place number two) brings many joys and yet many strains. . . . As I shall be mounting the campaign alone and without the usual party-machinery (which we totally reject) even without motor cars, I shall have to count on solidarity from my friends.*

She added that she was also taking ten weeks' leave of absence from her job in Brussels, despite being in the middle of fighting a discrimination case with EcoSoc 'a rather blatant and open case of repression and injustice'.[31] Funds were to be sent to her campaign HQ, which was Omi's small flat in Nürnburg.

With Vogt, Petra criss-crossed Germany to attend meetings in many towns and villages. As well as Vogt, at Petra's side on the platforms were Joseph Beuys, Czech exile Milan Horáček, and the recently expelled East German economist Rudolf Bahro. All of them, the following year, would become founder members of Die Grünen, when the temporary political alliance went the whole way to become a formally established political party.

What did SPV-Die Grünen get for its DM50,000 investment in the European elections? It got a nationwide platform for its campaign for a nuclear-free Europe of the Regions, a respectable 3.2 per cent of the ballot (900,000 votes) and an extremely welcome DM4.8 million in the bank. (The law governing elections in West Germany permitted a 'refund' of electoral expenses calculated according to the party's share of the vote.) Although the French Greens did better in terms of votes (they got 4.7 per cent) no green party managed to win seats, though in Italy, the Radicals, led by the flamboyant Marco Panella, won three seats.[32]

With Solange Fernex, leader of the French Greens and a stalwart anti-nuclear campaigner, Petra organized a demonstration against the unfair European electoral systems in the gallery of the EC parliament when it convened on 17th July 1979 in Strasbourg. The same day, representatives from the different national parties founded the Coordination of the European Green and Radical Parties. Roland Vogt offered to assume the secretariat and a commemorative picture was taken. The new transnational green family was in business. In the middle is Petra, holding a flower and smiling radiantly.

Notes

1   Petra Kelly, 'Outline of a comparative study of the development of the political strategy within various private European organisations which have since 1945 attempted to promote European unity', mimeo, Europa Institute of the University of Amsterdam (no date *c.* 1970).

2   Essay: (13 May 1968).

3   Carlo Weber, 'The birth control controversy', *The New Republic*, vol. 159, no. 21 (23 November 1968).

4   Essay: (no date, post-November 1968).

5 Bach (1973) p.25.
6 Chapters and Articles: in *Staff Courrier* (17 April 1973).
7 Speech: Galway, (19 October 1975).
8 Essay: (July 1973).
9 Chapters and Articles: in Economic and Social Committee (1975).
10 Speech: Dublin (19 November 1977).
11 Speech: Dublin (December 1978).
12 Petra Kelly, 'We have been making a kind of "Europe" but where are the Europeans?' memo to all concerned leaders within the European Federal Movements and in like-minded interested groups and organizations (13 March 1972).
13 Letter to Dr Mott (18 March 1972).
14 Mansholt (1974).
15 Sicco Mansholt, 'Les remèdes à la crise sont connus mais les Occidentaux sont sourds', CJN 153 (November 1974).
16 John Lambert, 'Mansholt – man of vision', *Irish Times* (3 October 1972).
17 Chapters and Articles: in *VISTA* (April 1973).
18 Essay: (July/August 1977).
19 Book: with John Carroll (eds) (1978).
20 In German in *FORUM E*, 1.2.3, 1978, updated in Book: (1984) p. 97ff.
21 Essay: (1969).
22 Hülsberg (1987) p. 74.
23 Hülsberg (1987) p. 62.
24 Hülsberg (1988) p. 59.
25 Speech: London (24 November 1979).
26 Parkin (1989) p. 114.
27 Petra Kelly & Roland Vogt, 'Ökologie und Frieden', in *FORUM E*, 1/2, 1977.
28 Kolinsky (1989) p. 100.
29 Book: (1984) p. 11.
30 Speech: London (24 November 1979).
31 Petra felt she had been overlooked for promotion to grade A6 and had activated solicitors to fight her case in the courts. Otto Kuby defended his decision, saying that however dynamic she might be, Petra's frequent absences put her at a disadvantage with her less talented but more present colleagues. However, she did eventually achieve her promotion.
31 Parkin (1989) p. 257.

5

JANUARY 1980
-TO-
MARCH 1983

THE GENERAL

On 3rd March 1979, shortly before the first meeting of SPV-Die Grünen, the youth organization of the Social Democratic Party (JUSO) held a discussion in Bad Mergentheim, near Würzburg, on 'Political education and the social standing of the soldier'. On the platform was Major General Gert Bastian, commander of the 12th Panzer Division, based nearby at Veitshöchheim. The talk turned around the longstanding difficulty of reconciling military discipline with the rights of an individual soldier in post-war Germany. At what point does following one's conscience become a breach of regulations? General Bastian expressed his concern over the impending decision that NATO would decide to base US nuclear weapons on German soil. The new weapons would, he felt, destroy NATO's strategy of deterrence – mutually assured destruction. For deterrence to work, parity of destructive power had to exist between the two sides, he argued, and the proposed new missiles would have a 'first strike' capacity which would not only destroy that parity, but also guarantee any conflict that did occur would be in the European theatre, with Germany and its East and West divide centre stage.

His remarks caused a bit of a storm. Bastian drew attention to himself again in July at a Rifle Club fête at Marbach. When the band began to play 'Badenweiler Marsch', one of Hitler's favourite marches, he had mounted the podium to demand that they stop.

However, it was not until after NATO's December 1979 decision to station the missiles if peace talks with the USSR in Geneva failed (the so-called 'double-track' decision), that Bastian finally composed his famous letter of resignation. He sent it to Defence Minister Hans Apel on 16th January 1980, stating the reason for his resignation to be the decision to deploy American Pershing II and Cruise missiles in Europe, particularly in Germany. The new American systems represented a major and therefore destabilizing escalation in 'first strike' ability. He accompanied his letter with an eight-page memorandum of his arguments.[1]

Apel was furious. This was not at all a useful thing to happen just before the Social Democrat government was due to defend itself in a difficult election, and the Christian Democrat candidate for Chancellor, Franz Josef Strauss, was poised to pounce remorselessly on any 'softness on communism'. Apel decided not to accept Bastian's resignation: 'We do not need any martyrs with a pension scheme.' Hoping to keep him quiet, Apel had Bastian removed from Veitshöchheim and given the command of a small desk in Cologne. To no avail. Within a week, the text of the letter and memo were published in the *Frankfurter Rundschau*, so most of Germany could read about how Major General Bastian felt the German people had been cheated of a proper debate about the dangers to Germany of the new missiles. Franz Joseph Strauss led the posse of MPs calling Bastian a security risk, and the press began to investigate the man behind the memo.

They found an enigmatic personality. As an officer, Bastian had an impressive military record, his meticulous attention to detail moving him smoothly up the promotion ladder – at least as far two-star general. But the quiet and precise Major General Gert Bastian was also a womanizer. Inside the army, his reputation as a Don Juan had got him into trouble more than once. An affair with the wife of a colleague in 1976, and then the rumour that shortly before he resigned the wife of a lieutenant had become pregnant by him (a rumour later confirmed by Petra to her confidantes) hinted that his chances of ending his military career on a high note were a touch diminished.

Looking further back, an even more interesting picture emerges, of a man who, far from being a leader, was actually a rather passive passenger of destiny. Born on 26th March 1923 in Munich, Gert Bastian was the son of a Brazilian-German father. His grandfather had emigrated to Brazil, married, made a fortune and lost it before returning to Germany. Alberto Bastian went along with his wife's support for Hitler and the Nazi Party. According to Charlotte Bastian, it was she who was the strong and dominant partner. She brought up her children – daughter Ruth and sons Ruy and Gert – to believe the Nazi ideals that children should be educated to be tough and the weak eradicated. She was particularly fond of Gert.

When Hitler invaded Poland, Gert Bastian was sixteen:

On September 1 1939 our whole school form, all the same age, were in Lower Bavaria on harvest work, picking hops, and I remember how the farmer came to the fields in the evening and said: War has broken out this morning. As for us we were firmly convinced that Germany had been attacked by a malicious, hostile alliance which wished to destroy all the achievements of the past years and they had to be defended. This was the picture held, without any doubt, by all my friends. And the very same evening we cycled to Munich to register at the recruiting office as volunteers for the Wehrmacht. But they were so sensible as to send us home again, telling us to finish school first. They didn't need to call up children yet.[2]

Two years later Gert Bastian volunteered again. In the meantime he had become active in the Hitler Youth organization.

Within a year of joining up, at the age of nineteen, he became *Gruppenführer* of the 45th Pionier-Bataillon, and by 1947 was second lieutenant of the 86th Panzerpionier-Bataillon: 'I saw action mainly on the eastern front, on the central sector between Orel and Kursk, once on the southern sector on the Don near Krivoi Rog, and finally in the invasion battle in Normandy, but that for a very short time.'

Bastian went to the Russian front in 1941. There, the 1935 Nürnburg 'Law for the Protection of German Blood and Honour' was being applied with increasing diligence; in March 1941, Hitler issued his 'Commissar Order' for the execution of gypsies, 'political enemies' and all Jews. The definition of political enemies was open to the widest of interpretations, and extended to all Russians, whom the

German soldiers were encouraged to see as *untermenschen* (subhuman). Behind the armed forces, special mobile security forces, *Einsatzgruppen*, were ordered to work with the army to round up and shoot Jews – down to the last child – in the towns and villages. At first the army objected (somewhat feebly) to the brutalities of the Commissar Order and the *Einsatzgruppen*, but they were overruled by Hitler himself. As Soviet Russia was not party to the Geneva Convention there was no need to observe the rules of war, he said. By the end of 1941, this method of slaughter was deemed inefficient and the building of the huge camp at Auschwitz commenced. Early in 1942, what Himmler called the Final Solution (the application of advanced modern science to the task of extinguishing all Jews in Europe) replaced the unsystematic *Einsatzgruppen*.[3]

Bastian must have been a brave and conscientious soldier. He was wounded three times, once by a Russian bullet through his upper arm, once by a splinter of grenade in his head and finally, on the western front, by six US machine-gun bullets through his upper body. He was awarded two decorations, the Iron Cross, first and second class.

While at the front, Bastian wrote letters home, with details, not of the horror and sadness of war, but of everyday things like the cost of schnapps and potatoes. In the film *The Generals*, made in 1986, Bastian recalls Operation Citadel – viewed by military historians as the most important battle of 1943 – but does not talk about the battle itself. Instead he gives details of a day spent before the battle with his brother Ruy, also a second lieutenant but in a different division.

Gert Bastian ended the war in an American prisoner of war camp at Regensburg, where he heard the news of Hitler's defeat:

The day of capitulation came and earlier the news that Hitler had fallen fighting on the steps of the Reich Chancellery. Later we found out he had committed suicide, and that was just another of those outrageous lies told to the soldiers right up to the end. At that time that was a very great shock to me. I recall very clearly the absolute despair which befell me, because, seen with the eyes of today, we had believed with a blindness which can only be described as manic that this ending could not come, that our admired Führer had to be right, had to remain the victor, and could lead Germany out of the danger of defeat. We believed this so firmly that we were protected against any better assessment. We were simply not open to it. And when this unavoidable event, the defeat, came about, the imaginary world we had constructed collapsed with a huge bang, and this was a terrible spiritual shock.

Bastian kept no diary during the war, and, on his return to Munich in 1945 he spoke to no one about his experiences except to say that he was lucky not to have been drawn into any atrocities, and lucky to come back. His brother Ruy and his school friends did not.

Bastian's reticence about the details of his war years, which he maintained during his relationship with Petra, is intriguing. In the film *The Generals*, members of Generals for Peace and Disarmament, the organization Bastian helped to found in 1981, spoke of their conversion to anti-nuclear positions. His seven colleagues chatted freely about their wartime experiences but not a surplus word passed Bastian's lips. Was this because he was the only German, and felt the whole load of shame for Nazi atrocities?

When faced with the truth after the war, German soldiers were said to have responded in two ways. Some were at once devastated, all previously held beliefs instantly destroyed. Others fought against the truth – it was a bloody lie, the bodies at Auschwitz were taken from the brutally bombed city of Dresden, and so on. According to his wife, Gert Bastian moved from the second position to the first in his time in Regensburg.

Before long, and by common consent, a collective amnesia descended over the German people. Soldiers, like former Nazi party members, rarely offered information about the extent of their participation, and were rarely asked to do so, even by their intimates. 'What did you do in the war Daddy?' was a question no child dared ask.

When he became involved with the peace movement, Gert Bastian met Heinrich Böll, who had also served on the eastern front, but who had never risen above the rank of private. Böll had tried to penetrate the amnesia through his writing. Although he had rationalized the cruelty he suspected was occurring at the time, Böll insisted that if the reality of the past was buried, then its lessons would not be learnt, but repeated. But Bastian's response was very different. He remained silent, and, when pushed (as he was when the media began to investigate his background) Bastian always maintained he had known nothing of the broader picture during the war.

There is a chance that Bastian *was* completely unaware of atrocities and had been only marginally involved in the army's disregard of the international rules of war. Perhaps life in the tank division was an insular one. But, in the circumstances, it seems a remote chance. Although official records and attempts to discredit Bastian when he resigned from the army unearthed no evidence to the contrary, if Heinrich Böll as a private knew something of what was going on, surely an ambitious and brave officer cannot have remained completely ignorant? Over two million Russian prisoners of war were taken and over ten million Russian civilians were killed. In addition Bastian's parents were well connected on the home front; Heinz Suhr recalls passing Gert Bastian's office in the Bundestag in April 1983, on the day the newspapers reported the discovery of what were first believed to be Hitler's diaries. Bastian was laughing. He was sure that Hitler kept no diaries, he said, because he knew Hitler's secretary very well; she was a close friend of his mother's.

In view of all this, Bastian's belief in Hitler as victor right up to the very last does not ring completely true. He must have been aware some time before he got to the US prisoner of war camp in Regensburg that the war was not going entirely Hitler's way. In July 1943 the Germans had mounted Operation Citadel, one of the most decisive battles of the war, in order to regain the town of Kursk, one of the few Russian gains in recent fighting. Unexpectedly, the German army experienced heavy losses and the Russians began to counterattack. A great tank battle took place; for the first time in the war, Hitler had to admit defeat, and by the autumn, the inexorable retreat had begun. By February 1944, Bastian's battalion had pulled back from the Krivoy Rog and was retreating towards Odessa. In April, his brother was killed in Rumania and buried in the churchyard of a village called Kapustaweshe. When her last letter to her son Ruy was returned with the words 'Return to Sender, Died for Greater Germany' written in bold red crayon, his mother placed an announcement in the paper saying he died for a cause. Gert Bastian was transferred to Normandy, where he was wounded once more before being captured and sent to Regensburg.

In March 1945, just before the war officially ended, Gert Bastian obtained leave to marry Charlotte Baronin von Stipsicz. She was from a Hungarian noble family and had met Bastian on one of his home leaves while travelling on a local train between Tutzing and Munich. Gert Bastian's mother did not much like her and doubted her skills as a housewife. When Lotte and Bastian married, she was already pregnant and when he finally returned to a shattered Munich in June, the newly-weds had to share a three-bedroom flat with his parents and eventually the baby. Occasionally Gert's sister Ruth and her baby would stay with them too. If Bastian did not share with Böll the same memories of the Russian front, he certainly experienced what Böll called the inevitable 'living kitchen stench' of 16 million families sharing 10 million homes.[4]

After the war, Bastian did not take up his studies again. The limited number of places in the universities were reserved for those less obviously enthusiastic about National Socialism, and, besides, Gert Bastian did not have a particularly curious mind. He trained as a bookbinder and got a job in a public works office. The job was not taxing, in fact it was boring, he remembers, so he had lots of spare time which he spent playing chess.

In 1954, the West's new security organization, the North Atlantic Treaty Organization (NATO), agreed to admit the German Federal Republic into its fold, and plans were drawn up for a German army which would not be a closed body or 'a collection of robots and functionaries with weapons' but *Staatsbürger in Waffen*, a citizens' army.[5] In an attempt to escape all echoes of the military past, the new German army wanted to close the gap between the ordinary citizen and the soldier. The guiding principle of the new soldier became known as *innere Führung* – literally meaning 'inner leadership'; from now on a soldier would be encouraged, indeed expected, to place respect for a higher moral leadership above military discipline. In the future, no soldier could claim as an excuse for brutality that he was following orders.

In July 1956 general conscription began and Gert Bastian was one of the first to sign up; 'I felt suitable for this profession.' He enjoyed being a soldier again, and later explained that he set great store by the *innere Führung* principle. As long as he could be a soldier out of conviction, he said, he was happy. 'And I think I was a good soldier in all my posts.'

He was obviously a very successful soldier. After being conscripted to the rank of lieutenant in 1956, Gert Bastian followed a smooth path of promotion – company commander, battalion commander, general staff officer, adviser on long-term planning in the Ministry of Defence, colonel, brigade commander, major general, and finally commander of the 12th Panzer Division, based at Veitshöchheim near Würzburg.

At the same time as he rejoined the army, Bastian joined the right-wing Christian Social Union (CSU), the Bavarian version of the Christian Democrat Party. In the early 1950s the CSU did hold some positions redolent of the National Socialists, including national-ization, but there was no sign of either violence or nationalism. 'If a German picks up a gun his arm should fall off' was a common refrain of its most dominant personality, Franz Joseph Strauss, during the years immediately following the war. But by the mid-1960s, both the CSU and the army were showing signs of falling into old bad habits. Rigidity and a narrow focus of thinking were leading, as was inevitable, to intolerance of anyone who might think differently. Strauss was becoming more extreme in his views and Bastian felt that some senior army personnel were becoming a little too fond of certain traditions. *Sture Böcke* he called them – 'stubborn rams', a pejorative term applied to old Nazis.

By 1965, when all twelve divisions of the new Bundeswehr were ready for service, Gert Bastian had left the CSU. He was involved in the discussion about how the *innere Führung* might actually work in practice. The then Minister of Defence, Kai-Uwe von Hassel, issued a memorandum entitled 'Bundeswehr and Tradition', trying to provide some guidance to soldiers as to how they might take a critical view of Germany's military past, yet find some inspiring and worthy models. One of the chapters addressed 'political participation and shared responsibility': 'He who follows a false tradition of the unpolitical soldier and restricts himself to his military craft neglects an essential part of his sworn duty as a soldier in a democracy.'[6]

Perhaps because of his own skirmishes with democracy within the army, Gert Bastian was greatly influenced by this memorandum, and found himself drawn politically to the Social Democrats through its sympathetic leader Willy Brandt, who became Vice Chancellor in 1966 and then Chancellor in 1969. Brandt had promoted a popular debate about increasing democracy everywhere – from political parties to the army – under the slogan, *mehr Demokratie wagen* (risk more democracy).

When Gert Bastian achieved his final promotion in 1976, he was criticizing with increasing openness the failure of internal democratic procedures inside the army. The *Sture Böcke* were gaining too much ground. Bastian's concern for democracy was fuelled by his fear of any situation which might allow Nazism to flourish again in Germany. His argument was that with more democracy and open debate, it would be impossible for Hitler's favourite march to be played at a fête, or for nuclear missiles to be placed on German soil. According to Dr Mott, the monkey on Bastian's back was the same as the one on Petra's. He remembers a long phone call with Bastian in 1992, in which Bastian discussed his worries about the rise of neo-Nazi activities. Despite Mott's best efforts to convince Bastian that nineties Germany was not the same as thirties Germany, Bastian apparently remained unreassured. Perhaps he knew from personal experience that most people are followers, not leaders.

In May 1980, the Bundeswehr organized a grand tattoo in Bremen to combine celebrations of 25 years of Germany's membership of NATO with the usual swearing-in of new recruits. The tattoo was meant to be a celebration of military comradeship and music. However, the decision to hold it in Bremen, with its fairly anti-military tendency, shortly after the controversial decision on nuclear weapons, *and* to invite the new President of the Federal Republic, Karl Carstens (an extreme conservative rumoured to have had pro-Nazi feelings during the war), was confrontational to say the least.[7] A bloody battle between police and anti-war demonstrators left many injured, nearly thirty seriously. There was widespread debate about the insensitivity of the Bundeswehr, despite its guiding concepts of citizens in uniform and *innere Führung*.

It was against this background that Gert Bastian finally resigned his commission in June, and embarked on a busy round of television and radio appearances, public meetings and interviews. His views resonated with the anxiety German people felt after the tattoo debacle and he became a star:

> *The ethical justification for a military force – that those people are protecting and defending what they love – is lost in the nuclear age*

*because nothing can be protected in a nuclear war. In fact, military
service in such circumstances becomes undignified and is a threat to
everyone. Abandoning the military, then, becomes a decision of reason
and is the only morally justifiable course.*[8]

The peace movement was ecstatic; a general in their team. Bastian
was courted assiduously and invited to lots of meetings, with his wife
Lotte more often than not in the audience. On 1st November 1980 he
found himself on the same platform as Petra Kelly. If anything his star
status was brighter than hers at the time and the topic they were
invited to discuss was 'Women in the Army'. They both agreed that it
was wrong for women to be in the army at all, but for very different
reasons, over which a brisk argument took place. Petra believed
women should not be in the army because they it would be wrong to
participate in any violent activities. 'The question is not should
women become soldiers, but how can men stop being soldiers?'
Bastian thought women should not be soldiers because they are
entirely unsuited for the job, both physically and temperamentally. A
real sexist comment and utterly naive, responded Petra.

But she was intrigued by this general who had resigned on
principle. And when they were introduced, he had kissed her hand;
despite herself, Petra was more charmed than offended by such
romantic gestures. She also found him very handsome and told
friends she thought he twinkled his eyes rather like Curt Jürgens, a
popular German filmstar.

On 16th November Gert Bastian invited Petra to the launch of the
Krefelder Appell, an initiative he had organized with other members
of the peace movement, calling for the German government to
withdraw its approval of the stationing of intermediate range nuclear
missiles on German territory. The objective was to collect as many
signatures as possible – within three years the Appell would amass 5
million.[9]

At once accusations began to fly that the Krefelder Appell (and later
the international grouping of Generals for Peace and Disarmament
which grew out of it) was, if not organized by the Soviet Communist
Party and the KGB, then full of its stooges, and Bastian was one of
them. Bastian always insisted he was never contacted at any time by
the East European secret services, something his wife confirmed. Yet

1949 – aged 2

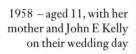

1954 – first day at school

1958 – aged 11, with her
mother and John E Kelly
on their wedding day

All the photographs on
this page taken in
Gunzburg, Bavaria

1963 – a 'night to remember' with Dion in the Roosevelt Hotel, New Orleans

1968 – at American University, Washington DC

June 1968 – the Vatican, with half-sister Grace and Pope Paul VI

August 1990 –in Dharamsala with Nima Chonzom,
the Tibetan orphan Petra started to foster in 1971, the year following Grace's death

1978 – in front of the European Commission's Berlaymont building, Brussels

1983 – Omi at home: the 'green granny' in her Nürnburg flat

September 1973 – Petra and Sicco Mansholt (left) at the United Nations, New York

December 1979 – with John Carroll (left) and Michael Mullen, (General Secretary of the ITGWU), at launch of *A Nuclear Ireland*

June 1980 – daffodils for co-members of *Die Grünen* executive board at a party conference in Dortmund

Gert Bastian, 1980

March 1983 – into the Bundestag.
From left to right, Gert Bastian, Petra Kelly, Otto Schily and Marieluise Beck

8 December 1989 – with Dalai Lama in Bonn. He was
en route to Norway to receive the Nobel Prize

Top Left: 25 September 1986 –
with Erich Honecker (left) and
Gert Bastian, in Cinema Kosmos,
East Berlin for showing of the
film *The Generals*

Bottom Left: August 1987 – with
(from left) the author, Solange
Fernex of the French Greens, and
Freda Meissner Blau of the
Austrian Greens at a European
Green Conference, Stockholm

LEFT: October 1990 – Gert Bastian at his
typewriter in the little study at
Swinemünderstrasse,Bonn

October 1992 – Memorial for the life and work of Petra Kelly and Gert Bastian Beetthovenhalle,
Bonn. Joschka Fischer: "Commemorating means remembering".

Petra Karin Kelly 1947 – 1992

it would be extraordinary if this was really the case; these organizations were meticulous in developing any contact which might be of use to them. It could be argued that he was already doing a fine job undermining Western defence policy on his own, but I feel about this denial of Bastian's, as I do about his 'luckiness' in the war – not entirely convinced.

Between his resignation and his encounter with Petra, less than a year had passed. His spectacular rebellion may have been prompted by the combined pressure from several directions: his sexual indiscretions; his genuine conviction that stationing Cruise and Pershings in Europe would destabilize the balance of power; and his distaste at the slowness of the army to turn soldiers into responsible citizens. But the dramatic leap of Gert Bastian from the Bundeswehr to the greens was perhaps less the conversion of a passionate idealist than the response of a pragmatist to the circumstances around him.

Nonetheless, Gert Bastian was enjoying his new life, and when he met Petra he was very attracted to her, at first in his usual predatory manner. Petra held a particular appeal for older men. Many young men were slightly (some seriously) alarmed by the power she exuded, but to older men the effect of her energy combined with her fragile vulnerability was electric. During the many interviews I conducted for this book, almost without exception the eyes of men over a certain age would become wistful as they talked of Petra. 'There was an intensity to that woman, and my God was she a woman. Who would want to talk to Bastian if she was around?' one confided.

In Bastian, Petra saw someone who certainly needed a stiff tutorial in feminism and non-violence, but she also saw someone from whom she could learn a lot, and perhaps most importantly of all, someone who had matched his personal actions to his beliefs. Bastian was quickly elevated to her gallery of heroes and heroines and joined the roll-call of examples in her speeches. But she was worried by the personal attraction she felt towards him. She told Roland Vogt about her feelings towards this man who was so much of the moment. To Erika Heinz she voiced her doubts about the wisdom or otherwise of getting more intimately involved with Bastian. 'He is kind, courteous and he can teach me so much, but, oh Erika, he is such a womanizer.'

For his part, Bastian had decided early on to add Petra Kelly to his collection of amatory campaign medals. She was physically most attractive, and her political certainty on so many topics filled in the gaps around his otherwise isolated anti-Cruise and Pershing position; at this time Gert Bastian wasn't at all anti-nuclear or anti-military in any broad sense. But this was not to be any ordinary campaign. Petra was not to be easily diverted into a little affair in which Bastian retained command.

As well as her fierce independence and tremendous ambition for the new political movement in Germany, Petra took a pretty radical stance as far as sexuality was concerned – and it had nothing to do with the 'free love' culture of her student days (to which she had never subscribed). For Petra, sex could only be part of a partnership forged on the much firmer ground of deep friendship and community of purpose. On this point, she was radically conservative. To sleep with someone with whom she had worked intensely, or with whom she had a close friendship (often the same thing) was as natural as sitting down to dinner, but to sleep with someone merely for sexual gratification was out of the question. Petra was attracted most to men she could meet on equal terms, and who were part of her larger world of work and politics. Much has been made of Petra's predilection for older men, with the assumption that this was part of a subconscious search for her biological father. While there may be some truth in this, the more prosaic explanation is that she found most younger men boring. Their experience was quickly mined. There were younger men in her life, like Roland Vogt, Lukas Beckmann and later Palden Tawo (with whom she worked on her last big campaign for Tibet) but her most significant relationships, the ones that marked and changed her life, were with older men, like Sicco Mansholt, Heinz Kuby, John Carroll and, finally, Gert Bastian.

When Petra met Gert Bastian she was still involved intimately with Roland Vogt and John Carroll, and, through the development of Die Grünen, drawing closer to Lukas Beckmann. When one of her secretaries asked how she could possibly cope with several lovers at one time, Petra responded that it was easy. What mattered most was to be free to love as she chose, and just as a mother could love equally all her children, so a woman could love equally several men.

Towards the end of the 1970s, Petra began to write and speak quite freely about sexuality. She was influenced by sources as diverse as Aleksandra Kollontai and Hindu and Buddhist writings. Some of her stoutest fans were startled by the way she brought sexuality into Die Grünen's electoral campaigns at the beginning of the 1980s. 'Even in progressive political circles I come up against barriers when I talk of religious character of love, and the erotic character of genuine religious feeling,' Petra would complain. 'The inner relationship between religious mysticism, spiritual love and physical eroticism derives from the fact that, by its nature, the true erotic transcends the confines of the ego, leading to a transcendental, mystic experience.'[10]

Aleksandra Kollontai, who died in 1952 and reputedly scolded Lenin for his chauvinism, provided Petra with the guidelines for her own sexual politics. 'Genuine love and freedom are the cornerstones of feminism. But a love based on solidarity, not the romantic ideal whereby we (the woman) must sacrifice all in the name of obtaining love.' Kollontai also said that the focal point of a woman's life must be her work, her own achievement and the self-confidence awakened by it. This gave the woman the power to love and be loved in an equal partnership. For Petra this was the only route to the essence of love – through a perfect meeting of mutual respect and desire – and the only way to protect herself from hurt. Through her voracious reading, Petra had discovered an extensive culture based on love. She became very attracted to the idea of replacing personal gratification in sexual relationships, with sustained erotic arousal. The mutual objective should be to give maximum pleasure over the longest possible time.

As Gert Bastian raised Petra's hand to his lips and gave her his special enigmatic lopsided smile, it is unlikely he had the remotest idea of what was about to hit him. Another little adventure, perhaps, with an appropriately exciting woman, while he was being courted for his opinion on the future of the Bundeswehr? No chance. Petra's politics – public and personal – were to hit him like a steam train.

A HOLY TRINITY

By the beginning of the 1980s, Petra had replaced her jaded Catholicism with a new and sustaining personal spirituality which (through Grace) brought together the holy trinity of non-violence, personal responsibility and truth.

Action from principle, the perception and the performance of right, changes things and relations; it is essentially revolutionary, and does not consist wholly with anything which was. It not only divides states and churches, it divides families; ay, it divides the individual, separating the diabolical in him from the divine.[11]

Petra's gods were Gandhi and Martin Luther King. Her bibles were Thoreau and Gene Sharp (an American expert on non-violent action).[12] Her spiritual companions were all the people who, like her, tried to put their principles into action. She cited them so frequently, she sometimes forgot her audience might never have heard of them. One of her favourite contemporary heroines was Dorothy Day, who in 1973 at the age of seventy-five was jailed for picketing with Cæsar Chavaz, the tireless campaigner for the rights of California's immigrant farm workers. For Petra, Dorothy Day summed up the practical consequences of her own personal and political philosophy: 'Through [Dorothy Day] . . . one comes to know the seriousness of the situation and to realize it's not going to be changed just by demonstrations. It's a question of risking one's life. It's a question of living one's life in drastically different ways.' [13]

By now Petra was living her own life in drastically different ways. She was trying, with increasing difficulty, to combine a full-time job with EcoSoc in Brussels with a full-time activist job in Germany and – as her reputation spread – in other countries. As the ambitions of the nuclear energy industry in Europe became clearer and NATO prepared to announce its decision to site first-strike nuclear weapons on European soil, Petra's radical and impassioned speeches made her the number one choice for everyone's conference and rally.

Nuclear technology represented for Petra the epitome of violence, to the health and safety of people and the environment – directly, because of the deadly material involved; and indirectly, because of the massive sums of money and technological expertise rerouted from life-affirming activities – not least alleviating poverty. And of course there was the link with Grace.

It had been assumed that the radiation treatment Grace had received was benign. But the more Petra discovered about such things, the more she knew that the calculations scientists made were more hit and miss than anything else. Even the baseline measurements for calculating the effect of different doses of radiation were to be doubted. They had been taken from the victims of the Japan bombings, but had not been established until several years after the event. The cancer Grace had suffered from was very malignant and notoriously resistant to radiation therapy, so even if there had been an aggravation rather than an alleviation caused by her treatment, the outcome would probably have been no different. But this did not change Petra's memory of the awful trauma of the treatment. During her final years, Grace spent a lot of time in hospital. She had several operations, including one in which her right eye was removed, and countless sessions of radiotherapy. Grace had coped with everything with a calmness which affected everyone who knew her: 'That child was always delightful, her name summed her up,' recalls Susan French, Petra's best friend at AU.

But if Grace had borne everything with remarkable equanimity, Petra had been deeply concerned by the lack of special facilities available for children with terminal diseases. Spending money on such facilities would be a waste, the authorities implied, because these children are going to die anyway.

One of Grace's favourite books at this time was *The Little Prince*, Saint-Exupéry's story of the little prince and his strange planet with its three volcanoes and a proud flower.[14] Grace and Petra would read this book together and make up their own strange planets, where children were always happy and safe. Out of these moments grew the idea of the *Kinderplanet* (children's planet), a special hospital unit where children with cancer could get not only treatment but also live full and satisfying lives, with, wherever possible, their family nearby.

To raise money for this project, Petra had set up the Grace P. Kelly Foundation for the Support of Cancer Research for Children in 1973. The foundation described itself as a Europe-wide citizens' action group studying the connection between children's cancer and the environment (particularly the nuclear industry) and developing a project to establish a model psychosocial children's health care centre – the *Kinderplanet*. Wherever she travelled, particularly in Europe or the United States, Petra visited centres dealing with children suffering from cancer. The foundation committee met at least once a year. Petra was chair and members of the board included Omi, her mother, Sicco Mansholt and Bruce French as well as friends of Petra in Brussels. For several years John Carroll acted not only as general secretary but also took the minutes in a large looping hand. It was very much a family affair.[15]

In 1976, during the anniversary of the explosion of the first nuclear bomb over Hiroshima, Petra was invited to Tokyo to speak at a world conference against A and H bombs. The sight of Japanese children moving through the peace parks to place wreaths made up of thousands of paper cranes inside the statue of the Children of the Atomic Bomb had moved her enormously. This statue is in memory of Sadako Sasaki, a little girl from Hiroshima who died of leukaemia in 1956. She had come to symbolize all children who died as a result of the nuclear bombs which fell on Japan. According to Japanese tradition, anyone who folds one thousand paper cranes has a deep desire fulfilled. Sadako died after she had completed only 644.[16]

Anti-nuclear campaigning was one of the strongest, but not the only strand in Petra's political bedrock of non-violence. To Petra's mind, the entire world was, quite simply and quite clearly divided into that which denied life (was violent) and that which affirmed life (was non-violent). People and their activities were all subjected to this classification.

If non-violence could be used to analyse the world as it was, and also to describe the sort of world greens wanted – 'a gentle Europe in a living and loving world' – non-violence was also the method, the *only* method, by which it could be achieved. Of this Petra was convinced. The route to peace had to be peace. For many members of the peace movement who had not read their Thoreau, non-violence simply meant not hitting back when the police clobbered you on a demo. It was interpreted in a negative or at best a passive sense – it was about *not* doing something. For Petra it meant a continual living *active* affirmation of life. Non-violence was different from religious pacifism, she said, because it was not simply about not hitting back, but about seeking opportunities for dialogue or taking actions which would liberate people from the violent system (of thinking) which prevented them from seeing the power and the rightness of non-violence. If there had been any sort of tradition of non-violence in Germany, Petra frequently argued, then the Third Reich would have been impossible.

The Petra who was intellectually attracted to Thoreau and Gandhi was also the Petra who had suffered a great deal of pain. She had had so many operations to remove stones from her kidneys that metal sutures were needed to close her wound. And the heartache of Grace's death was a constant companion. Because she knew only too well what it was like, Petra would go out of her way to avoid pain, both physical and emotional. At times she would go to extraordinary lengths to escape from a painful situation, and had been known to faint rather than attend a meeting she knew would be unpleasant. Lukas Beckmann recalls that 'there seemed to be a total connection between her mind and her body'.

Because of her frail appearance and her fainting fits, Petra earned a reputation for physical weakness. It was widely reported that she suffered a heart attack in 1982, but this was not true. Apart from being slightly enlarged (as an athlete's might be) Petra's heart was in good shape. Genuinely troublesome kidneys notwithstanding, she was capable of great physical endurance. Petra set herself gruelling schedules, forgot to eat properly, and sometimes so overextended herself that she would collapse and need to rest for a couple of days. But mostly she was exhilarated by periods of intense concentration and activity.

If she inspired protective behaviour because of her physical insouciance, then this suited Petra very well. The more responsibility for the practical side of her life that she could abdicate to others, the more pleased she was. This not only left more time for other things but it also bound others to look out for her, care for her – to be there. Except when she was working at night, the thing Petra feared most of all was to be alone; and when she was asked in a newspaper questionnaire about how she wanted to die, Petra replied with two words – 'not alone'.

War-mongering, nationalism and the proliferation of nuclear arms and power were obviously violent. But so too were the systems of democracy which did not allow the views of non-violent people to be represented and respected. Petra referred constantly to the importance of people being able to take responsibility for their own destiny. Working in Brussels she had seen how the strategy of 'leading from the top' was hopeless. And as most European citizens were at best uninterested in what was happening in their continent, the few who were intent on steering the European project could do very much as they pleased. In the 1979 European elections, Petra strongly promoted the idea of a decentralized Europe. She went further than the federalists by talking of sub-national regions as the only organizing unit which made sense if people were to be genuinely in control. Although it remains an irritatingly vaguely developed concept, all European green parties echo this call for a Europe of Regions to this day.

The EC also taught Petra that most people in power – particularly those with a modest amount of power – are not overkeen to fight for any sort of justice that might imperil their job. She could see that Sicco Mansholt had been able to intervene on her behalf not only because he was supremely powerful, but also because he was only a few months away from his pension. These insights confirmed her ambition to become a different kind of leader. She did not want to 'lead from the top' but to lead by her example and inspiration, demonstrating by taking personal action as well as explaining what could be done. 'Power to, not power over' was one of Petra's favourite slogans.

Petra was quite genuine in her view of herself as one of many dissidents, not a leader of them. In her candidature to be a speaker of the first executive of the newly-founded Die Grünen in 1980, she styled herself as a dissident within the EC administration. As one of only six per cent of women in the administrative grade, she saw herself as rallying to student leader Rudi Dutschke's famous call to seek change through 'the long march through the institutions'. But Petra knew it was not a matter of only one or two dissidents making it. Sicco Mansholt again proved that. That was why the promise of the growing green movement in Germany excited Petra enormously. She could be one of them, part of the great family – the mass of people who would change the world because they themselves had changed. Change from below, not from above.

But if revolution lay with the individual, Petra also remained convinced about the value of going straight to the top. By bypassing the hierarchy and directly approaching Robert Kennedy, the Pope and German Chancellor Kurt Kiesinger she had obtained, respectively, help with her scholarship, a special audience and blessing for the suffering Grace, and a plane ticket in order to visit Grace in Germany at Christmas 1968. International Week had been launched on a tidal wave of letters, and the cages of Brussels bureaucracy were

rattled by her directness. Petra obliged people to react to her. For her
the high ground of truth, saying it clearly as she saw it, was the most
powerful place to be.

When asked to describe herself, Petra would reply with a laugh, 'I
am intuitive, intense and subversive.' For her intuition she thanked
Omi and her mother and her intense concentration she said she owed
to the nuns at the Englisches Institut. But like everyone, after a
certain age, Petra's character was shaped beyond her family – by the
people she met, the experiences she had and the books she read – and
it was here, in the wider world, that Petra had learnt what she called
the 'subversive power of truth and love'.

THE NAME, THE SYMBOL AND PETRA

After the 1979 elections to the European parliament, Petra's
relationship with her native Germany reached a significant turning
point. For several years and with increasing frequency, she had been
travelling back to Germany for demonstrations and meetings and to
visit Omi, Gracie's grave and friends. Omi's flat became her German
base, with Omi herself providing the secretariat, not only for the
Grace Kelly Foundation but for Petra's political activities too. It was
Omi's address which appeared on her fundraising and election leaflets.
Omi would answer the phone, clip newspapers and open and sort the
growing mail bag, as well as accompany her granddaughter to
meetings and demonstrations. 'She is,' Petra told Pastor Jörg Zink
when she introduced him to Omi 'my mainstay and my refuge.' By
the 1982 election campaign for the Bavarian parliament, Omi had
become famous as the 'green granny' at Petra's side.

When Die Grünen rented the office in Friedrich Ebert Allee in
Bonn in the spring of 1979, Petra's base began to move closer to
political centre of Germany. She was not finally to move back until
she was elected to the Bundestag in 1983, twenty-three years after she
left with her family for the United States, but if her job was in
Brussels and her heart with Omi and Grace in Bavaria, then from
1979 onwards Petra's political soul began to operate out of Bonn.

After the 'exemplary non-violent resistance' shown by the French
and German farmers at Whyl in 1975, the demonstrations at nuclear
sites had become more violent:

*By the winter of 1976, Grohnde and Brokdorf in the north became the
site of very violent police confrontations – and federal police helicopters,
dangerous chemicals thrown by police, bayonets and wire cutters, chains
and gas masks became the order of the day.*[17]

The very military style of the German police and their heavy tactics
during the demonstrations was, in the minds of many young people,
an uncomfortable evocation of the Nazis. 'Europeans of all classes,
ages and persuasions have one thing in common – an historic memory
of the deadly experience of brute and futile military power,' wrote
Petra.[18]

Consequently, at the end of 1979, when NATO unveiled its plan to
station Pershing II and Cruise nuclear missiles on German soil, the
two parts of the anti-nuclear movement, those against the missiles and
those against the power stations, came together. The military style of
the baton-wielding policemen did not discourage the opposition, it
united it, and helped to fire a debate about the very soul of modern
Germany.

Whatever the facts behind the German government's attempts to
paint the Krefelder Appell as an enterprise of the Central Committee
of the Soviet Communist party, it very quickly became the focus for
the whole German peace movement. Within months of the first
appeal, a million signatures asking the government to refuse to allow
nuclear weapons on German soil had been collected. German people
had been reminded how vulnerable they were to the superpowers, and
how difficult it was for them to assert their opinion as a nation.
Heinrich Böll and many leading writers and intellectuals joined in the
campaign, and the author Günter Grass, who was a member of the
SPD, followed up his vigorous campaigning with a book *The Rats*,
which poignantly evoked German misery at the time.[19]

The Appell held several meetings, including a Hiroshima Hearing
in Dortmund on 21st November 1981, followed by a huge concert
with over two hundred international personalities. Harry Belafonte
and Coretta Scott King joined many others to speak and sing. Also
there was one of Petra's favourite singer-composers, Konstantin
Wecker (who was later to compose a special song for her memorial).
A bestselling record was produced, and on her way home from
Dortmund with her friend Erika Heinz Petra passed over all the

participants lists with some of the speeches, poems and other contributions from the hearing. 'Here, get more, make it all into a book!' Surprised, Erika did, but in her typical self-effacing manner, insisted it be published as edited by Petra. Petra relented but added the inscription 'Thanks to my friend Erika Heinz. Only through her untiring direction was this book possible.'[20]

In April 1981 the rumbustious German anti-nuclear campaigning was given some gravitas by an assembly of scientists and military and peace strategists gathered at the invitation of the University of Groningen in Holland. The meeting was co-organized by Admiral Gene La Rocque, formally a very senior member of the Pentagon staff and the infamous Nuclear Planning Group (NPG), and since his retirement, Director of the Washington-based Center for Defense Information. It was the secret NPG which determined US and NATO nuclear strategy, and (after La Rocque's retirement) had taken the decision on deployment of cruise missiles in Europe. Therefore La Rocque spoke with some authority at Groningen: 'Some military men feel that a nuclear war, once begun, can be controlled and limited even within the theatre, but I have never seen a reasonable plan to control a nuclear war.'

The mobilization against the weapons during the next two years gathered momentum all over Europe. In Germany a series of rallies and marches marked the 'hot autumn', with its climax in October 1983, when Admiral La Rocque was invited to speak in Bonn before a huge crowd of around 350,000, with, amongst others, Willy Brandt, Heinrich Böll, Arno Guthrie and Petra. La Rocque was impressed with her:

She gave a wonderful rousing speech, and the audience responded enthusiastically. Afterwards we had dinner, Guthrie, Bastian, Petra and me. She was a sort of controlled firebrand, disciplined but about to explode anytime – on a messianic mission to save the world from itself. But she saw it from all angles. I saw it mostly in military terms, I would never have related the environment to the military.

Waves of peace marches and actions in Germany (including an amazing 100-kilometre human chain stretching between two US Army bases in Stuttgart and Neu-Ulm) were matched by similar events in other countries. Petra spoke at many of them, sometimes sharing the platform with Gert Bastian. In all her speeches she included an ardent plea that humanity and human rights be deployed in the pursuit of peace. In London in 1981 she ended a speech at a Campaign for Nuclear Disarmament (CND) rally with the words of Martin Luther King: 'I believe the unarmed truth and unconditional love will have the final word in reality.'[21]

In August 1981 Petra returned to Japan, invited by Gensukium, the Japanese Socialist Party, to mark Hiroshima Day. Since her first visit to Japan in 1976, Petra had remained in friendly contact with Ichiro Moritaki, Emeritus Professor at Hiroshima University and a leading anti-nuclear campaigner, and she was anxious for her new friend Gert Bastian to experience Hiroshima, to visit the radiation victims and see the Peace Park which meant so much to her.

In December of the same year she took Bastian to visit the American Berrigan brothers, two of the heroes in her non-violent hall of fame, who had been found guilty of burglary, criminal conspiracy and criminal mischief after their action in the Pennsylvania draft office the previous year. Bastian had been invited to speak with Petra at a Washington meeting on 'NATO Missiles: a European Perspective'. The day before, he had also joined Petra and British Labour MP Jo Richardson on a platform at the Cathedral of St John the Divine in New York. 'It is wrong,' emphasized Gert Bastian (still not entirely convinced by non-violence) 'to say we are anti-American and pro-Soviet. We have reached the point where more weapons do not mean more security, they mean more instability.' Petra spoke of the powerful combination of feminism, ecology and non-violence: 'In an atomic age you do not have an enemy, you can only have neighbours.' All three speakers spoke of the need for the anti-nuclear movements in different countries to build up their contacts in order to improve their effectiveness. Bruce Kent, former chair of CND, remembers that from about this time a sort of international 'anti-nuclear mafia' developed, with regular contacts sustained between key members of the movement. Petra became a pivotal point in the communication network. Alongside the growing network of European green parties, this was exactly the sort of international collaboration she had discussed endlessly with Heinz Kuby and other European federalists; she wanted to make sure the transnational movement became a reality.

Back in Germany, as activity intensified in the broader peace movement, and all other German political parties remained disinclined to provide any opposition to the impending arrival of the missiles, so the momentum behind Die Grünen began to gather steam. In the October of 1979, by just scraping over the 5 per cent threshold, a green list had already won four seats in the *Land* (regional) parliament of Bremen. This gave a great boost to the November meeting of SPV-Die Grünen which prepared the ground for turning the informal 'political association' into a formal political party to be called simply Die Grünen. Since the 1979 European elections, membership of the new political alliance had soared from 6,000 to 16,000 and some of the money from the European elections had been used to establish a framework for a national party. The date for the founding conference was set for 12th/13th January 1980 in Karlsruhe.

The congress was chaotic. Although Petra and her ringing advocacy for the new party to be 'beyond the politics of the left and right' had been prominent at many stages of the process so far, primal forces were locked in battle at Karlsruhe. There was a straightforward struggle between traditional conservative and socialist opinions as to which of them should possess the new party's soul. Lukas Beckmann remembers asking the caretakers of the hall to stop the clock on the Sunday because he was fearful people would start leaving for their trains before any compromise had been reached. Eventually Herbert Gruhl, former CDU MP and leader of the conservative greens and Jürgen Reents, a journalist from Hamburg who was a leader of the left, were forced to sign a piece of paper on which were written four words: ecology, social-responsibility, grassroots-democracy and non-violence. These 'four pillars' were to become legendary, and quoted at the time as the key to Die Grünen's success; however, they would turn out to be too fragile an intellectual support system for the huge and variegated body which they were eventually required to prop up.

That the party had actually come into existence and would contest the elections to the federal parliament due in October left Petra absolutely elated.[21] With her indefatigable faith in the intrinsic good sense of human beings, she felt confident that, once everybody started working together, the various factions would soon achieve the same synthesis of ideas as she herself had done. In her address for the election of the new party's three speakers in March 1980, she made a point of supporting the four pillars and underlined her commitment to a new sort of party organization – an 'anti-party'. That autumn Petra told *The Times* that she was happy that large numbers of the 'undogmatic left' should join the greens, including communists, as the party must draw on the best of Christian, Marxist and humanist philosophies. [23]

But many others were not happy. Within a few months the not so undogmatic Marxist left had begun to organize around a newspaper called *Moderne Zeiten*, in a manner which strongly resembled a party within a party. Calls that their membership be rescinded led to the party holding a tribunal; Petra was amongst those who argued strongly – and successfully – against the expulsion of the Marxists. Several years later, as she and I took a break during a hard day's campaigning in London during the 1984 European elections, she confessed this was one of her greatest political mistakes. When she had worked in the EC, and been active in the young federalist movement, she had found the Marxist-oriented people to be amongst the most kind and thoughtful and later, in the anti-nuclear movement, they were usually the most dedicated organizers. Because she herself had examined Marxist doctrine and dismissed it as inadequate to the purpose of social change, she imagined anyone with half a wit would do the same. It took Petra a long time to grasp the fact that, just as stoutly-held ideological beliefs could close the minds of the right, so they could blinker the left. In 1980, Petra could not yet believe that anyone would join Die Grünen who did not agree that the new green politics went *beyond* the old ideologies.

Like many of us, Petra found it difficulty to explain succinctly the philosophical change which lay behind the green slogans. There is an inevitable time-lag before new concepts and their special language become common currency. While trying to explain to uncomprehending journalists what green politics was all about in a crisp quotable phrase, Petra reached hopefully for the words 'feminism, ecology and non-violence'; but this invariably met with blank stares from newsmen hewn out of the rocks of left-right politics. 'A sort of emancipatory socialism' she would sum up rather desperately. Ah! Now, they understood – green politics was socialism plus a bit extra. But of course she did not mean that at all. What Petra was talking about was not social*ism* with a green stripe, but the emancipation of old social*ists*. She expected them, whether inspired by Marx or Willy Brandt, to be drawn to green politics as they realized that social*ism* had not worked.

And the way things were going, in terms of both extra-parliamentary and electoral activity, she might have been forgiven for thinking the emancipation of the old lefties would indeed be accomplished in short order. After Die Grünen was formally established as a nationwide political party, events moved so fast that little time could be spent worrying about the internal divisions in the party. A general election was due in October 1980, and two more congresses were held, one in Saarbrücken and one in Dortmund, to elect the executive of the new party and cobble together a programme. Petra was chosen as one of the speakers of the new party and photographed waving a daffodil by a German press not quite able to believe the informality of the meetings, in which tough debates took place while children and dogs wandered freely about.

Despite the daffodils, the symbol which Die Grünen adopted was the one which Roland Vogt had proposed for the European election campaign – the sunflower. Petra explained that it was derived from the Danish anti-nuclear symbol, the smiling sun which came to say 'Nuclear Power? No Thanks?' in so many languages. 'It stands for our commitment to live with the earth, to live with an ecological sense, to try to help the flowers live. Because if you help a flower live, you're helping people live as well.'[24] In the meantime Die Grünen had entered another *Land* parliament, this time winning six seats in Baden-Württemburg.

As it turned out, the 1980 federal elections were a non-event for Die Grünen. They polled only 1.5 per cent, less than half the votes they had won in the European elections. Because the ultra-conservative Franz Joseph Strauss was the right's candidate for the Chancellorship, potential green voters decided either to stick with the Social Democrats or voted tactically for the centre party (FDP) to ensure he did not succeed. Petra had personally fought Strauss in a ferocious and energetic campaign in their common *Heimat* of Bavaria, exhausting herself and everyone around her. She blamed her lack of success (with some justification) on the Bavarian vilification campaign against the Greens, blatantly egged on by the Catholic Church, but the main reason the voters did not support the Greens was that they agreed with her about the unthinkability of Strauss being Chancellor. Behind Petra's bitter disappointment over the election result was the fact that it meant she would have to go back to the cloistered tedium of the EC bureaucracy in Brussels. The double life and gruelling commute was not over yet.

As the star turns of the movement, 1981 was a busy year for Petra and Bastian. Bastian continued his campaigning for the Krefelder Appell, and became involved in Generals for Peace and Disarmament, an international grouping of retired senior military officers initially brought together by a Gerhard Kade, a German historian and political scientist from Hamburg University. With the membership of Die Grünen increasing rapidly, Petra, along with the rest of the executive, was kept very busy dealing with the organizational nuts and bolts of running the party, its finances and its congresses. The 1981 Die Grünen conference in Offenbach agreed a Peace Manifesto, which Petra had helped to draft. In the section entitled 'Neither to the East, nor to the West, but loyal to one another' there was little sign of the 'one-eyed pacifism' which Petra hated so much. The manifesto was reasonably even-handed in its criticism of expansionism and bloc mentality in both the United States and USSR and made clear that human rights and peace were two sides of the same demand. Towards the end there was a quotation from Henry Thoreau: 'If, however, the law is so promulgated, that it of necessity makes you an agent of injustice against another, then I say to you – break the law.' [25]

By 1982, little *frissons* of fear had begun to enter the hearts of several Western governments as they read the documents of this increasingly popular new political party. The traditional Easter peace marches in Germany attracted massive numbers of people that year; one hundred thousand attended the Krefelder Appell rally and concert alone. Also in 1982, Die Grünen entered three more of the ten *Länder* parliaments. In Hamburg in June, and Hesse in September, not only did the greens win seats but they ended up holding the balance of power. This unleashed a storm of reaction inside the party, as arguments raged about whether the greens should form coalitions or not, and, more fundamentally, what would happen if Die Grünen should win seats in the federal parliament?

Franz Joseph Strauss started a campaign to have the party banned. He doubted its constitutional legitimacy, referring to a clause in the

German basic law which required a party to demonstrate its legitimacy not only as far as organization and membership were concerned but also by ensuring that 'its public appearance guarantees the seriousness of its political goals'. Petra herself summed up how many people saw the public appearance of Die Grünen:

We've got back-to-the-land romantics, and drop outs, young anarchists, mature Christian pacifists, utopians, socialists, dogmatic conservatives who think animals are more important than people, old aunts who like gardening. We have big regional differences to resolve. The Hamburg Greens are obsessed with abolishing the police force, while in Bavaria the Greens rather like the police – macrobiotic food is their thing.[26]

On leave of absence from the EC again, Petra was once more campaigning in her own *Land* of Bavaria, where elections for the state parliament were due on 10th October. Just to complicate matters and heighten the tension, on 1st October the Social Democrat government had fallen when its coalition partner, the centrist FDP shifted its support to the CDU, thus making Helmut Kohl Chancellor. Federal elections were anticipated in the spring of 1983, and all the attention of the German and international press homed in on the amazing growth of Die Grünen. Could it be that this anarchic, anti-nuclear rag-bag of a party would not only end up in the Bundestag, but also have the power to make a governing coalition with the SPD? To keep the door open, just in case, Social Democrat leader Helmut Schmidt (Willy Brandt's successor) began to mince his words about the Greens, saying that although he was worried about some of the extremist elements of the party, he admired the idealism of Petra Kelly. It was always politically safe to admire Petra.

But Petra made it very clear that this possibility was not on her agenda: 'If the Greens were to start sending ministers to Bonn, they would no longer be the party I started to build up.'[27] 'Even if we hold the balance of power in the Bundestag, or lower level parliaments, there's no possibility of our going into any cabinet. Some people say that's not being responsible, but they're wrong' she told the posse of reporters following her around Bavaria.[28]

Petra's diary for this campaign started in the middle of July. She travelled relentlessly (usually with Omi, sometimes with Bastian) between campaign events, interviews and executive meetings. With Manfred Coppik, another green refugee from the SPD, Petra had just edited a book of essays about the ideas behind the new movement, so meetings were organized to promote it.[29] Shadowing her campaign was Helmuth Weiland who was making a film of her life for German television, and Pierre Salinger, former press secretary for President John F. Kennedy, turned up to find out for ABC and America just what the leader of this 'freewheeling radical party called the Greens' really thought. Adding to the general mayhem, the European Workers' Party, which is linked to the United States-based Lyndon LaRouche organization, began its campaign against Petra during this election. LaRouche's 'intelligence gathering' organization regarded Queen Elizabeth II as a drug smuggler and Henry Kissinger as a Soviet agent, while the European Workers' Party had a record of harassing prominent German political figures, including Willy Brandt.[30] They would disrupt Petra's meetings with aggressive heckling: 'What did you do in bed with Sicco Mansholt?' 'I think nuclear power stations are better constructed than you.'

The demands on Petra were constant, and, as usual, she tried to do everything; neither Bastian or Omi were able to prevent her from overdoing it and she collapsed at the end of September. But within a few days she felt well enough to rejoin the campaign trail for the last week. Die Grünen polled 4.6 per cent, infuriatingly short of the five per cent needed to win any seats, but a tremendous score for the greens in the up to now unfertile political soil of Bavaria. When the result was announced, pictures of Petra weeping in the arms not of Omi but of Gert Bastian were broadcast all over Germany. This time, Petra did not go back to Brussels. She extended her leave of absence by another six months, and started to prepare the campaign for the federal elections due to be held on 6th March 1983.

Back in Brussels, where many of her colleagues had been reading with interest about Petra's rapid rise to fame in Germany, a question about the legitimacy of her leave was put to the Commission. EcoSoc issued a terse reply which pointed out that she was entitled to such leave under article 40 of the staff regulations, which included leave on personal grounds when the member of staff concerned was a candidate for elective office.[31]

INTO THE BUNDESTAG

In 1981, Achim Schuppert, a newly-qualified doctor and supporter of Die Grünen, was offered the opportunity to rent a large farmhouse in Irlenbusch (population 200), to the southwest of Bonn. Schuppert called the Die Grünen offices in Bonn to see if he could find some courageous and convivial soul to share with him. Lukas Beckmann called back, and the two men shared the house until 1985. The huge old farmhouse became a gathering place for many of the greens, and a place Petra would often stay when she was working in Bonn. Here, plans were laid, strategies elaborated and ideas discussed late into the night. Schuppert's fiancée, Irmgard, still a medical student at the time, liked to study in a room overlooking the drive and would watch the comings and goings of what Petra called the 'core group'. These were the early party founders who had stayed with it through thick and thin and who were still working long and hard hours, largely at their own expense. 'We grew together, thought alike, voted alike at conference and could almost put words into each other's mouths,' Petra used to say.

Irlenbusch became a safe haven for Petra, a place where she could, from time to time, even relax. It was at this time that she drew closer to Lukas Beckmann. A quiet, private man, he was also amused by the way Petra would negotiate her personal relationship with Vogt, Carroll and Bastian as openly and freely as she discussed political and organizational matters. Eventually, in August 1982, after a visit to the theatre and supper with some friends, they became lovers, to the intense annoyance of Gert Bastian. He had seen it coming and would jealously phone Petra, especially when he knew she was staying at the farm. He was not an enthusiastic subscriber to Petra's philosophy of personal relationships, and remained intent on having her all to himself. Bastian had just begun to feel confident that he had finally displaced Roland Vogt and John Carroll, so Beckmann constituted seriously unwelcome additional competition.

Some people have suggested that Lukas was Petra's true 'grand passion'. Heinz Suhr remembers Beckmann being a perfect foil for the torrent of ideas and energy that she generated, and Beckmann remained one of the few people whose advice and political judgement she respected. But they were two strong and completely different personalities. Although it was usually Beckmann she would call when she collapsed from overwork, and he would promptly turn up and ferry her to a clinic, he was not interested in abdicating his own political activities to adopt the role of her protector. Once, when she overslept at Irlenbusch and woke to find Beckmann had left for the office without her, she decamped to the Hotel Eden in Bonn in protest. But, to her irritation, it was not Lukas Beckmann who raised the panic when she could not be found the following evening, but Gert Bastian – all the way from Berlin.

By the end of 1982 Gert Bastian was more than in love with Petra. Their regular encounters on public platforms since the end of 1980 had soon been augmented by planned meetings, where she pursued her campaign to complete his personal transformation from a military man with doubts about the latest nuclear weapons system to a full-blown pacifist who could quote Gandhi and Martin Luther King as easily as she could. After a while the meetings became assignations. Freimut Duve remembers one of the first. Duve and Petra were returning from a peace rally late one night in the summer of 1982. Both were due to stop over at Hannover, it being too late to make connections, he for Hamburg, she for Bonn. Although she told Duve she would be staying with friends, at the station Duve spotted Bastian, lurking sheepishly behind a pillar, carrying two plastic bags.

Bastian had fallen in love with a passion he had never experienced before. He was transported by sexual bliss and political fervour. He had lost control and did not mind a bit. He sought to be with Petra at every opportunity. He let his hair get longer and, from time to time, forgot to put on a tie. But even though Gert Bastian was confident enough to announce on German television during the October 1982 Bavarian campaign that, yes, he could publically confirm that he and Petra were intimate friends, and furthermore it could be also be said openly that his wife was most understanding about it, Petra's affair with Lukas Beckmann continued until the following year – after Die Grünen had entered the Bundestag.

Intensely jealous, Bastian knew desperate measures would have to be deployed if he was to have Petra all to himself. It was during this period that Bastian began to take on the role of protector by adding himself to Petra's retinue on a regular basis. Omi was not always up to the gruelling travelling schedule, and certainly not able to help Petra when faced with rough crowds or disruptive hecklers, so she welcomed having Bastian around. In December, when Petra went as planned with Omi to Stockholm to receive the Alternative Nobel Prize, Bastian went too. By the beginning of 1983, he had allowed himself to be persuaded to run for the Bundestag on the Bavarian list.

During the 1983 campaign, Petra had one of her boldest and best ideas. The party would organize an international hearing on the legality of first-strike weapons of mass destruction, in the same city where Hitler had promulgated his infamous Nürnburg Law in 1935 and where the 1945-6 military showtrial of senior Nazi officers had been held. 'It is most unlikely we shall be confused with Hitler,' Petra assured her colleagues. With her keen eye for anniversaries she suggested it be held on the 40th anniversary of the night Goebbels screamed in the Berlin Sports Hall, 'Do you want the total war?'

The trial, covered by a stunned press, became the launchpad of Die Grünen's campaign for the federal elections. It opened with Petra quoting Robert Jackson, the American Associate Justice in 1945: 'If certain acts in violation of treaties are crimes, they are crimes whether the US does them or whether Germany does them, and we are not prepared to lay down a rule of criminal conduct against others which we would be unwilling to invoke against ourselves.'

In the dock were the nuclear powers of the USA, USSR, Great Britain, France, China and India, as well as all countries who were secretly in possession of nuclear weapons, charged with 'denying the fundamental principles of international law and human rights'. The Federal Republic of Germany was charged with (among other things) being in breach of its own Basic Law. Petra plundered her extensive list of international contacts to bring together an array of international lawyers, peace experts and doctors to join their German counterparts as jury and witnesses. The accused were found guilty on several counts, and the jury's final declaration ended by stating 'Not violence and weapons, but reason and trust must determine the fate of our planet.'

Petra spent most of the Bundestag election campaign in Bavaria. Because the party had a two-year limit on holding national posts, Petra and Bavarian colleague Dieter Burgmann were replaced as speakers by Wilhelm Knabe, an expert on forests, and ex-communist Rainer Trampert from Hamburg in November 1982. Nonetheless

Petra remained the person the press, particularly the international press, wanted to speak to most. She was charismatic, emotional, knowledgeable and spoke almost perfect English. Knabe and Trampert were too similar to the other serious and earnest party leaders. The main part of the campaign involved the deployment of what was called a green caterpillar, but which was actually a bus, weaving its way around Germany carrying well-known rock bands and other musicians, actors and comedians to the local meetings. These were staged with a mixture of political speeches from green politicians, music and plenty of satire on all that was pompous about normal German political life. Die Grünen election broadcasts were also very different from the grey-suited seriousness of the other parties: one showed an ordinary German couple on the doorstep of their home, firmly refusing to accept delivery of a stamped, addressed Cruise missile.

On election night, Sunday 6th March, 1,500 greens and their guests packed into the conference hall at Bad Godesburg in a southern suburb of Bonn. The rock bands were there too, but silent. The German computerized system which brings reliable estimations very quickly after the close of the polls was showing the early figures. A sweat-drenched and exhausted Petra Kelly stood beside Lukas Beckmann waiting for the results to appear. When first estimations came at 6.20p.m., it looked as though the greens would not make it over the five per cent threshold. At 7.15p.m. Petra appeared before the cameras, convinced that it was all over, to denounce the 'lie' on which the victory of Helmut Kohl and the CDU had been built. Then at 7.39p.m., the result was confirmed. With around 5.5 per cent of the vote Die Grünen had won 27 seats in the German federal parliament. Petra was in; and so was Gert Bastian. The hall exploded with noise, and the party to end all parties began. 'It's fabulous,' Petra managed to say into the microphone before the tears of relief began to flow and she turned away to be engulfed in the arms of her friends. This time it was all over. She would never have to go back to Brussels again.

Notes

1   Gert Bastian, 'General Bastian zur Lage', in *Neue Politik*, 25 Jahrgang/11 (15 February 1980).
2   Walter Heynowski, Gerhard Scheumann and Gerhard Kade, *Die Generale*, (Berlin, Verlag der Nation, 1986); (English film version distributed by ETV Films Ltd, London).
3   Stone (1980) p. 160.
4   Watson (1992) p. 150.
5   Craig (1990) p. 245.
6   Craig (1990) p. 148.
7   Craig (1990) p. 251.
8   Spretnak and Capra (1984) p. 44.
9   Wasmuht (1987) p. 247, footnote 154.
10 Book: (1984) p. 111.
11 Thoreau (1983) p. 395.
12 Sharp (1973).
13 Speech: Sydney (July 1977).
14 Saint-Exupéry (1974).
15 Today, the Foundation has about DM500,000 and 320 members. At a meeting held in Würzburg on the 1st October 1993, the first anniversary of Petra's death, the Foundation decided to push ahead with the fundraising (including a calender and another art auction) and, with facilities much improved in most of West Germany, it was decided to investigate the possibility of siting Grace Kelly's Kinderplanet somewhere in East Germany.
16 Essay: (1-9 August 1976).
17 Essay: (March 1978).
18 Essay: (July 1982).
19 Craig (1991) p. 313.
20 Book: Kelly (ed.) (1983).
21 Speech: London (24 October 1981).
22 *Earthwatch Oregon* (June/July 1979).
23 *The Times* (16 September 1980).
24 *Earthwatch Oregon* (June/July 1979).
25 'Peace Manifesto', Federal Executive of Die Grünen (1981).
26 *The Sunday Times* (3 October 1982).
27 *The Economist* (10 July 1982).
28 *US News and World Report* (1 November 1982).
29 Book: with Coppik, (eds.) (1982).
30 *International Herald Tribune* (3 July 1986).
31 Official Journal of the European Communities, No c275/7 (18 October 1982).

MARCH 1983

-TO-

DECEMBER 1985

THE ANTI-PARTY PARTY

However disappointed they might be that the Christian Democrats had won the election, most of the greens celebrating at Bad Godesburg were profoundly relieved that Die Grünen had not ended up holding the balance of power. After the *Länder* elections which had led to the Greens 'tolerating' a minority Social Democrat government (in Hamburg) or negotiating for a coalition (in Hesse), huge arguments had broken out in the party over what it should do if they found themselves in a similar situation after the federal elections. When it became clear that the Christian Democrats had won comfortably and that the Social Democrats would be joining the Greens in opposition, there was widespread relief that this particular argument could be shelved, at least for the moment, and all immediate effort directed to some serious celebrating.

No one was more relieved than Petra, who had argued hard against coalitions. 'Parliament is like the marketplace for us, or the building site, where we can spread the information. Parliament is not our goal, only part of our strategy.' This irritated the pragmatists in the party who had hissed that if Die Grünen persisted with this sort of nonsense, 'We will slide into a minority sect faster than we can talk about it.'[1]

But the dispute over whether Die Grünen should, or should not,

make coalitions did not go away. It got worse – a lot worse – and became very tedious for all but the most partisan participants and a handful of masochistic political scientists. On the one side the pragmatists lined up; they believed that coalitions (especially in local parliaments and councils) provided the chance to put green solutions to current problems into action – and show they really worked. They became known as the *Realos*. On the other side were those who maintained that Die Grünen's primary role was to provide a fundamental opposition to the entire system. They styled themselves the *Fundis* and were a confusing mixture of the Marxist-inspired left and the more spiritually oriented greens. Petra liked to see herself as independent of both factions. She believed the Greens should only make partnerships under very specific circumstances. For her, political coalitions should be seen in the same light as the relationship between men and women, only worthwhile if they were negotiated from a position of mutual respect and equal strength: 'and it will be years before we are ready to do that,' she said shortly after the Hamburg result. 'If the Social Democrats switch off all atomic power stations, stop stationing the missiles and start building ambulances, then we can talk.' She also remained convinced that Die Grünen must continue to be involved in movement activities, that there must be no separation of roles. 'If the Party ceases to be a movement it is nothing.'[2]

At Bad Godesburg on election night, Petra had expounded to the press on the possibilities of the next few years. She was confident the Green Party could form a strong opposition group with the Social Democrats:

We will be able to come to an agreement with them on ecological problems and the missiles if they opt for our strategy on non-violent struggle. If Hans Jochen Vogel [then SPD leader] really wants to stop the stationing of the Pershings in West Germany next autumn, he can come with us into the streets to give more weight to his opposition to deployment.

But of course this was not to be. Joschka Fischer, another Die Grünen MP elected to the Bundestag that night, was dedicated to coalition building wherever possible and was in the middle of negotiations with the Social Democrats to participate in the government of the *Land* of

Hesse, but generally speaking, the Social Democrat Party was very doubtful of the wisdom of being seen to be too close to the chaotic and inconsistent Greens.

Petra's comments on election night showed that however she might protest her independence, she was, in truth, firmly in the *Fundi* camp. *Realos* like Fischer believed that the Greens should set up hurdles for the Social Democrats – hurdles carefully angled in terms of policy, but hurdles it could jump nevertheless. Once over, the next hurdle could be discussed. When Fischer eventually became Minister for the Environment in Hesse he agreed with his SPD partners that there would be no expansion of the nuclear plant at Hanau. For him this was the first hurdle to be cleared on the path towards closing it down. Petra was furious; for her this was supping with the devil with no spoon at all. From then on she called Fischer the Atomic Minister. 'There are certain topics – the right to life and the right to a safe environment, that are not negotiable.' Until the SPD, or any other political party could clear – in one go – the hurdles of: non-violence as a strategy; rejection of civilian or military use of nuclear weapons; no employment at the price of health; parity of men and women in political positions; and a decentralized, renewable energy policy, there could be no deal.

Refusing to compromise on principle and combining the role of party and non-violent activism was what Petra meant by an anti-party party. She took this idea from a Hungarian philosopher Gyorgy Konrad, who described 'antipolitics' as a moral force. 'Antipolitics strives to put politics in its place and make sure it stays there, never overstepping its proper office of defending and refining the morals of the game in a civil society – where a civil society is the antithesis of a military society.'[3] Kondrad, of course, was writing in a totalitarian state, and Petra rather distorted his point when she transposed it too literally to the situation in Western Europe, where politics is everything to do with give and take, and refining the moral framework in which the political system works is the job of a civil society. In Hungary the conditions necessary for operating a civil society were absent.

By transposing Konrad's point to refer to a political party, Petra had given Die Grünen the double role of defending the highest moral standards *and* of behaving as the antithesis of any other political party.

She was right in one sense. Party politics did need a fairly serious overhaul, both in its morality and its organization; this the anti-party party slogan conveyed to great effect – particularly when the Greens played a central role during their first term of office in the investigation into corrupt laundering of donations to other parties through the Flick company. But to ask any political party to compensate for the imperfections of society was perhaps to ask too much.

But these complications were still in the future. In March 1983, as a radiant Petra walked arm-in-arm with Gert Bastian at the front of Die Grünen's colourful parade through the Bonn streets to her seat in the Bundestag, everything seemed possible. Walking beside her was Otto Schily, the civil rights lawyer and Marieluise Beck, a schoolteacher. With Petra, they would be the speakers of Die Grünen's first parliamentary group. Everyone held a seedling tree in a plantpot to place on their desks, symbols of new growth, not just for the environment but for German politics. Over her shoulder Marieluise Beck carried a branch of a pine tree, shrivelled and distorted by acid rain. This she presented to the newly sworn-in Chancellor Kohl, who was too relieved to have won the election to be anything but jovial about the whole occasion. And it was a remarkable moment. After a tremendous fight to escape the traditional seating arrangement, whereby the parties are fanned around the semicircular plenary chamber from left to right, the Greens had agreed to be seated in pairs in a thin row between the two major parties. Apart from Otto Schily and Gert Bastian, who remained attached to shirts and ties for anything remotely resembling a formal occasion, colourful casual clothes predominated. All around them the other members blended into the otherwise grey and austere surroundings. Like a warning of excitements to come, the bright, lively stripe of the new green *Fraktion* (parliamentary group) reached back from the central speaker's podium like an exclamation mark.

As Petra took her seat at the front, Willy Brandt came up to shake her hand. His fear that when she left the SPD she would take with her what he called the 'lost children' of the country's political system had been realized.

Moving Petra and her already substantial archive from Brussels to Bonn was a happy but complicated operation, not helped by the fact that Petra and Gert Bastian departed in the middle of it for a lecture tour of the United States. Mrs Kelly came over from America and stayed most of the summer to help out, and a fleet of cars and vans brought Petra's furniture, books and papers to Swinemünderstrasse. 'It was a nightmare!' Mrs Kelly remembers with commendable good humour. 'And as soon as we'd finished I went to Nürnburg to move Omi from her apartment to a new one with an elevator. What a summer!'

Petra had persuaded Martha Kremer, a secretary in Brussels, to come and work with her in Bonn, and Kremer and Mrs Kelly spent weeks getting everything unpacked and onto the shelves which lined most of the walls of the house – in the rooms and down in the cellars. Just as they thought they were nearing the end, Lukas Beckmann turned up with all Petra's files from the new party office.

The parliamentarians' offices were in large tower blocks not far from the Bundestag chamber. Petra's office was on the seventh floor of the Tulpenfeld building, along with the other speakers and also Bastian. Stepping out of the lift in search of a particular MP's office, it was easy for visitors to be confused over which corridor to take. Unless, that is, it was Petra you wanted. In no time her papers had overflowed from her office, the extra filing cabinets and pile of archive boxes in the corridor indicating unmistakably where she was.

On her first day in her new office, Petra sat for a while taking it all in. At last, the double life was over. She was no longer an anonymous civil servant in the bureaucracy of Brussels; from now on she would be the political servant of anyone who aligned themselves with her principles and her cause. To the door of her office she carefully taped the pictures of her two guiding political stars – Martin Luther King and Rosa Luxemburg.

But the real world of anti-party politics beckoned. From day one the meetings of the *Fraktion* group became marathon debates until the weakest gave way to the strongest. As part of the brand new green theory of organizing, it had been decided that the *Fraktion* meetings would be open to the press and public. This meant that the new MPs, plus their *Nachrücker* (successors who would 'rotate' into office in two years' time) discussed their business under the lights and microphones of the world's media. Because many members of the *Fraktion* had never met each other before and all were new to parliamentary life, it was rather like going through adolescence in public. Everyone was self-conscious, unsure and intolerant. Very quickly personal relationships degraded. Petra was upset; what was happening in the group was a long way, she said, from the 1980 Saarbrücken programme which declared that the new political movement would be 'based on human solidarity and democracy among its members and on the rejection of a performance and hierarchy-oriented approach governed by rivalry hostile to life'.[4] The anti-party party had fallen at its own first hurdle.

Particularly difficult for Petra at this time was the matter of 'rotation'. This was the system whereby each Green MP should hand over their parliamentary seat to another party member after two years; the Greens believed this was the best way to avoid being 'corrupted' by power. Petra supported the principle, but the decision that this should take place halfway through a term of office was proving 'politically disastrous and is unacceptable, from a human point of view, to both members and substitutes'.

By January 1984, life in the parlimentary group had become so grim that Gert Bastian demanded 'fundamental structural improvements'. The parliamentary group was unable to work efficiently he said, because the party failed, or refused, to provide them with the means to do so. Lack of professional staff meant that important green policy work was not being done. The informal working groups of the party were simply not up to the level of research needed by the parliamentarians. Bastian directly blamed the chaos on the colonization of the party organization by former communists. They were, he said, trying to replace the green concepts of ecology and non-violence with 'outdated class struggle notions' and, he feared, a 'violence oriented as well as a strongly anti-American bias' was becoming explicit. If, Bastian concluded, these deficiencies were not remedied, he would resign from the group and work as an independent member of parliament.[5] One month later he did so, saying that he felt funding two academically qualified assistants did not amount to resolving the structural, material and psychological difficulties of the group.[6]

Petra and Die Grünen were finding out in the most painful of ways that internal democracy requires not just good will, but good structures and rules. Just as it only takes one car driving on the wrong side of the road to wreak enormous havoc, so a small number of people can bring to its knees an organization which does not have the constitutional means to prevent it. Freedom to think differently was fine in theory, but in practice some qualification was needed, and Petra was not alone in finding it difficult to come to terms with this.

When Bastian resigned, the press reported the whole argument in great detail under the headline 'Climbing out of the green hell'. Much was made of the rancour and spite now seething in the anti-party party. However, Bastian's resignation and the explicitness of the reasons behind it were not entirely prompted by a climax of pique. After all, he had known what he was getting into when he agreed to stand for parliament. There was a strategic reason too. Access to parliamentary committees and speaking time in the chamber is calculated according to the percentage of seats your *Fraktion* holds. The minimum number of seats required in order to qualify as a *Fraktion* at all was, at that time, 25. By resigning from the group, Gert Bastian left Die Grünen on the borderline, so giving Petra more space for manoeuvre. Should she resign too, then they would be in trouble. The general had taken a strategic tumble onto his sword so his love might fly more freely.

But the first year was not all internecine strife. To begin with at least, the continued fight against the stationing of the missiles glued everyone together. Petra opened her maiden speech in the Bundestag on 4th May 1983, with a quote from Rosa Luxemburg: 'If we are asked to raise the weapons of murder against our French brothers, then we shall cry, "No! we will not do it." ' She went on to give 'this high house of many men and few women' a complete tour of the principles which govern her policies, and to demonstrate how profoundly violence shapes society. Weapons of mass destruction are linked to 'structural and personal violence' – including rape in marriage. She listed all the allies of the greens in the campaign against the stationing of the missiles, including peace movements, US senators and congressmen, as well as *Solidarnosc* in Poland and the East German Swords into Ploughshares movement. She closed by warning that 'when justice becomes injustice, resistance becomes a duty'.

Throughout her time in the Bundestag, Petra was remorselessly and sometimes rudely heckled, particularly by CDU and CSU members, for the speed and tone of her speeches. Later on, she participated less in the house, preferring to devote more time to other parliamentary procedures such as preparing questions. She summed up the hostility of the whole environment by the fact that the microphones were permanently tuned to a man's voice, so when a woman spoke she sounded unnaturally shrill. It was a small but significant battle won when the microphones were automatically retuned each time a woman spoke.

But in the main, for now, times were good for Petra and Die Grünen. The Greens were new, the press was watching closely, and all political parties were jittery about the coming 'hot autumn' and the mounting protest against the arrival of the Pershing and Cruise missiles. The first weapons were due to arrive at the end of the year, but not before a parliamentary debate and vote in November. In May, the European Nuclear Disarmament movement (END) held its annual conference in West Berlin, and on the 12th, Gert Bastian, Petra, Lukas Beckmann, Milan Horaćek, Gabi Potthast and Roland Vogt crossed to the vast and bleak Alexanderplatz in the centre of East Berlin to unfurl a large banner with the banned slogan of the East German peace movement, 'Swords into Ploughshares'. They asked to see Erich Honecker, president of East Germany, but as he was out of town they circulated a declaration which asked both governments to work together for peace not war. For this, they were promptly arrested, but as soon as the police realized they had members of parliament on their hands they were hastily returned over the wall to the West.

Although it got widespread and approving publicity, this action was not universally popular inside Die Grünen. The left-wing Greens, feeling confidently in the ascendent in the party organization, issued a statement which claimed that any criticism of East Europe removed pressure from the West to disarm. Petra's co-speakers Otto Schily and Marieluise Beck agreed. But the Alexanderplatz action was vindicated when Erich Honecker wrote to Petra and her colleagues agreeing with the proposal for a nuclear-free zone in Central Europe, and inviting a delegation to return for a meeting. The date was set for 31st October.

Meanwhile, Petra was pushing the anti-missile argument in the Bundestag: 'I think the politics keep getting clearer. You create the enemy that you need.' Shortly afterwards, she was in the parliamentary delegation when US Vice President Bush visited Krefeld, to commemorate the 300th anniversary of the emigration of Quakers to America. The irony that the Quakers had left Krefeld because of persecution for their pacifist views was lost on George Bush, but not on the peace movement which assembled to make its protest felt. The event was marred by *Autonomen* (anarchists) who threw stones at the presidential limousine. Later on it was revealed that a federal intelligence agent had acted as *agent provocateur*, but not before wide divisions were exposed within Die Grünen, between those who saw violent activists as part of the same movement and those who did not. Petra was very clear where she stood: 'We know that the violence of the state and the politicians is much greater, yet I cannot say that the violent people are part of the green movement.'[7]

At Petra's insistence, a delegation from Die Grünen's parliamentary group went to New York and Washington in July to meet government officials, defence experts and to forge closer relationships with the diverse but active green movement in the United States. With the three parliamentary speakers were Roland Vogt, Gert Bastian, press speaker Heinz Suhr and Manon Maren-Grisebach of the party executive. The whole itinerary was prepared by Petra. Talks were held with officials at the Foreign Relations Committee (which exposed the extent of anti-Soviet paranoia in the State Department) and plans were laid with the US peace movement to run parallel actions in both countries that October. On 10th July Petra was invited to appear on NBC's 'Meet the Press', a programme with a particularly tough format; four journalists line up across the studio from the guest and take turns to fire questions. Dressed in a T-shirt bearing anti-nuclear slogans Petra gave a sparkling performance during which she displayed a knowledge about weapons systems and foreign policy which clearly surpassed that of her interlocutors. Once the show was over she received the ultimate accolade – a spontaneous round of applause from the studio crew, the first time in the many years the show had been on the air that this cynical and worldly bunch had been moved to such a gesture. One of the journalists, Robert Novak, moved across the studio to shake her hand with the words 'I wish you were on our side.'

That summer all efforts went into preparing for the 'hot autumn', with the highlight being carefully planned blockades of the missile sites at Mutlangen, near Stuttgart, and Bitburg in the hilly region near the border with Luxemburg. At Mutlangen, the demonstration was low-key and quiet. The police kept their distance and the press recorded Petra, wearing an army hat woven with flowers, sitting with Gert Bastian, Anne-Marie and Heinrich Böll, Günter Grass, Lukas Beckmann and others, including visiting Americans Philip Berrigan (the protesting priest), Anne Montgomery (a nun), Daniel Ellsberg (who leaked the

'Pentagon Papers' on top secret decision-making on Vietnam) and Ed Hedemann of the War Resisters League. Petra had urged them to come over to prove that the Greens were not simply anti-American.

Then came the news of a heavy police presence at the Bitburg site. More people were needed. An overnight caravan of ten cars reached Bitburg early on a windy, cold 3rd September to join the 900 people already there. During the day several thousand more people arrived. The police were indeed heavily armed, with dogs and water cannons, and as soon as the demonstrators began to move towards the base entrance to try to sit down the police dragged them off the road and threw them into a ditch. When the numbers of demonstrators began to swell, the dogs, which had bitten two demonstrators the previous day, were in a frenzy of snarling excitement within a metre of the faces of the sitting demonstrators. Finally came the rough arrests and the water cannons. It was, remembers Ed Hedemann and Daniel Ellsberg – both veterans of many a protest – a terrifying and painful experience.

When the dogs moved in, Petra had to move out. Despite her admiration of Rosa Luxemburg and Dorothy Day, it was impossible for her to sit still in the face of the threat of physical pain or violence. For all her convictions about the importance of non-violent direct action and the solidarity of the affinity groups, she became anxious and panicky, and Gert Bastian had to take her away to a nearby hillside from where she could watch.

The year sped to its climax. Petra returned with Gert Bastian to the United States for a lecture tour which included a debate at Columbia University on American missiles in Europe with Robert Jastrow, the man who drafted Reagan's famous Star Wars speech, and a visit to the War College in Washington. While in Washington Petra also made a triumphant return to American University, which had to hire the church across the road to cope with the huge numbers who wanted to hear her speak. In Philadelphia, Petra was presented with the Peace Woman of the Year Award, before returning to Germany for another round of peace demonstrations which culminated in the huge October rally in Bonn.

At that rally Willy Brandt declared that, after all, the SPD should oppose the new missiles. Daniel Ellsberg, who had spent some weeks in Bonn advising the Greens, had argued that Brandt should be on the platform of the rally as it was very important to gain the support of the Social Democrats. Others were not so sure. Lukas Beckmann for one. He held up a banner reminding the crowd that it was the SPD who had agreed to the missiles in the first place. Petra gave Brandt no quarter either: 'It is absurd when Brandt says no to the missiles but yes to NATO.' The SPD position was equivocal to say the least; despite Brandt's words, the Social Democrats supported neither Die Grünen's demand that the debate on the stationing of the missiles be moved to the autumn, nor a proposal to parliament that a referendum be held on the matter. Opinion polls suggested that over three-quarters of the German people, if not yet ready to leave NATO, were clearly opposed to the missiles. In the Bundestag Petra argued that the referendum would give the German people the opportunity to express this view officially. In a state of near-panic, the SPD held an emergency conference the weekend before the final Bundestag vote at which they decided they would oppose the stationing of the missiles in the following week's debate.

For the Bundestag debate itself on 21st and 22nd November, the Greens invited representatives of the Hopi and Navajo Indians to observe, and in her speech, Petra reminded the chamber that it is from native Americans that the peace and environment movement has gained much inspiration. 'The time when the trees begin to die is the time for action', she said, and welcomed the Indians as 'ambassadors of survival'. An all too appropriate air of menace was added to the occasion by the presence during the debate of several special policemen, and Petra ridiculed a government intent on deploying atomic weapons for being frightened of the possible actions of a handful of democratically elected members of parliament. Before her speech Petra had held up a poster with the words 'Will you say you didn't know?' – the central question after the liquidation of the Jews during the Second World War. Now she said: 'When it is said that the peace movement is a fear movement, I reject that. The few who sit at the government table make us afraid – *they* are the fear movement . . . they manufacture fear.' Petra called for a vote against nuclear missiles with no 'ifs or buts. The generation living today has to decide whether we want to be the last generation of humanity, or the first to reach unity of humankind.' Knowing the vote would be lost, she ended by calling for civil disobedience, arguing that there is a law higher than civil law and that even governments can make mistakes.

Most of the SPD voted against deployment, but, as expected, the governing coalition had a comfortable majority. The missile deployment started immediately and, despite agreeing to a series of actions and a hearing on social defence to coincide with the next elections to the European parliament on 17th June 1984, the mufflers of what was to prove terminal apathy descended on the peace movement. In January 1984, some initiators of the Krefelder Appell edited out from a press statement a condemnation of the Soviet Union's decision to deploy short-range missiles. This prompted Petra and Gert Bastian to resign. The Appell did, after all, hold a frank pro-communist point of view.

THE GERMAN QUESTIONS

On a visit to her old school in Günzburg in 1982, Petra had been told by the nuns that Joseph Mengele (who fled to South America after the war) had visited the town in 1959 to attend the funeral of his father. He had even been hidden in the very convent where Petra had gone to school, and most of the town knew he was there. This incident, said Petra, was symbolic of the state of mind of many Germans who conceive the Nazi atrocities to be a type of 'accident' which should no longer be discussed. 'Maybe he did some bad things,' she quotes one Günzburg citizen as saying, 'but what the Americans and the British did at Dresden wasn't so great either.' This sort of moral obtuseness, Petra said, is a crucial failing of the Germans. Mengele, was not an 'accident'. He belonged to the mainstream of prevailing moods, attitudes and scientific philosophy of his nation during Hitler's regime, and the only way to guarantee that such a climate could never flourish again, she was sure, would be to remember and mourn forever.[8]

In many of her speeches Petra touched on the debate which had risen and fallen since the end of the war about how Germany, or rather the Germans, might learn to live with the grim legacy of their past. She would recall that she had been in America when she was confronted 'with Anne Frank, with Auschwitz, with Bergen-Belsen, with Treblinka, with Buchenwald, with Ravensbrück, with fascist crimes, with Dachau, with the "silent consenting" of the German people', and was pleased when in 1978 the debate was popularized through the televising in Germany of the American series, *The Holocaust*. This was watched by millions, which cannot be said of the *Historikerstreit*, a dense argument conducted by German historians on screen and in print during the 1980s, which took the debate into previously unplumbed depths of obscurity and tedium. It was certainly the US series which many young people thought about when the chance came to campaign against the new missiles or support the new political party with its policies of non-violence and ecology. Here, at last, was a chance for their generation to refresh the pages of Germany's history books by taking responsibility for a life-affirming future, a chance to make it possible to be proud of being German. For many, Petra epitomized this new hope. She was a young woman, obviously immensely knowledgeable but not frightened to bring passion, emotion and, above all, frankness into the dustily earnest, but still uneasily guilty, world of German politics. Petra was certainly a charismatic person, but what her audiences appreciated most was her total honesty. Whether they agreed with her or not, they had no doubt she was speaking from the heart.

Sadly, Petra was in a minority in understanding the wider historical role of Die Grünen. As her disaffection with the party increased, part of her refusal to submerge herself in the detailed debates about organization and policy was her feeling that it was impossible to sustain an overall vision at the same time. On their part many of her colleagues failed to appreciate that when it came to sustaining the faith of the party's voters, inspiring and trusted figureheads are more important than amendments to motions at conference.

The policy for a Europe of Regions which had been elaborated for the 1979 European elections, was particularly important for Die Grünen. Petra campaigned strongly on the relevance of such a policy to a permanently divided Germany. The aim was to create a number of *ecologically* determined regions shaped around, rather than separated by, natural features like a river or a mountain range. By replacing old state boundaries, determined by the history of people, with new ones, determined by the future needs of the environment, the whole question of two Germanies was lifted into a different arena.

Unfortunately, the debate inside Die Grünen about whether West and East Germany should be reunified or not became separated from the larger debate about an *ecological* Europe of the Regions. It was dragged back into the stranglehold of history, with the arguments for Die Grünen's official policy (against a united Germany) based explicitly on fear of a large, strong German state.[9] Although the party claimed it had made no difference to the way their policy towards East Germany (*Ostpolitik*) was developed, one of the Die Grünen MPs in the parliamentary working group on the subject was Dirk Schneider. He was was later exposed as an agent of the STASI.

Consequently, when the Warsaw Pact began to crumble at the end of the 1980s, Die Grünen's alternative vision for Germany in an ecological Europe of Regions was sparse and not terribly coherent; as far as policy was concerned, the Greens were caught as much on the hop as the other political parties – and NATO, which, despite possessing the biggest security budget in the world, had not developed one single strategy for handling an outbreak of peace. However, as Petra pointed out with more than a little *schadenfreude*, if NATO had taken their intelligence from the *opposition* groups in the East, they would at least have had an earlier warning of the collapse of the Warsaw Pact. Lack of democracy does not prevent people from thinking, and many people in East Europe had been aware for some time that their leaders were out of control.

The same weekend as the blockades at Bitburg and Mutlangen, members of the East German peace movement set up a line of candles between the US and the USSR missions in East Berlin. For this simple gesture, many were beaten up and imprisoned, and one, an East German journalist, Roland Jahn, was put on a closed train and sent to the West. From him, Lukas Beckmann obtained the names and addresses of the key people in the East German peace movement. The meeting with Honecker was fast approaching and Lukas, Petra and the others wanted to be as well prepared as possible.

The 31st October finally arrived – and while they waited to meet Honecker, Petra began to feel faint. Tired because she had just returned from a visit to Moscow, she was gripped by one of her panics, not in fear of physical pain as at Bitburg, but by a sort of stage-fright which would overwhelm her when she felt out of control of the situation. While they had been in the United States it had not happened. There she had known her way around the politics and the psychology of the political leaders, so it had been alright, she had been in control; but this was different. She knew so little about East

Europe, she had no idea about Honecker's life and personality, and mistakes might lead to misery for the imprisoned activists.

So it was with both astonishment and relief that she found Honecker not much less nervous than she was. Provocatively wearing a T-shirt emblazoned with the banned *Schwerter zu Pflugscharen* slogan she promptly tackled him with questions about the imprisoned peace activists. Honecker turned pale, quite unused to such direct criticism or frankness – outside Moscow it had probably never happened to him before in his life. Lukas handed him a hastily drafted 'Personal Peace Treaty': 'We hereby undertake: definitely to rule out the mutual use of force; not to regard each other as enemies and to reduce antagonism; to support the start of unilateral disarmament.' Honecker took out his pen to sign his name at the bottom. At this point the head of the central committee of the East German Communist Party leant forward to suggest that the last point concerning unilateral disarmament just might pose a slight problem with the Kremlin. Honecker hesitated, then signed after the first two points. It was clear that the East Germans were 'not exactly ecstatic' to act as host for Moscow's planned response to the Cruise and Pershing missiles.

That evening, the Western Greens went to meetings in several homes of leading East German activists, including Bärbel Bohley, Rainer Eppelmann and Gerd Poppe. Vera Wollenberger, a gentle woman who, with Poppe, would become one of the eight members of the East German green and democratic alliance (Bündnis 90/Die Grünen) when it was elected to the Bundestag in 1990, remembers these and subsequent meetings very well. 'Petra was brilliant, she could talk all evening and it was so interesting and useful for us.' From that first night onwards, Wollenberger joined the others on Petra's mailing list and received lots of letters, documents and cuttings which Petra thought might be of use. 'This continued even after I myself became a parliamentarian. In fact, she must have been already dead when the last letter, with some cuttings about Latin America, reached me.'

These encounters set the pattern for Petra's personal *Ostpolitik*. Meetings were arranged with both state officials and independent peace activities, the latter taking place openly and if possible with formal permission. This forced the East German government to acknowledge the right of such groups to exist. Sometimes the West German Greens were prevented from crossing the border, but when

Honecker wrote asking her to obey East German law and not to contact the dissidents, she refused. When she was unable to visit the 'subversive kitchens and small living rooms', where the non-violent revolutions of 1989 were planned, she wrote letters to everyone, and when she could get into the East, she never went empty-handed, bringing documents, books, parts for broken printing presses, paper and photocopying machines, which Gert Bastian would hide in his car and reassemble on the kitchen tables. Marianne Birthler, now a speaker on the executive of Bundnis 90/Die Grünen remembers that Petra would often bring presents for the children as well. 'These were not just any toys or things, each gift was chosen specifically for each child, and wrapped and labelled personally by her.' Our loyalty, Petra would say, is not to the blocs but to each other.

Petra developed a particularly close friendship with Bärbel Bohley. The two women were very much alike: small, blonde and full of nervous energy and tension. When Mikhail Gorbachev's *glasnost* and *perestroika* began to rattle the bars of East European communism, the old bears, getting nervous, began to clamp down on the freedom of the dissidents. Bärbel Bohley and several of her friends were among those put in prison. Greeting him with a smile at the reception held to mark Honecker's first official visit to Bonn in 1987, Petra gave Honecker a present. 'It is a painting, a present for the wall of your office,' she said. He was bemused. 'It is by my friend whom you have imprisoned because of her political activity,' Petra continued. 'Does this look like the work of an enemy of the State?' Bärbel was released, but the repression did not stop. On 26th November 1987, police raided the *Umweltbibliothek*, an 'environmental library' in the basement of the Pastor of the Church of Zion's house in East Berlin. Here meetings of people concerned with every aspect of the environment, from its flora to the democratic rights of its human fauna, had taken place for some time, but this was the first time the police had searched and confiscated material from church premises. Petra wrote an open letter to Honecker, and was refused entry to East Berlin. The following month she was also refused a visa to attend the Glasnost Press Club in Moscow.

Then, on 17th January 1988, during an officially sanctioned demonstration in East Berlin to commemorate the anniversary of Rosa Luxemburg's murder by army officers in 1919, more than one hundred dissidents were arrested and accused of 'treasonable

connections', 'riotous assembly' and 'actions detrimental to government activities'. Among them were Bärbel Bohley, Werner Fischer,
Vera Wollenberger and the songwriter Stephan Krawczyk and his
wife Freya Klier. Petra once again sent letters and telegrams of
protest to Erich Honecker, and on 3rd February addressed the
Bundestag during a topical debate on the events in East Germany.
Despite all this, Bohley, Fischer and some others were expelled to the
West. Several were happy to stay, but Bohley and Fischer wanted very
much to return to the East. In the meantime, they stayed for a while
in Bonn with Heinz Suhr and his girlfriend Renate Mohr, while Petra
provided them with everything from toothbrushes to a trip to Paris.

After a few weeks, Bohley and Fischer went to London to stay with
friends while Petra continued to petition Honecker until finally she
met him in May, at a congress on Nuclear Free Zones in East Berlin.
Ignoring all the protocol, Petra went straight up to him and
demanded an entry permit for Bohley and Fischer. Perhaps overcome
by the directness of her approach, as he so nearly had been once
before, Honecker agreed on the spot. Going to the top, it seemed,
could still work.

Most of Petra's *Ostpolitik* was conducted on a personal basis, with a
very small group of active supporters, like Elisabeth Weber, Lukas
Beckmann, Milan Horáček and Heinz Suhr around her. In general,
the rest of Die Grünen, both the parliamentary group and the
executive, were too much engaged in the arguments between the
Fundis and the *Realos* over strategy, or struggling with the increasing
power of the left-wing *Fundis* who were more and more openly
supporting the use of violence to achieve their ends. It was easy for
Petra to get expressions of solidarity from green conferences or
meetings, but attempts to obtain significant sums of money for the
East European democracy movements were repeatedly unsuccessful,
and Petra was furious when the Die Grünen executive refused to
invite the East European dissidents to their 1988 conference on
Europe.

It was in the subversive kitchens of East Germany therefore, that
Petra listened and watched the revolutions of East Europe take place.
'What we are witnessing,' she wrote happily, 'in these November and
December days of 1989 is a true non-violent revolution taking place
in the streets – it is a colourful, a creative, a happy a friendly and soft

revolution!'[10] Late in the day, but eventually, Gorbachev, Honecker, Kohl and other old bears from both East and West Europe began to realize that revolutions cannot be managed from the top. Once thousands of East Germans started to bypass the tightly-guarded border between East and West Germany via the frontiers of Czechoslovakia and Hungary, Gorbachev and Kohl, as well as the citizens of East Germany, knew it was nearly over. When Gorbachev visited East Germany on 7th October 1989 to celebrate the official 40th birthday of the state, newspapers showed pictures of him escaping his security men and stepping into the crowds to shake hands. Reporters speculated that in his private meetings with Honecker and other officials Gorbachev probably told them that the game was up and that Soviet soldiers would not back the East German government any more. But they did not hear his words to the crowd. 'If you want democracy, take it – now!' he had whispered over and over again. The message went back to the subversive kitchens and was translated; Gorbachev, in effect, had promised that if East Germans took to the streets, he would not send in the Soviet tanks.

It was all they needed to know. 'We are the people and we are one people' was the slogan of the crowds which took to the streets in Leipzig, Dresden and Berlin. The government floundered in chaos, and the wall was gloriously breached on the night of 9th November. On 1st December, Petra wrote jubilantly: 'Now in Europe it has become true – that which Martin Luther King Jr had often talked about – "We are caught in a network of mutuality. We are tied in a single garment of destiny. What affects one directly, affects us all indirectly!" '[11]

If the personal and public politics of Petra Kelly had an apogee, it was on 6th December 1989. At the invitation of the citizens' action groups in East Germany (with everything, including a Bundestag car, organized by Petra) the Dalai Lama broke his journey to Oslo (where he was to collect his Nobel Peace Prize) in order to visit East Berlin. By chance, it was the very day the communist government finally fell. Under the equally watchful eyes of the still-manned security towers and his own political advisors, the Dalai Lama passed through Checkpoint Charlie and stood beside the wall with Petra, Gert Bastian and a small group of dissidents. Bärbel Bohley passed him a candle and the group stood briefly in a circle before visiting a Jewish old people's home and attending a meeting of the round table of the citizens' action movement at the Dietrich Bonhöffer House. 'A very frank and sincere exchange of views then took place between people who had toppled the repressive regime in their own country with a peaceful revolution, and the spiritual and political leader of the Tibetan people, whose forty-year struggle for freedom and determination is still going on,' remembered Petra.[12] Petra knew that the Dalai Lama felt as she did; he told her this meeting was one of the most moving of his life. But its inspiration and its symbolism did not endure for very long; everyone's dreams were soon to be crushed by the stampede towards German unity and the exit of Die Grünen from the Bundestag. In his subsequent autobiography *Freedom in Exile*, the Dalai Lama's advisors had obviously prevailed on him to rewrite this story as a brief moment with an 'old woman', a candle and a prayer for peace on the West side of the wall.[13] But for a while the magic was there, and the events of 1989 caused even the most cynical old *Realo* to feel a rustle of life in their long-dead faith in humankind's ability to take more than one hurdle at a time.

IN THE BUNDESTAG: TIBET, NEUTRALITY AND THE UNDERDOG

Formally, Petra's agenda in the Bundestag was set by three things: the foreign affairs committee on which she sat; by the timetable of outside events, like an election, Spain's accession to NATO or the Single European Act; and any current affairs which demanded a reaction from, if not her committee, then from her personally.

When it came to getting the best out of the Bundestag, Petra's hard apprenticeship in Brussels stood her in good stead. She became one of the most diligent and effective green MPs practising a *Realpolitik* to obtain cross-party support for motions before they entered the official process. Inevitably, by the time many of them were put to the vote, they were much watered down versions of her original proposals, but sometimes, as in the case of Tibet, she achieved a great deal.

On the foreign affairs committee Petra was well respected. Freimut Duve worked on the committee with her and remembers her as very effective: 'She was very well prepared (sometimes too well prepared with too much detail) but would usually stick to getting over one point or one resolution.' Frieder Wolf, her parliamentary assistant for five years, agreed. 'She was very direct in her questions, extremely well informed and efficient – if a bit polemic. Her very human approach made her disarming.' Petra was also a member of the sub-committee on arms control. In 1984 she expressed concern about arms, including chemical weapons, going to Iraq. At the time, this was denied, although a few chemicals were put on the banned list. Consequently, when it was revealed during the Gulf War that German chemicals had been used on the Kurdish people, Petra was withering in her attacks on Hans-Dietrich Genscher, then Germany's foreign minister. She was also instrumental in persuading the foreign affairs committee to expand the remit of its humanitarian sub-committee to include human rights; in parliamentary terms, this was a considerable coup.

Apart from her committees there were two other parliamentary tools which Petra (and the other members of the green *Fraktion*) used a great deal – *kleine Anfragen* (minor questions, requiring a written reply) and the *grosse Anfragen* (major questions, requiring a reply in the chamber). Altogether, in her eight years, Petra tabled over 140 *kleine Anfragen* (plus many more smaller written and oral questions) and eight *grosse Anfragen*. These confections of often detailed questions around a single topic took a long time to prepare – sometimes over a year – and with the help of experts, Petra put together two on children with cancer, two on nuclear arms and one each on: chemical weapons; women and human rights; uranium; and women car-workers.

A glance through the official records of the Bundestag and her own file of press releases, reveals that the bulk of Petra's parliamentary work was with military issues (particularly nuclear), the concerns of the Grace Kelly Foundation and equal rights for women. But of the many other topics she covered, a few stand out: Tibet; the threat to Ireland's neutrality of the Single European Act; Yugoslavian dissidents; and the predicament of aboriginal people, particularly in Australia and North America.

Otto Schily used to be irritated by what he saw as a complete lack of logic in the way Petra conducted her foreign policy. And in a way he was right. Her agenda was set far more by the events swirling around her than by a long-term strategy. Whenever Petra touched the lives of other people – whether by reading the thousands of letters they wrote to her or by meeting them on her travels – she would pick up their concerns and make them her own. Her commitment to representing the unrepresented she portrayed as part of her political principles, but it was as much driven by a compassion she was incapable of controlling as anything else. If you accepted Petra as a magnet of non-violent principle trailing through the iron-filings of human misery, then it was possible to see a pattern in her work; the causes which stuck were the ones nearest to her – literally and symbolically. Ireland and Tibet, for example, symbolized for Petra the state as underdog; both had entered her life at a personal and a political level; in each case a matter of high principle was at stake; and she felt that her intervention could make a difference. And when in her travels at the invitation of others she fell upon German shame at Guernica, the health or land-rights of Aboriginal peoples, or the persecution of dissidents in Yugoslavia, she had no option but to become involved.

Though she herself was often reluctant to classify her concerns – to her they were all equally important – she would not hesitate to nominate Tibet as the campaign nearest to her heart. Freimut Duve, who published one of the three books Petra edited on Tibet, points out that many Germans have a great affinity for the country. They are not necessarily drawn by the general theory of Buddhism or anything like that, he says, but the concept of a rocky centre of the world – 'a place beyond' – has all the sort of philosophical and emotional elements Germans find attractive. Here was a place where people *knew* about the relationship between earth and God.

Petra's connections with Tibet date back to 1971, the year after her half-sister Grace died. Still in deep mourning, Petra began to foster a Tibetan girl, Nima Chonzom, who lived in a refugee settlement in Dharamsala, Northern India. No one, not even Petra's mother or the Dalai Lama, knows exactly why Petra chose a Tibetan child. Her interest in eastern philosophies had been kindled at American University by Professor Said, but the most likely explanation is that Nima was close to Grace – in age and looks.

Certainly a great affection grew between Petra and Nima, and through her visits to Dharamsala Petra developed a great affinity, with Tibet and its peoples.[14] Empathizing with their pain at being separated from their place of cultural and spiritual belonging – their *Heimat* – she felt for the exiled Tibetans, and shuddered at the stories they told of Tibet's invasion and annexation by China and the persecution of the people who remained. She would often use the word holocaust to describe what had happened – what was still happening – to the people of Tibet, and in the prevailing international climate where principles of international law and human rights were viewed almost exclusively through the filter of relative economic power, she saw the issue of Tibet as a 'touchstone of morality in international politics'.

In 1985, Petra and some other sympathetic parliamentarians were approached by lawyers working for the Tibetan cause in Germany. It was through them that she made contacts with the Tibetan government in exile and eventually the Dalai Lama. Stephen Batchelor, an expert on Tibet who often attended the visits of the Dalai Lama to Europe, describes the Dalai Lama as a kindly, sometimes impulsive man, who finds all westerners, particularly women, strange – 'though considering he was projected onto the world stage from a narrow closed upbringing he has done remarkably well'. Petra was impressed by how liberal and well informed the Dalai Lama was, but the sometimes reactionary views of the 'aristocracy' surrounding him irritated her. Often she would take the Dalai Lama's sleeve and try to separate him from his entourage so they might speak frankly together. It was clear they had a warm relationship and, recognizing her restlessness and anxiety perhaps, he would tell her, 'Don't worry, I will meditate for you.'

Wherever he went, there were certain people the Dalai Lama would always notice – not the main people, but someone quiet and still on the fringes of the group whom he would then approach and greet personally. Once it was a cameraman on a film crew who was startled to find himself given this special attention, but Stephen Batchelor remembers the Dalai Lama also singled out Gert Bastian.

Petra started to write letters about the Tibetan situation in the summer of 1985, and followed up with a *kleine Anfrage* on international law and human rights in relation to Tibet in 1986. A group of concerned people, including several Tibetans living in Germany, began to gather. Before long the hypocrisy of the German government proved to be as annoying as that of the Chinese. When the Chinese Foreign Minister Xy Xuequain had visited Bonn in March 1987, Petra had made her views clear, but was disgusted when

Helmut Kohl visited Tibet the following July and declared that 'Tibet is part of the Chinese polity; this fact is recognized by all the countries of the world.'

It was with relish that Petra made public the results of a study she had commissioned from the federal parliament's research service. She had asked them to investigate what arguments support the contention that the integration of Tibet into the Chinese state was not valid in international law. They had concluded that when Tibet was forceably annexed by China in 1959, it had been an independent state.

In August 1987 the Dalai Lama met MPs, including Petra, and other supporters to discuss his five-point peace plan which he planned to present to the US Congress a few days later. At the same time, from Tibet came reports of violent clashes with several deaths. Petra initiated an emergency Bundestag debate on what was described as the worst unrest in Tibet in 28 years. She was shocked, Petra told the chamber, to discover that the Bundestag had not once addressed the situation in Tibet since 1949, and welcomed the support she had had for her demand that the house discuss the violation of Tibetans' human rights. In contrast to Chancellor Kohl's crude remarks in July, she said this was 'a positive experience and a sign of a new, honest application of human rights policy in the German Bundestag'.

On 15th October, a motion submitted by Petra and supported by all the parliamentary groups called on China to respond positively to the Dalai's Lama's efforts to bring about a constructive dialogue. It was passed unanimously. A historic moment in the Bundestag, Petra noted, with Vice President Stücklen moved to point out after the vote that 'miracles still occur in parliament'.[15]

In Dharamsala in 1988, Petra had discussed the idea of an international hearing on Tibet with the Tibetan government in exile. She would invite not only the expected 'old Tibet hands' but the voice of real Tibet; its people and its culture must be there too. So the programme had to include eyewitness reports of repression and violation of human rights from Tibet, the experience of refugees and an evening concert performed by Tibetan and other Asian artists. A nightmare of logistics. One Tibet 'old hand' who was there was Lord David Ennals, a British Labour peer who has campaigned strongly for Tibet for many years. He remembers a tremendously inspiring occasion: 'She had obviously gone to boundless trouble to bring together Tibetans with moving human stories to leaven all the dry talk about treaties and parliamentary resolutions.' And it had worked. All the participants, even those who had been campaigning for many years, felt their commitment to the country and its people deepened and revitalized, and went home with more than a one-page declaration and a fond memory.

Then, at the beginning of June 1989, Chinese troops opened fire on the students campaigning for more democracy in Tiananmen Square, Peking. Speaking to an emergency motion on 15th June, Petra told the Bundestag she regretted the weakness of the German government's response to the massacre, feeling that economic liberalization in China had for too long been mistakenly interpreted as evidence of more profound changes in human rights. She cited the unchanged repression in Tibet as evidence, where martial law (or more accurately an extension of it) had been declared in March. This motion and another on 22nd June, both urging economic sanctions, were passed unanimously, but with minimal practical effect.

Inside Die Grünen, Petra's championing of the Dalai Lama and his quest for international support for an independent Tibet did not meet with unqualified approval. For some, including several regional parties, the Dalai Lama was an object of ridicule, and certainly could not be seen to have legitimate claim to the leadership of Tibet. The Tibetans were backward, both religiously and socially, Petra was told, so should not be supported, and, as an atheist party, it was wrong for the Greens to support a religious leader. She countered by asking: 'Did we ever ask how religious the mothers of the Plaze de Mayo were, before supporting them? Did we ever ask how often the people of Nicaragua went to Mass, or how often the people of Chile took Holy Communion?' No one responded.

She was disappointed too in the response of the peace movement at the time of the massacre at Tiananmen Square. In Hungary, thousands had turned out to demonstrate at the gates of the Chinese Embassy, while in Bonn only a dozen assembled in protest. In a robust open letter to the German peace movement, Petra wrote 'There was no wave of protest in our streets, nor did thousands of people gather in the Hofgarten in Bonn or march to the Chinese Embassy in Bad Godesberg. There were no large-scale manifestations of the united left!' Could it be that the peace movement was 'one-eyed' about human rights too? She signed her letter 'with sad greetings from Bonn during the summer recess'.[16]

Two months later, Petra was in Prague for the enormous party thrown to celebrate the free elections in Czechoslovakia. After his election as President, one of Václav Havel's first gestures had been to invite the Dalai Lama on an official visit to Prague – the first head of state to do so. 'It is possible to be two steps ahead of everyone else,' said Havel. 'Many more pragmatic politicians had warned me that China would be upset. As it turned out, China did not invade us in retaliation, nor did they cancel any contracts. But the Dalai Lama was subsequently received by many other heads of state.'[17] Looking at a scene very different to the one she and Omi had witnessed in August 1968, Petra hung a Tibetan flag from her hotel window overlooking Wenceslas Square as the Dalai Lama set off through the crowds on his state visit to the president's country residence. In October, when the two German parliaments celebrated the first anniversary of the abolition of the German Democratic Republic by holding a joint session in the Reichstag in Berlin, the Dalai Lama was received by German president Richard von Weizsäcker.

One other country which occupied a special place in Petra's heart was Ireland. When she took her stepfather's name, she also took a strong affection for the country of his family. This was cemented during her relationship with the Irish trade union leader John Carroll and her frequent visits to speak in the 1970s. Apart from her political connections with the country, Petra also developed a deep love and respect for Irish culture and had a fine collection of Irish folk music. Although Petra had a reputation for never taking a holiday (not strictly true, she took holidays but took work along with her), when she did have a break it was often the peace and gentle pace of Ireland she sought. In a bed and breakfast tour of the west coast of Donegal in the summer of 1984, she introduced Gert Bastian to the country she had learnt to love, and they returned several times to this area, sometimes staying in a house belonging to Heinrich Böll and his family. The Irish also had a special affection for Petra too. Her public visits were invariably treated as major news items; when she was in Dublin, Jury's Hotel would give her a free room, and in restaurants complete strangers would insist on paying her bill.

It was the defence of Ireland's cultural richness and its precious neutrality to which Petra leapt in 1987. Freda Meissner Blau, who in May 1986 made European headlines as a green candidate for the Austrian presidency, frequently said that Petra was one of the few people to have a really complete understanding about neutrality and its potential as a strategy for peace. *Real* neutrality Petra defined as positive, active non-violent theory in operation at the level of the state.[18]

Petra thought Irish neutrality was gravely menaced by the Single European Act – a sort of 'dry-run' for the Maastricht Treaty in which the Commission managed to prise an early slice of sovereignty away from member states without, as it turned out, most of them being aware of it.

Several people in Ireland felt the same way as Petra and decided to challenge the government's right to ratify the Act their *Taoiseach* (prime minister) had signed back in February 1986. The Single European Act, they argued, contained commitments to 'consistency' in foreign affairs and a determination by the signatories 'to maintain the technological and industrial conditions necessary for their security'. As other European states were variously involved in NATO and the Western European Union, ratification would therefore contravene Ireland's constitutional commitment to neutrality. In a smart bit of legal footwork, fronted by Raymond Crotty a senior lecturer at Trinity College Dublin, the Irish opponents sought a High Court injunction to prevent ratification of the Act before the deadline of 1st January 1987, and after a bit of a scuffle in the Supreme Court, they succeeded. This left the government two choices: renegotiate the Act or hold a referendum. They chose the latter.

A very unequal contest began, in which the government stated the choice as Europe – Yes or No? and reminded a worried and confused Irish people that 1/13 of the country's income derived from the EC's structural funds. 'A "No" vote would end EC grants,' was the campaign slogan.

In the face of this sort of blackmail a serious discussion about the principle of neutrality did not really stand a chance, but the battle was engaged with vigour nevertheless. Quickly the Campaign for Irish Neutrality and Independence recruited Petra, and she gave their campaign a headline-guaranteeing start by accusing the government of lying to the Irish people. 'The Irish would be very good Europeans if they remain neutral . . . [the Prime Minister] is completely wrong when he says the Act cannot be negotiated. The United Kingdom and Greece renegotiated their EC entry terms twice.' [19]

The impending arrival of Petra Kelly to launch the 'No' campaign unnerved the Irish government. Knowing her power to win headlines, it hastily moved its own campaign launch to the same day. Geraldine Dwyer of Irish CND remembers the delightful contrast between the 'No' campaign launched by a bright, combative, fast-talking Petra and a respected local priest, and the 'Yes' campaign which fielded two defensive-sounding middle-aged men in grey suits. The press gave Petra top billing and she went on to make similarly provocative speeches in Cork before returning to Germany from where she sent the campaigners piles of information, including the response to a *kleine Anfrage* she tabled on the subject. The final vote may not have been in doubt, the No campaigners explained, but thanks to the 'value added' of Petra, the opening skirmish had definitely been theirs. 'She was an MP from abroad, attractive, very articulate and knowledgeable – a good counterpoint to the usual representation of greens as ayatollahs and isolationists,' said Anthony Coughlin of Trinity College.

The plight of the 'Yugoslav Six' came to Petra's attention through an invitation she had accepted to speak at an international conference of socialism and freedom in Cavtat, Yugoslavia in October 1984. She turned up equipped with a T-shirt bearing Rosa Luxemburg's 'Freedom to think differently' slogan in Serbo-Croat and met one of the six, Vladimir Mijanović. A tall, bearded man, Mijanović has the agitated perpetual motion of a long-time underground political activist. He and five associates had been arrested and charged with holding 'Free University' meetings between 1979 and 1984. They had already been in custody, where Mijanović had been force-fed while on a hungerstrike. Now they were on parole, pending trial. Mijanović was well aware that international attention for the trial could be instrumental in influencing its outcome, so he was delighted when Petra agreed to help. Between October and the start of the trial on 5th November Petra sent to everyone she could think of an appeal for letters, petitions – anything – to demonstrate to the Yugoslavian authorities that the world was watching.

When she herself turned up in court on the first day, Mijanović was amazed. The tiny courtroom had been besieged by people trying to get in, and although she had lost some buttons from her shirt and her arm had been twisted, she had made it. In the event, three of the accused received reduced sentences, two were released because there was not enough evidence to convict, and the case against Mijanović (who had to be removed from the court for repeatedly asking witnesses questions which 'involved criticism of the regime') eventually fizzled out. The presence of a foreign member of parliament alongside the human rights organizations, Mijanović felt, had sent a special signal to the authorities, and he never forgot Petra's efforts on his behalf. When his first daughter was born in July 1992 he named her after Petra, who was delighted and sent presents. That Petra should die before she met her namesake causes Mijanović great sadness.

As part of her anti-party party strategy, Petra liked to invite people to come to the Green parliamentary offices in Bonn and take advantage of the facilities. Renate Mohr, who was in charge of the public relations side of the *Fraktion's* press office at the time recalls that sometimes this would lead to an embarrassment of people for whom she would have to find a corner of a desk, but that it could also work very well, with some visitors staying for several months to work on one of the *Fraktion's* projects. Amongst Petra's most frequent guests at the Bundestag were representatives of aboriginal peoples. Renate Mohr remembers one particular occasion in 1984 – 'in the days when the press still used to turn up to our press conferences' – when, as part of their campaign to obtain the right of Indian nations to issue their own passports, some American Indians passed through Bonn on their way to a human rights conference in Geneva. After the press conference, Petra and Renate accompanied the Indians to a nearby café, forgetting that it was Mardi Gras – carnival season. Into the café came some people dressed as Napoleonic soldiers who instantly and merrily seized upon the bewildered Indians as fellow revellers while Petra danced around shouting 'No, no no! They are *real!*'

Milo Yellow Hair, of the Oglala-Lakota Indians of South Dakota, spoke for several tribes when he came to the Bonn memorial. 'The spark that was given to us by their sympathy in action will continue because, like a lonely voice in the forest who hears the falling tree and who speaks to it, so spoke these two . . . in our nation we called her *Shante washde* – the good hearted woman – and for that we will always thank her.' [20]

One of the least well-known but arguably the most important aspect of Petra's work in the Bundestag was her office's massive 'outreach' work. A very large amount of information poured in to Petra's office. To the unsolicited and routine flow of documents and press cuttings which she kept on file she added what she called 'counter-information' by maintaining a worldwide network of trusted contacts who could offer useful perspectives on any event or issue. This 'counter-information' network she saw as one of the 'cornerstones' of her parliamentary work. 'If you want to stay honest in politics you have no choice but to handle all information, inquiries and subjects very conscientiously.'[21]

Petra did not just absorb all this information before consigning it to her files, she also made it work. As she ploughed her way through it all she would mark pages to be copied and sent out again to others who might be – or in her mind ought to be – interested. Terminally suspicious of computers, Petra had a card index of her several thousand contacts. In addition there were the hundreds of letters she would get each day. Some she replied to simply, others inspired her to prepare a *kleine Anfrage* or a simple written question. 'Fortunately,' said Frieder Wolf, 'she gave lots of speeches, so there was always something to send out, but she liked to add a personal note.'

The extent and importance of this outreach was not generally appreciated. It is true that journalists would find the stuff she sent out so excessive they would frequently file it directly in the rubbish bin. The strongest and kindest encouragement never persuaded Petra of the average reporter's resistance to more than one side of A4. 'I refuse to play their game,' she would reply. 'I will not encourage them to substitute dramatic headlines for in-depth reporting.' Friends and colleagues would also be irritated by yet another call to action for a cause which was already close to Petra's heart but still far from their own – irritated by the guilt that went with putting it into the pending tray – because Petra's causes, if sometimes untimely, were always just.

But apart from cynical reporters and jaded activists, the bulk of Petra's mailshots hit targets who were deeply grateful. For all the people trying to work for the environment, human rights and against any sort of injustice who were not close to the epicentres of global power politics (and in some cases not even close to a library) to be on Petra's mailing list was a lifeline to inspiration, information and hope.

In their small but precious corner of the planet, a piece of paper from a member of parliament in Germany was a very powerful weapon.

THE POLITICAL IS PERSONAL

When Die Grünen made its triumphal entry into the Bundestag, letters of congratulation from all over the world poured in; some were simply addressed to 'Petra Kelly, Germany'. But not all the messeages she received were supportive. Some time before she took her Bundestag seat Petra had already discovered that to become a public figure is immediately to attract envy as well as adulation, and also sackfuls of mail from all manner of people, from distressed souls troubled by a neglectful spouse to the full-blown viciousness of the seriously deranged. Achim Schuppert remembers Petra bringing back to Irlenbusch piles of letters from people full of misery – they were being persecuted by their neighbours, they were being followed, they were being betrayed by their friends and family. In short they were surrounded by treason. Only Petra could help and it was urgent. As a doctor, Schuppert was able to make at least a stab at differentiating the psychoses and the paranoia from the genuine, but Petra was incapable of this. Not only did her boundless compassion for other people get in the way but so too did the fact that much of what she read about in these letters had already happened to her – and in some cases was still happening. She *was* being watched and followed, she *was* being threatened and it *was* increasingly hard to know who she could trust. Where, she asked, is the difference between their madness and my reality?

'If being a celebrity has changed me,' she once told me, 'it was not the direct effect of fame itself – inside I feel no different – it is because I have had to adjust myself to the effect it has had on other people.' She was talking not only about the public response, but also the response of people close to her. 'That is the hardest thing.' More than once, Petra was disconcerted to turn up for what she thought would be a private evening with friends, only to find that the friends had arranged to show-off to half the neighbourhood that they were personal friends of the famous Petra Kelly. Instead of being able to enjoy a relaxing evening she was expected to perform – exhibiting evidence of both her fame (names dropped, important meetings mentioned) and her intimacy with the host. Failure to deliver on either count meant an resentful erstwhile friend who would soon be denigrating her behind her back. At the time when she needed most support, the number of intimate and trusted friends with whom she could genuinely relax in total confidence shrank to a handful.

Petra was also being followed and harassed by the strange European Workers' Party, which made a point of targetting certain German political figures. However hard Petra and her staff tried to keep her itinerary secret, Petra's tormentors would invariably turn up at airports with offensive banners to greet her and see her off.

In June 1982, after she had spent two weeks on a speaking tour of the United States, during which she had been almost continuously harried, an article about Petra appeared in Lyndon LaRouche's paper *New Solidarity* under the headline 'Did you see this whore on television?' Tucked away in the middle of the article which suggested the peace movement intended to 'provide cover for President Reagan's assassination', was a direct reference to Petra's relationship with Gert Bastian: 'Kelly's special project deployment is the recruitment of aging military officers to the peace movement.'[22] Petra decided to use this article to fight back. Proving a connection between LaRouche's organization and the harrassment she had experienced in the United States and from the European Workers' Party in Germany might be difficult, but she felt the article was a good place to start.

Petra telephoned Bruce French, by now teaching and practising as a lawyer in Ohio, and asked him to start proceedings against *New Solidarity*. He did so, but the case dragged on, mainly because Petra could not get to New York for the hearings. Then, in 1985, when Die Grünen agreed to guarantee 100,000 DM to help her fight, Petra turned for advice to Ramsey Clark, a civil-rights lawyer who had been John Kennedy's Assistant Attorney General; she was set on getting the best possible lawyer to help her deal with the LaRouche machine. An ardent anti-nuclear and human rights campaigner himself, Clark agreed, not because he liked libel suits (on the contrary he disapproved of libel laws altogether), but because he knew and admired Petra and had experienced himself the misery of being persecuted by LaRouche's organization. He knew too that if Petra persisted, the defence lawyers would be certain to make detailed enquiries about her private life in court. At best she would be put embarrassingly on the defensive; at worst, she could be humiliated. In November 1985, Petra informed the New York court of her decision to discontinue the case.

Aside from the harassment by the European Workers' Party, Petra also experienced the not unusual array of threats and intimidation often suffered by public figures – sufficient for the West German police to list her as a top security risk. Although she would feign an insouciance about security, and at times could be very careless, Petra lost her confidence in travelling alone and had her house in Swinemünderstrasse equipped with a double alarm system. While many people were genuinely concerned on her behalf about the intimidation she received, few understood how deeply she was affected by it. As a result she was sometimes accused of over-reacting.

Many felt she overreacted when *Penthouse*, the soft-pornography magazine, produced a calender with caricatures of VIPs (including the Pope and Mrs Thatcher) in which Petra was portrayed drinking at a bar, nude except for a holster and two pistols. Petra was outraged. 'This picture makes a unity between pornography and militarism, a picture of a person [who has] for many years struggled for the dignity of women . . . true disarmament and for human rights in many parts of the world.'[23] No sooner had she escaped from the *New Solidarity* litigation than she began an action against *Penthouse* which drizzled on until the end of 1988 when she finally lost.

However right she may have been in principle, many of her colleagues and even close friends, thought that in pursuing *Penthouse* as well as meticulously sending in corrections to inaccurate press reports, she was wasting her time and her energy. But she could not help herself. How the world outside reflected her was how she judged herself, so if the image was not correct, she was cut to the quick. She reacted not out of vanity as many assumed; she had to set the record straight because she did not have enough confidence in herself to trust others to see the real Petra beyond the pastiche.

By the summer of 1984 the threads which had bound Die Grünen and Petra together were already beginning to loosen; each held impossible expectations of the other. In her bitter assessment of the first year in the Bundestag, Petra wrote of the way the *Fraktion* had failed personally and politically to live up to even the principles it had set itself in its founding documents, never mind her own hopes for it.[24] She was right of course, but because the party was without proper structures, it was incapable of doing much about it. They, on the other hand were disappointed that Petra's actions inside the group did not entirely match up with her promises to the peace movement. Her power to move thousands at the anti-nuclear rallies had not survived the transfer into the chamber of the Bundestag, and she had quickly tired of the grinding meetings which often lasted until late at night.

When Petra had risen to her feet to give her maiden speech on 4th May 1983, many expectations had accompanied her. The peace movement hoped, and the other parties feared, that all the respect and authority she had commanded on the demonstrations would reverberate around the chamber, reducing by comparison all arguments for the missiles to impotent squeaks. But in the Bundestag the magic did not happen. She seemed more tiny among the 512 MPs than she did among the hundreds of thousands in the street. And although she delivered her usual passionate defence of non-violence it took the government about two minutes to realize that she was not, after all, dangerous. She might be able to rouse rabbles who were willing to be roused, but in the chamber her splendid rhetoric did not possess a logic sufficiently tight to resist the eager unpicking fingers of the sceptical.

But perhaps the most important rock on which Petra stumbled was the promises she had made to the peace movement. These she had reiterated at a press conference on the day Die Grünen entered the Bundestag. She had personally guaranteed all the safeguards that would keep the party 'different from all others' – solidarity, direct democracy, rotation. Yet she had been among the first to break ranks on many of the principles. When the press office refused to put out every release she sent to them, she simply bypassed them and circulated the releases directly. Bored and frustrated by the *Fraktion* meetings and their tendency 'to spend a tremendous amount of time discussing futile details and minor problems in mammoth debates and to concern itself far more with internal difficulties than with the matters of life and death because of which over two million voters elected us to parliament', she simply withdrew and focused on what interested her.[25]

Again, she was often right. The *Fraktion* would meet every Tuesday, sitting late into the night but allowing domestic quibbling to push serious political debate to the end of agenda, with important matters often going undiscussed. The length and inefficiency of these meetings made it difficult for parliamentarians to be ready for their committees on Wednesdays and the plenary debates on Thursdays without working through the night.

Die Grünen's more pragmatic activists, if they did not share Petra's notion of anti-politics, and particularly disliked her refusal to contemplate coalitions, certainly agreed with her about the need for a more professional and efficient party organization. But they were essentially out of the game because, as most of them were elected members of national or local government (many already involved in coalitions), rules forbade them to hold posts in the party's organization as well. That left the field free for the 'cadre politics' of the left-wingers, who at federal and *Länder* level were dominant in the party organization. Because they were remorselessly opposed to any sort of charismatic leader, and hated Petra's insistence that the Soviet Union be criticized as much as the United States, they grasped every opportunity to 'cut her down to size'. Consequently, when gratuitously unpleasant attacks on Petra occurred, motivated by little more than spite and envy, neither the official party machinery nor any faction moved to defend her.

The last straw came in 1985, when Petra became the only member of the first *Fraktion* to refuse to rotate. Although there was wide agreement that the whole rotation arrangement was not working, everyone went along with it – some because they were glad to get out, others because they had decided that, tactically, this was the best way to get back into the Bundestag in 1987 when the rotation rules would be rescinded. Petra, on the other hand, decided to go to Bavaria and ask her local party to use its power to overrule rotation. This required a 70 per cent majority at a regional conference held in Aschaffenburg in July 1984. Purity of principle prevailed among the Bavarian delegates and they rejected her appeal and asked her to rotate, as agreed, in March 1985. Much sniping, only slightly behind her back, suggested that Petra had a 'Lady Di complex – wherever there is a camera, you will find Petra Kelly.'

Marieluise Beck remembers that no one believed Petra would rotate. 'It was ridiculous that she should not have some sort of mandate, but after she had been so outspoken, it was difficult not to go ahead. The party was too simple-minded in those days to accept someone as different.' So when Petra wrote a letter to the parliamentary group in January 1985 announcing that she would stay on, it did not come as a surprise. Her closing plea in her letter revealed she understood very well how much her decision would upset her colleagues:

> *Knowing full well that this will not be made easy for me in the time ahead and that I must be prepared for animosity in many instances, I nonetheless hope that I shall not be punished with isolation and restrictions in my existing area of work. I therefore ask you not to make it humanly and politically impossible for me to stay on in the parliamentary group.*

But from this point onwards, the ways of Petra and Die Grünen increasingly diverged. The party never really forgave her, and her enemies amongst the left-wing greens missed no opportunity to remind everyone of her treason. Party conferences, always hard but exhilarating occasions, became a misery for Petra. Averted eyes greeted her more often than friendly smiles. She turned up less and less for the *Fraktion* meetings, preferring to concentrate on her own particular interests and to use the large numbers of invitations she received from overseas to escape from 'the green hell'.

Gerlind Bode, who now runs an umbrella group for organizations working with children with cancer, worked with Petra during this difficult time. She remembers that Petra was enormously insecure:

> *At times she was so afraid, she became almost paranoid. She felt everyone was out to get her. Of course there had been a big change – the Greens were not very nice to her any more, apart from a small group. We would try to sit her down and persuade her that it would work out, but all of a sudden it had become very personal. She had the feeling that no one was helping her any more, she had no real friends.*

Notes

1 Wilfried Krestschmann quoted in the *Guardian* (6 October 1982).
2 *Guardian* (30 November 1982).
3 Konrad (1985) p. 83.
4 Essay: (3 March 1984).
5 Gert Bastian, letter to Die Grünen im Bundestag (9 January 1984).
6 Gert Bastian, letter to Die Grünen im Bundestag (9 February 1984).
7 Spretnak and Capra (1983) p. 71.
8 Speech: Los Angeles (25 September 1987).
9 Kolinsky (1989) p. 148.
10 Essay: (1 December 1989).
11 Essay: (1 December 1989).
12 Book: with Bastian and Aiello (eds.) (1991) p. 324.
13 Batchelor (1994).
14 Petra never visited Tibet; her applications for a visa were repeatedly refused.
15 Book: Paige and Gilliatt (eds.) (1992) p. 141.
16 Essay: (July 1989).
17 Havel (1991) p. 100.
18 Speech: Lund (2 July 1988).
19 *Irish Times* (28 April 1987).
20 Beckman and Kopelew (eds.) (1993).
21 Book: Paige and Gilliatt (1992) p. 123.
22 *New Solidarity* (18 June 1982).
23 Speech: Athens (21 November 1985).
24 Essay: (3 March 1984).
25 Essay: (3 March 1984).

7

September 1985
-to-
October 1992

'I HAVE TO KEEP FLYING AS I FIND THE GROUND ABSURD'

If 1985 was not the most miserable year Petra spent in the Bundestag, then it was only because 1986 was worse. Faced with the hostility of her colleagues over her decision not to rotate, Petra dealt with adversity as she usually did – and worked even harder. The permanent exhaustion this caused only made matters worse. It exacerbated her *angst*, and made her feel more insecure than ever.

During 1985, Petra had managed to travel abroad quite frequently, mostly to the United States, but she travelled much less in 1986. More time was devoted to writing and she prepared two books, one on Hiroshima and the other on children's cancer, and contributed more chapters and articles for other books, journals and newspapers (mostly in German) than at any other period of her life.[1] For most of the time, in public at least, she managed to appear confident and happy. In Dover to speak at a conference of the European greens in March 1985, during a period when the 'torture the celebrity' campaign in Die Grünen was at its height, she was even able to laugh and joke with me about the awfulness of it all. Later, her *angst* would overwhelm her until she could scarcely get out of bed. In the middle of September, with some colleagues to stage a 48-hour occupation of the German embassy in Pretoria in protest against Germany's economic links with South Africa, she once more lost her nerve and had to be taken out through the back exit. By the time we next met at a Die Grünen conference on Europe in November 1986 in Köln, she was in a terrible state, looking exhausted and ill. Without even greeting me, she started to whisper from behind her hand about all the dreadful fights going on inside her party. It was as if every harsh word spoken had damaged her physically as well as emotionally.

As far as the state of her party was concerned, much of her anguish was well founded. In December 1985, the Greens in Hessen formed a governing coalition with the SPD, and leading *Realo* Joschka Fischer was sworn in as Minister of the Environment, a step which was welcomed by most of the party membership and their supporters. Petra issued a press release to point out that as he was now responsible for running the nuclear power plant in the *Land* he was as much an atomic as an environment minister. But the *Tageszeitung* was jubilant, and pictured Fischer at his swearing-in ceremony (wearing a pair of trainers): 'The long march through the institutions – one made it!' Perversely, a Die Grünen conference held a few days later elected an executive dominated by the left-wing *Fundis* whose leader, Jutta Ditfurth, had accused Fischer of siding with murderers.[2] Subsequently, what Petra called the 'Holy War . . . fostered by the mullahs of the two camps' abandoned all remnants of restraint and waged their war as publically and in as unholy a manner as possible. Only after the nuclear reactor at Chernobyl exploded in April 1986 was a truce called, and unprecedented unity reigned for the run up to the Bundestag elections at the end of January 1987.

By the time these elections took place, Petra's dependence on the now ever-present Gert Bastian was almost total. When first elected to the Bundestag he had rented his own flat in Bonn near to the university, but in 1984 announced he was giving it up: 'It's OK,' he told everyone, 'when I'm in Bonn I can stay with Petra.' As Bastian often complained about how difficult it was to live and work closely with Petra, this move confused many friends; but to warnings from Roland Vogt and others that he should keep his flat and his independence he replied sharply, 'I can handle it.' At first, when Bastian went to Munich to visit his family and friends, Petra would go with him as far as Nürnburg to visit Omi, or stay on her own in Bonn. By 1986, she could no longer stay anywhere alone; the very thought made her anxious – ill even – and before Bastian could leave he had to organize for someone either to be with her or to telephone her regularly. This was a very different Petra from the person who once so cherished her freedom and independence.

In many ways, Gert Bastian did not appear to be entirely unhappy with the way things were at this time. Both publically, and, it seems, privately, he was loving and devoted at all times, and even when things were at their most difficult, he would willingly join forces with Petra's staff and friends to support her. And things did get very difficult. Petra's *angst* caused her to feel panicky and fearful at times of stress, but deep exhaustion would degrade her anxiety into a paranoia which encompassed even those closest to her. Petra's friend, Gerlind Bode, remembers being unpleasantly surprised when she first came to work in Petra's office in 1984 at how 'unfairly the group acted with each other, and how they hurt each other. It was true that Petra was a special person, she was so energetic and wonderfully creative and, yes, it was not always easy to work with her, she sometimes did not do things correctly and so forth, but because she was special we always tried to protect her from the group.'

Matters got worse after Petra refused to rotate and the group's hostility began to extend to her staff: ' "Oh its Petra's people again," they would say, when we asked for more paper, more postage, because she mailed letters into the whole world. No one did as much work as she did.' Andrea Shalal-Esa, now a correspondent with Reuters news agency in Washington, remembers the difficulties of this time too, but also that it was interesting, exhilarating and inspiring work. Others have less pleasant memories and quite a few lasted only weeks before giving up. Some even formed a club for what they called 'those who have been hurt by Petra'. In all, during her eight years in the Bundestag, and including the ubiquitous North American politics students on six-month 'locums' in Europe, around thirty staff are reputed to have passed through Petra's office.

For much of the time though, Petra's staff did not see her. When parliament or committees were not sitting she would work at home, coming into the office late in the evening to go on working through the night. In the morning her staff would find notes stuck everywhere and to everything – desks, walls, even lampshades. At her most anxious, she would rifle through drawers and wastepaper bins, leaving accusatory notes about documents lost or wrongly thrown out. Sometimes, staff protest resulted, and a demand for an office meeting was made, but Petra wouldn't come. She couldn't face the unpleasantness and sent Bastian instead. At other times, if there was a birthday or other cause to celebrate, it was Petra who organized the party and presents.

Ingrid Aouane, who worked with Petra at the party office prior to the 1983 election, then rejoined her staff in 1987, remembers the ups and downs of working with Petra. 'There were often disputes at the office; for example she would take things home and then forget and accuse people of losing them, so no wonder she lost staff. There were those who could put up with it and those who couldn't.' Tswang Norbu, who worked with Petra in 1990 laughingly agrees. 'She was not easy to work with, that is true, but I've known a lot worse.' Those who knew her well understood that behind the difficulties lay a caring and compassionate woman, and, like her longest-serving member of staff Frieder Wolf, they felt a deep loyalty to both her and her work. Martha Kremer, who came with Petra from Brussels to be her first parliamentary assistant, recalls that it 'took a long time to recover from working with Petra' but she remained a close friend and still sits on the board of the Grace Kelly Foundation. (After Petra's death, when she was helping Robert Camp to transfer Petra's papers from Swinemünderstrasse to the archives, Ingrid Aouane found pinned to a cellar wall a painting her son had given to Petra over ten years previously. 'He had written on it "For you Petra Kelli" – with an i at the end; all wrong, but she had kept it and I find that great.')

For the January 1987 Bundestag elections the Bavarian Greens made a point of giving first place on their list to Hannelore Saibold, the *Nachrücker* who had been denied her seat when Petra refused to rotate. Petra was selected for fifth place and -unless the Greens polled significantly better than 1983 – she would be lucky to win a seat. On the night of the election the Greens gathered to await the results in the Biscuithalle, a disused ceramics factory in Bonn. For once, Gert Bastian was more anxious than Petra and refused to accompany her. When I met her there, Petra was with her mother and stepfather, and though desperately tired was quite optimistic about the result, which as usual came through very quickly. Chancellor Kohl's government had survived – so no need to worry about coalitions – and the Greens had done better than anyone imagined. Die Grünen polled 8.2 per cent of the vote – over 3 million votes – to win 44 seats, 25 of which would be taken by women, one of them Petra. For the first time in the history of the Bundestag a parliamentary *Fraktion* would have a majority of women. In Bavaria the Greens had won seven seats. Petra was delighted. Thank goodness, she told me, I can keep my office and go on working. Around us the celebrations began in earnest. The Greens were back in the Bundestag, with a substantially increased vote but, for Petra, the contrast with 1983 was stark. Then she had been the centre of everyone's attention. This time it was the chief mullahs – Otto Schily for the *Realos* and Jutta Ditfurth for the *Fundis* – the press wanted to hear from. After a couple of interviews, Petra and her parents left the Biscuithalle to return to Swinemünderstrasse and Bastian.

After she was returned to the Bundestag, Petra was able to manage her *angst* rather better. Since Bastian had moved into Swinemünder-strasse she felt much safer, and now that her office and her job were secure for the next four years she felt a huge burden had been lifted from her. Her harassers left her mostly in peace, and even the personal attacks on her from within the party had diminished. She began to feel and look a lot better, to travel again, and to take up the campaign for Tibet seriously. There were even moments when her faith in the parliamentary system was restored. In response to her persistent campaigning DM2 million had been allocated to research into facilities for children with cancer and the Bundestag passed unanimously her motion on Tibet and human rights violations. Petra regained her equilibrium, and as the revolutions in East Europe moved out of the subversive kitchens and into the streets, her spirit discovered how to fly again.

Although Petra was regaining her confidence, the Die Grünen train was still bucketing down the track towards the end of 1990 when it would lose all its seats in the Bundestag. The end of 1987 was an indication of the troubles which lay ahead. Prompted by the tenth anniversary of the bloody autumn of 1977 (when the kidnapping and murder of German industrialist Martin Schleyer and the highjacking of a Lufthansa aircraft in Mogadishu had been followed by suspicious group suicide of members of the Red Army Fraction then in prison) Antje Vollmer, a theologian and Die Grünen MP had launched a debate about a *possible* amnesty for any terrorists who renounced violence. In October Jutta Ditfurth, speaker for the party executive, created a considerable commotion by calling for an *unconditional* amnesty for all 'political prisoners.'[3]

The commotion turned to uproar, when, one month later *Autonomen* killed two policemen during a demonstration at Frankfurt and one of Ditfurth's co-speakers Regina Michalik called for a broad show of unity with the *Autonomen*. Petra threatened to resign over this. She was already seething after a party conference at Oldenburg had rejected a proposal to establish a foundation in the memory of recently deceased Heinrich Böll: 'The arguments used by the Greens in the debate against the personality and works of Heinrich Böll reflect an intellectual and cultural indigence that is incompatible with the Green claim to a more human state.'[4] Petra was furious that after his death Böll should be denounced 'by certain grass-roots vigilantes' as a 'chauvinist', a 'super-father', and a 'naive sentimentalist' while the same people had felt him good enough to be included in party campaigns and events when he was alive.[5] The growing anti-intellectual climate in the party and now frank support for violence was, she said 'tantamount to political bankruptcy'. Why, I asked her around this time, do you not do as Gert Bastian did and leave the party and sit as an independent? 'I couldn't,' she replied, 'I've been in this from the beginning.' For all her exasperation, to Petra Die Grünen was like a child which would, she was sure, one day grow up and start to behave better.

In December 1987, away from the press, the party held an emergency 'burying the hatchet' meeting. On the wall of the room was a wonderful cartoon of two brawling green frogs watched happily by the three other parties drawn as vultures. Sustaining the imagery of the zoo, one state representative accused the Bonn leadership of being a theatre of monkeys; their performance was jeopardizing the party and losing members. The two factions agreed a paper presented by a conciliatory group led by Antje Vollmer. Almost immediately supporters of the group were designated as a third faction and dubbed the *Neutralos*.

Sadly, the *Neutralo* group came too late for Petra, and working closely with Antje Vollmer would be very difficult. Petra was now fully immersed in her own interests, making a great deal of being 'independent of the factions', and the two women could hardly have been more different in style and personality. Where Petra was impulsive and passionate, Vollmer was reflective and a skilled political tactician. As far as policy goals were concerned few differences existed between them, but Vollmer had been openly critical of Petra – for her refusal to rotate in particular and for the weakness of her strategic thinking in general.

Petra did have a problem with strategy; she was not good at understanding the way power worked, either in the real world or inside an organization. Petra would dismiss Die Grünen's internal arguments as 'boring and useless, because if you want to build up a movement to challenge the establishment, you can't keep on having arguments about who's got the power in the party'.[6] But ignoring power did not make it go away. One of the problems with non-violent theory, which made it so difficult for Petra and many others to deal with it on anything but the most general terms, was that it was not entirely realistic about power or about the psychology of people faced with violence. Petra waxed lyrical about the beautiful act of non-violent resistance by the students and intellectuals in China for example, but only by writing-out of her mind's script the subsequent brutal suppression by the Chinese authorities.

In the public arena, however, it was not Petra's lack of engagement in the details of policy or organization which really mattered, as she more than made up for that with her strengths. Her warmth and translucent honesty combined with her formidable knowledge and breadth of experience to make her the most powerful communicator of green ideas to the widest of audiences. Where Petra's disregard for strategy really tripped her up was in failing to secure her survival as a force to be reckoned with inside Die Grünen. No matter how many members agreed with her basic principles and greatly appreciated her powers of communication, by becoming isolated from them as they wrestled with the banal everyday grind of putting green politics into practice, Petra was loosening the threads of their loyalty.

By now, Die Grünen was preparing for their 1990 elections. Many constituency parties, including Petra's local party in Bavaria, had replaced the two-year rotation rule with one which limited candidates to two terms of office. This made her ineligible for selection for a third term. The neighbouring *Land* of Hesse, fiefdom of Joschka Fischer, did not have such a rule, so Petra decided to try her luck there. Her first attempt to win a place was in May in the *Wahlkreis* (electoral district) of Fulda, but faxing her nomination papers at the last minute from Tokyo did not impress, and, described as a 'personality almost never present' she was beaten for fifth place on the list by East German author Freya Klier. An invitation from Bündnis 90 – the alliance of dissident groups in East Germany – to take second place in Sachsen-Anhalt also foundered when its alliance partners, the East German Green Party, applied their rule that no West Germans should be parachuted into East German seats.

But if Petra's personal strategy for these elections was a mess, then so was that of her party. At a press conference to mark the ten-year anniversary of the party's founding, two of the speakers (both women) came to blows over their different interpretations of the party's achievements. The largely personality-free slate of Green candidates gave the SPD's stars a free run of whatever television coverage the opposition parties got. And, crucially, Die Grünen was caught out by the stampede towards German unification. The party had decided to make global warming the central theme of its campaign. Unsurprisingly, at the end of one of the most astonishing years in German history – a year which had seen free elections in East Germany; Chancellor Kohl's 'purchase' of East Germany from Gorbachev for $8 billion; the end of the post World War Two division; and the first joint meeting of the two German parliaments in Berlin's Reichstag – Die Grünen's sudden concern about global ecological problems fooled no one. The policies were not wrong, but the moment was. All but the most loyal voters deserted the Greens.

Die Grünen failed to win any seats with 4.9 per cent of the vote in the West, while Bündnis 90/Die Grünen won eight seats with 6.1 per cent in the East. Petra was not the only person to note that if she had been near the top of some list somewhere – anywhere – her personal vote might have been enough to take the result over the all-important five per cent threshold. Nevertheless it was clear, she said, that the 'margin of mercy' the voters had given Die Grünen had finally come to an end. In *Taz* Joschka Fischer described what had happened as not so much a 'shot across the bows, [as] a direct hit.' He deplored the way the party had ignored the 'laws of political physics' by taking a low profile and ignoring the importance of personalities and a strong party structure. 'These are the three main reasons for the catastrophic

defeat last Sunday. The debacle is essentially of our own making and
its seeds were sown years ago.'[7]

THE PERSONAL IS POLITICAL

Within thirty-six hours of the election, Joschka Fischer and Antje
Vollmer, leaders of the *Realo* and *Neutralo* faction respectively, held a
press conference to reflect on the reasons for Die Grünen's poor
result, and to pose a question about its future: 'Does society want to
keep its own party to cope with its biggest problem in the future (the
relationship between ecology and peace), and is Die Grünen capable
or willing to offer that help?' A new Die Grünen stripped of its
ideologies and reformed structurally, had to move fast, they said, but
they were optimistic that this could be done.[8] Thus they began the
final battle with the unreconstructed left-wing of the party.

Petra was not so optimistic about the future of the party:

> *The defeat . . . has left most of us sad and stunned and somewhat bitter
> and unfortunately, it has also left us, as ever, divided! I believe we have
> not so much failed in political terms, but most of all we have failed in
> human terms . . . The Green Party has a very small chance to learn
> from its past mistakes and to begin accepting the fact that political
> programmes are communicated to others by persons, by human beings
> made of flesh and blood, each of us with our strengths and weaknesses,
> each of us with our pluses and minuses.*[9]

Before she moved out of her office at the end of December, Petra
communicated her distress by phone and by fax to every corner of the
world. To the startled editor of a *Los Angeles Times* syndicated column
she wrote:

> *There is at the moment very little hope about the Green Party staying
> together. The coming weeks will determine if the Green Party still has a
> national future in Germany. After eleven years of dedicating all my
> efforts, my health and all of my private life to the development and
> strengthening of the Green Party – it is all the more painful for myself.*

For all her misery at losing her office and the horrendous task of shifting three-and-a-half rooms of files and archives out of the Tulpenfeld building, this was not despair speaking. It was much more like the old pugnacious Petra simply communicating her latest joy/hurt in lurid detail. She was preparing a contribution to a book of mine at the time, so we spoke together quite frequently and, amidst all the anger and disappointment about Die Grünen, she explained she was already looking for writing and other jobs – would I promise to let her know if anything turned up? Petra was in a crisis but she was in reasonable control. While we spoke, Gert Bastian could be heard in the background steadily filling boxes with books and files, and she would interrupt our conversation from time to time to redirect some file or another or to seek from him confirmation of what she was saying. As most of Petra's friends and colleagues to whom I have spoken over the last year all claim to have had one of Petra's last phone calls from the Bundestag, it must be assumed that Bastian completed his task virtually singlehanded.

One reason Petra was in relatively good form was that, despite her disappointments over the performance of her party, she herself had had two reasonably good years. She had been able to concentrate on issues which mattered most to her, especially Tibet, East Germany and the Grace Kelly Foundation, and in March 1989 she became Chair of the German Association for Social Defence. Here she could develop a policy area to which Die Grünen was not, she felt, paying sufficient attention. She also published three more books, two with Gert Bastian on Tibet and a second collection of her speeches and essays entitled *Mit dem Herzen denken* (Thinking with the Heart), and she received more invitations to speak and write than she could possibly accept. Overseas her standing remained high – in the autumn of 1991 she was named one of the 1000 makers of the 20th century by *The Sunday Times* (to her delight profiled on the same page as John F. Kennedy). In addition, the ordinary German public still appreciated her: they loved her frankness and courage in debate and wondered why she had dropped out of sight recently.

Although Petra continued to criticize from the sidelines, she had managed to steer reasonably clear of the ructions going on inside her party. A sort of truce had been called between Petra and the parliamentary group, whereby Petra exercised what she called 'civil disobedience in my own party' and they left her free to work in her own way. The only fly in this ointment was the persistent refusal of the press to give what she called serious coverage to the issues that mattered most to her. They were only interested in the spinning-top of power politics in Bonn and Berlin; and, to her great irritation, now she was marginalized inside Die Grünen they were not even interested in her opinion about the party. The exception she always made to this criticism was the international press. For them she still had the only 'name recognition' that mattered, so they usually turned up to her press conferences.

There were two other reasons why Petra seemed to be coping with the dreaded moment of finding herself jobless and officeless. After reading an article about *angst* in *Emma* magazine, Petra had begun to understand she suffered from a genuine illness which could even be treated.[10] 'This is what I've got,' she excitedly told her mother, Erika Heinz and others, 'it's what's been wrong with me all these years. It's why I feel so nervous and frightened that no one will help me.' She bought books about it, even tabled a *kleine Anfrage* about it in August 1990, and promised her mother that as soon as she had a minute, she would seek help.

But she never did. For the moment at any rate she felt no urgency. One month before the Tibetan hearing in Bonn in April 1989, she had fallen in love with a young Tibetan doctor. Palden Tawo, married with three children, was charismatic, energetic, a leader of the Tibetan community in Bonn and he was working closely with Petra on the hearing. All the ingredients for passion were in place, and the affair, although brief, was conducted with Petra's usual great intensity. After the deaths of Petra and Gert Bastian, the general opinion was that Bastian had not been concerned by this affair, and that it was of no significance. It was even reported that when the relationship began to fizzle out, Bastian had contacted Tawo to urge him to go on seeing Petra so he might have more time to himself. But this is not strictly the whole story. When the affair started, Bastian had really suffered. He phoned and drove all over Bonn to try to find out where Petra was. Then, when the possibility arose that Tawo would leave his family for Petra, Bastian made a bargain; he would tolerate the affair if only she did not leave him. He even drove her to meet Tawo (she could not drive). But by November 1990, when the three of them travelled together to the United States, the affair was beginning to draw to a close.

Eventually the dawn of 1991 cast its harsh light on the difficulties of life beyond the Bundestag. All Petra had was her massive archive (much of which had had to be stored in a furniture repository as the little house was packed to bursting point with books and papers) and a pension of one month's pay for each year she had been an MP. The office, the staff, the photocopying service, the free telephone, the travel expenses and the research facilities were all gone, but the requests for information and the invitations kept on coming. Petra sent Heinz Suhr a photograph of three large plastic washing baskets stacked high with mail. 'Look,' she wrote on the picture, 'this is what was waiting for me after only two weeks – 350 letters.'

When the eight East German MPs of the new parliamentary group, Bündnis 90/Die Grünen were installed in their offices, Petra tried to establish some formal arrangement which would help her manage her still formidable workload. Heinz Suhr had joined the new group as press speaker and proposed they might formally appoint Petra as an honourary (i.e. unpaid) international consultant, but this was rejected. When the argument of her international importance was used, the reply from both the new *Fraktion* and the party executive was; 'If she is important in America or India, then let them pay for an office.'

The party was having to go through a period of readjustment. Failing to reach the five per cent barrier in the West had lost the party a lot of money, and nearly 300 staff had to be laid off. But however poor it was feeling in morale and bank balance, the meanness of Die Grünen to Petra at this time illustrated one of the biggest failings of the German Green Party – one that had brought it the strongest criticism from their sister parties in the rest of the world – its parochialism. Die Grünen was not really interested in the international vision of green politics. Petra had been one of the few not only to understand the importance of the international dimension of green politics, but also to go out of her way actually to help worthwhile causes wherever and however she could. The dissidents in East Germany and the Tibetans were the best-known examples but there were many others. Gerald Häfner, a Bavarian colleague of Petra's, remembers visiting Indonesia, where he met – illegally, as was so often the case – disaffected intellectuals and writers who were trying to found a green party. 'This was a crime in Suharto's "controlled democracy". The people I met had succeeded, despite tremendous difficulties, to send two letters asking for support to the die Grünen offices, but had received no reply. They sent a third letter, this time to Petra Kelly direct, and received a reply immediately.'

Petra was special, she was different and she was difficult, but it was all of these things *together* which had made her – and Die Grünen – great, so the party looked deservedly small-minded when its inability to accommodate her was exposed to the full glare of publicity after her death. In defiance of this mean-spiritedness, Heinz Suhr, to his eternal credit, slipped Petra a key to his press office so that she and Gert Bastian might use it at night and during the weekends.

If the practical side of working from home was bad, the psychological adjustment was also difficult. Petra no longer had the status of MP, and because she held no position in her party either, several platforms were no longer available to her. In Germany her easy access to members of government was cut off overnight, there would be no more invitations to important state events. In other countries the usual protocol afforded to visiting parliamentarians, which provided her with so many contacts and so much information, would no longer be there. Gone too was the diplomatic passport which eased her passage across difficult borders. The media rarely canvassed her views and getting articles published became more difficult. For the first time for many years, Petra's destiny was back in her own hands, and she didn't know what to do with it.

Brushing aside all counsel that she should take some time out to pause, think and look around before making any decisions, Petra immediately gave in to all the old anxieties about how she would earn her living. How could she possibly go on contributing to the support of her grandmother and Nima, never mind pay the postage and telephone bill? As usual, her anxieties were relative. She had substantial savings and the Bundestag pension was sufficiently generous to last well over a year without too much scrimping. But, objectively, she was jobless, and something had to be done. First, she decided, she would run for one of the two speaker posts on the party executive at its first all-Germany conference at Neuminster at the end of April. That would give her a platform again. The worries about money she solved by signing a lucrative contract with a private television channel, SAT 1 (best known for broadcasting soft pornography) to moderate six programmes on the environment to be broadcast weekly, starting in January 1992. When asked why she was working with this particular channel when she had been known for her strong stand against pornography, she replied that someone had to try to reach the sort of audience which watched it. Many felt the truth to lie in Petra's anxiety about money and a job being more powerful than her dislike of the channel.

Petra decided to stand as party speaker because she was genuinely fearful Die Grünen would split. Integration was needed and she felt it could only be done by someone genuinely independent of all factions. However, there were two other candidates for the post of female speaker, Christina Weiske from the former East Germany – and Antje Vollmer. Lukas Beckmann was horrified when he heard who was standing. It could hardly be conciliatory and integrating for the party if Petra and Antje stood against each other. But his efforts and attempts by others to persuade Petra to try for an ordinary seat on the executive rather than for a speaker's post failed. 'Remember, you will have to speak for all the party, not only for yourself,' Beckmann warned Petra.

This time Petra did not listen to Lukas Beckmann, nor did she do her usually thorough research. If she had done, she would have noticed that several thousand Greens now sat on local councils, and that most members and supporters wanted Die Grünen to be a political party which actively sought and participated in power – if necessary, through coalitions.

Petra might also have thought twice about an open letter she wrote to the party in February 1991. In it she explained how she thought things had gone wrong, and even though much of what she wrote was true, a little reflection might have suggested that this was perhaps not the moment to rake it all up. She concluded her letter by saying that although she said she did not reject outright the possibility of coalitions with the SPD, she thought they were a long way off:

Today's Green Party has no room for tactical coalitions with the PDS [the new incarnation of the old East German Communist Party which won 17 seats in the Bundestag in December 1990] that party which lacks credibility. Nor can we allow our party to be brought to heel, becoming the springboard for the SPD, nor should we become a sort of Green FDP . . . As far as I am concerned, the most important and most

credible coalition partners of the Greens continue to be the committed
human rights groups like Amnesty International and pioneering ecology
groups such as Greenpeace. These are the people who we, the anti-party,
must be sure not to disappoint.[11]

For a political party struggling to move forward after a thumping
electoral defeat, a call for a return to the 1970s was not what they
wanted to hear.

Leo Cox, Secretary of the European Greens attended the
Neumünster conference as an observer. Before her speech he saw
Petra sitting apart with Gert Bastian, drafting and redrafting her text.
In the end, Cox remembers, it was not a particularly good speech, she
was tense and lacklustre, but still the result of the vote shocked
everyone. Weiske got 344 votes, Vollmer 263 and Petra 39. The last
thread of loyalty between Die Grünen and Petra Kelly had snapped.

PetrandGert

In 1991 a change took place in the relationship between Gert Bastian
and Petra, but it was so subtle that no one really noticed it at the time.
Only later did Petra's friends realize that they had seen less and less of
her during the last months of her life. If they phoned, it was usually
Bastian who answered. A call from the couple came, more often than
not, from him, not Petra. At the very time when Petra should have
been out and about, keeping up her political contacts and enjoying
more time with the people she loved, she instead retreated further
behind the lace curtains of Swinemünderstrasse and let her protector
put up more barriers around her.

Friends like Achim and Irmgard Schuppert say that, however busy
she was, Petra always remembered birthdays, sent gifts to their
children and had time to visit; reunions, celebrations and intimate
evenings with friends used to mean a lot to her. Towards the end of
her life, however, although she still sent the presents, she rarely had
time to visit or to be visited. Dinner appointments were made with
difficulty then often cancelled shortly beforehand. Even when
Schuppert wanted to do something for the Grace Kelly Foundation,
Petra sounded enthusiastic, but never got round to setting a date. In
the last year it was always Bastian who phoned but it was about

himself he talked. 'I am in despair, I do not know how I will continue.' The problem, he explained, was that Petra did not earn enough money. Gert Bastian phoned one of Petra Kelly's friends, Christiane Gollwitzer, three times in the last month of his life. Again he spoke about himself and his tiredness. Was there, he asked, a life after death?

The mounting despair of Gert Bastian, together with less direct contact with Petra, did not ring bells of alarm with friends at the time. As far as they were concerned, these were only variations on themes which had been playing for nearly a decade; the more desperate tone of these variations was imperceptible. Petra had suffered crises of *angst* before and the complaints about money were constant, as were Bastian's gasps of frustration about life with Petra. The two still travelled a lot, had enough money to stay in comfortable hotels, and gave all appearances of caring deeply for each other. Furthermore, for too long offers of help or advice as to how the situation might be alleviated had been rebuffed, so friends listened and sympathized, said they were there if needed, and left it at that.

More than once, Bastian had asked psychiatrist Horst-Eberhard Richter for advice about Petra's *angst*. An expert on anxiety neuroses, Richter had advised strongly that Petra should obtain professional treatment. He himself had once spoken directly to Petra about this possibility, but she was feeling fine at the time so brushed the suggestion aside. Richter believed (as did Petra's mother) that Bastian was the only one who had the power to persuade Petra to seek help. But Bastian never did. The advice he was looking for was how he, Bastian, could look after her, not how she might be persuaded to seek help elsewhere. This of course was one of the worst things he could do. As Richter told him, you cannot be partner and therapist at the same time.

Looking back, perhaps, it was particularly unfortunate that, not only did the personality and soaring intellect of Petra eclipse that of the *sorgfältig* (meticulous) but pedestrian general, but the conspicuousness of her *angst* also detracted the attention of friends and observers alike from contemplating any internal fears that Bastian might have. While the storms of Petra's rage or excitement and the sun of her joy left no one with the slightest doubt about how she felt, the barometer of Bastian's emotions rarely moved off middling; he was renowned for the evenness of his temperament. Nobody suspected that where Petra expressed, he might repress.

Petra's *angst* was entirely understandable; she was, Richter said, a textbook case. From the moment she left the safe, ordered and loving confines of her convent school and Omi, her life had been a story of separation – from her culture, her father, her sister and her family. Her kidneys had taught her all there was to know about physical pain and at times she had been so intimidated she had even learnt what it meant to fear for your life. In all that has been written about Petra since she died, no one has expressed surprise that she should have achieved so much *despite* these hardships.

Instead, most of the surprise has been saved for Gert Bastian. It was a wonder, everyone said, that the kind, courteous Bastian – 'my gentle general' as Petra called him – had put up with the volatile and demanding Petra for so long. It was assumed that the early passion he had felt for her and for the cause which had brought them together, had long since been replaced by a sense of duty – loving duty, but duty nevertheless. It was even rumoured that he was impotent. People imagined he stayed, shouldering the most mundane tasks, because he was an honourable man and because Petra had so often said 'I cannot manage without Gert' he believed it to be true.

Intimates saw a relationship which had plenty of ups and downs, with rows and reconciliations, but, they said, no more than many marriages, and Bastian seemed quite happy in his role. A journalist with an office overlooking the road leading to the Bundestag, reflecting on the regular sight of Bastian plodding along under the weight of all Petra's bags, while she danced around him, touching his arm and talking incessantly, thought it served as the perfect metaphor for their personalities and their relationship.

Bastian had courted Petra with the skill of a military strategist. It had not taken him long to work out that if he wanted her as a lover, he would have to become a close political ally, and that the weakness in her defence was her anxiety about being alone. But, of course, Bastian had not bargained for falling in love. Petra was great fun to be with; she was gentle and loving, he found the storms and calms of her different moods exhilarating, and she had introduced him to a passion he had never experienced before. But most of all he was touched by the depth of her beliefs and the courage with which she promoted them. She had an inner strength and a certainty which he said reminded him of his mother – although he always stopped his comparison there. From the army, Bastian had learnt the importance of following orders, but from Petra he had learnt the importance of saying 'No.' If Gert Bastian had not been quite so lucky as he claimed at the Russian front, and he had indeed put obedience to orders above morality, then perhaps Petra came to represent a great deal more to him than anyone ever realized. It is conceivable that in the depths of Petra's moral convictions, Gert Bastian saw the chance of his own redemption. If, through her, through following her orders, he could say 'No!' often enough, perhaps he might be absolved of his sins.

Although he was careful not to show this dimension of his feelings for Petra (and to begin with he may not have been aware of them himself) it is difficult to find any other explanation for the way Bastian's love for Petra became so obsessional. She was obsessive about her work and he became obsessed with her. By 1983, he was accompanying her as much as he could, for which both Petra and her usual travelling companion, Omi, were eternally grateful. Omi was getting old and tired and beginning to feel out of her depth, both with the intensifying campaigning as Die Grünen got nearer to the Bundestag and the growing ugliness of Petra's harassers. Gert became Petra's knight in shining armour, leaping to her aid and defence. As time went on he also became her business manager, deploying his skills as an organizer to her chaotic schedule. It was the perfect job for an army tactician and – although he was an MP himself – he was much happier making himself indispensable to her.

Petra was grateful, but as always took everything that was on offer – then looked for more. Gert always seemed to have more to give. Others would set limits. Frieder Wolf worked with Petra for over five years, dealing with her foreign affairs work but refusing to be involved with other work (like the Grace Kelly Foundation) going on in her office: 'You had to set your own boundaries, or you couldn't survive.' Lukas Beckmann, if travelling with Petra, would warn her that if she turned up at the airport with more than one bag, he would go home. She obeyed, but began to travel less with him and more with Bastian. When Petra panicked just before meeting Erich Honecker, Beckmann told her bluntly that if she felt faint she should leave the room and he would get a doctor. Fear of missing the meeting helped her control her nerves, but when the same panic gripped her in the German embassy in Pretoria, Bastian spent hours trying to sooth her – without success. Achim Schuppert recalls one winter when Bastian phoned him from a motorway café halfway between Munich and Bonn. Earlier, Petra had called Bastian, tearful and frightened, begging him to come, but snow meant that his journey would take longer than he thought. Would Schuppert go and see she was alright? When Schuppert got there, Petra was fine. With hindsight, some friends now wonder if Bastian, by being so solicitous, so immediately responsive to her smallest request, had actually aggravated Petra's nervousness and insecurity. Had he perhaps done so on purpose in order to increase her dependency on him? Erika Heinz and others recall many occasions when Bastian would hold Petra back saying no, don't go, you can't go alone, wait, I'll come with you, it will be safer. 'He took responsibility for everything – even crossing roads.'

For all their sympathy with her extreme nervousness about her personal safety, it nevertheless came as a great shock when some of Petra's friends found out that Gert Bastian had brought his guns with him when he moved in with her. She had indeed received menacing phone calls and even death threats. More than once the bolts on car wheels were loosened, and in hotels and meeting rooms she would be followed into toilets and shouted at over the partitions. Parcels with odd or obscene gifts would be sent (once in New York the police bomb squad carefully dismantled a box which had been delivered to the meeting hall where she was due to speak, only to find it contained some black underwear). Lukas Beckmann remembers one night in Bonn when a terrified Petra called him because someone was rattling at her windows and letter box. He rushed over, only to find that whoever it was had moved over to his own house, from where his partner was now telephoning in a panic. At one point Petra was even listed by the Bonn police as their top security risk but she had refused their (armed) protection because her commitment to non-violence was stronger than her fear. So why did she allow guns into her house? Lukas Beckmann recalls borrowing Bastian's car to take Petra to a meeting in Duisburg in 1987. Rummaging in the glove compartment for a map he had found a gun, and was disconcerted to find Petra surprised, not that it was there at all, but that it was in the car instead of at home. Bastian took it with him to protect her she explained.

Some weeks later, Beckmann brought the matter up again when he was visiting her at Swinemünderstrasse. Petra said 'I must show you something,' and took him upstairs to show him the gun lying between some sweaters and scarves in the top section of a cupboard in the spare bedroom, which was known as 'Gracie's room'. That she should tolerate, never mind welcome, a gun in the room dedicated to her dead half-sister was an indication of how deep Petra's dread of being alone and vulnerable had become, and of how far she was from persuading her general to adopt non-violence for his own political creed. However much he parroted her words on the subject, he was never to be convinced by them.

Living secretly with guns while continuing to preach non-violence is perhaps the saddest example of Petra's struggle with the continual conflicts between her principles and the reality around her. She needed protection, and (apart from the politically unacceptable police) Gert Bastian and his guns were all that was available to her, so she had little choice but to take the whole package. So amazed were Petra's friends that she should compromise her most strongly held and most loudly proclaimed principle in this way that they failed to see the desperation which led her to do it. Moreover, beyond that desperation they failed to see the flabbiness of her protector's principles. It was she who became a little diminished in their eyes, while his reputation as a decent, honourable man remained intact.

Many people did wonder why the proud, handsome general should abdicate his own political career to become Petra's bag carrier, but it was widely assumed that he did so from a mixture of love and a recognition that she and her work were more important. He was an awkward public speaker (he always sounded as if he was on the parade ground) and could never be accused of being an original thinker. Lack of curiosity throughout his life meant he had read little, so Gert Bastian's intellectual landscape was pretty barren. After the first excitement of his resignation and the campaign to prevent the stationing of the missiles, he really had nothing much else to say. In 1983 his book about his views on German security policy was published. Reviewers thought it mundane and it was never translated.[12] So, by linking himself closely to Petra, Bastian could get the best of both worlds; his own limitations would be camouflaged and he could bask vicariously in her stardom. From most angles, it seemed like a good deal; he looked after the behind-the-scenes details she hated so much and she provided the script and the glamour. And it worked. Right up to and including the Bonn memorial, Gert Bastian got equal billing with Petra Kelly.

Managing Petra's bureaucracy, and appearing on her arm at big occasions – visits of heads of state, press balls, major overseas engagements – gave Bastian pleasure, but with the politics he could not be bothered. Although he enjoyed the status which went with being a member of the Bundestag, Gert Bastian seemed less interested in human exchanges and debates. Certainly he was tired – Petra's schedule was a tough one – but at almost every meeting, remembers Renate Mohr, about five minutes after everyone settled down to business, Bastian would doze off. Lukas Beckmann used to joke that he sometimes had the impression that Bastian slept right through the 1980s; at conferences, in meetings, at any get-together or discussion, whenever he looked, Bastian seemed to be sleeping. Even when Bastian accompanied Petra to Mohr's flat on the night Bärbel Bohley and Werner Fischer were expelled from East Germany – an evening of high drama and excitement – within minutes he was asleep in his chair.

Friends point out that it was around the time Bastian left the Bundestag (he did not stand in the 1987 elections) when he ceased to exist as a separate person in the minds of many of them. Petra had become PetrandGert. When together, it was she who would invariably do all the talking, turning to Bastian for confirmation or to bracket him (always affectionately) with her and what she was saying. He could rarely interrupt successfully, but when he did, she would soon cut across his words as if impatient with the slowness of his speech. Anyone who commented on this (and many did) found they both would laugh and exchange loving looks to show they were both quite happy about it all – they were a team. Petra frequently emphasized in a loving way that she could not manage without Bastian's constant support, and even private exchanges casually overheard did not reveal any serious strain in their relationship. 'Oh Gert,' she would say, squeezing his arm, 'I don't know how you put up with me.' He would reassure her that everything was just fine.

From time to time, Bastian would comment to friends on the pressures of being close to Petra, but they took it with a pinch of salt.

After all, all his actions showed him trying to get closer to Petra, not further away. When he resigned from the *Fraktion* in 1984, he gave up his flat and stayed at Swinemünderstrasse when he was in Bonn. Instead of encouraging Petra to do more on her own, he went out of his way to increase her dependency on him. In 1989 Petra's affair with Palden Tawo gave him the perfect opportunity and excuse to escape, but instead he used it to tie her to him ever more tightly. In the last year of their lives, they scarcely passed one day apart. 'I don't know how she could bear it,' said Marianne Birthler. 'He was like a coat, he was always so close to her.'

But Bastian had become truly indispensible as a protector from real and imagined harm. Petra also enjoyed his companionship; the rumour that he was impotent was, her intimates confirm, false. Right up to the end of their lives, private photographs show them having great fun together, and the house was littered with the loving notes that they left for each other. But with Gert Bastian, Petra could not soar like Jonathan Livingston Seagull. Unlike her other lovers, young and old, he was without real passion and imagination. He wrote her intense love letters ('I cannot bear it when you smile for him and not for me') but he did not have the poetry of Heinz Kuby, the intellect of Mansholt, the charm of Carroll or the spirituality of Tawo. Petra's lifelong search for a 'soul mate' with whom she could discover the essence of love and fly high above the absurd ground had not been successful. The price of keeping Bastian as a 'close political and personal companion', was that she must be tethered – practically, emotionally and intellectually – to his ground.

Certainly Petra could not manage alone. Who else would live with her and keep her safe? Her friends were busy with their own lives, Omi was too old and she felt estranged from her family. Although she and her mother phoned each other often, they saw each other rarely. Petra's parents had never been entirely at ease with her politics so, although their love was never stinted, they were unable to provide the unconditional and uncritical approval that Petra craved from them.

Furthermore, neither John nor Marianne Kelly liked Gert Bastian. When Major General Bastian had first met Lieutenant Colonel Kelly, Bastian had been reluctant even to shake hands. 'I don't like mixing with junior ranks,' Bastian told a mutual friend – who later related the conversation to John Kelly. At Kelly family get-togethers Bastian would go out of his way to avoid John Kelly and would irritate everyone by 'pulling rank' and taking the leading role. Marianne Kelly once had to sit furiously silent while her daughter's elderly lover proposed the toast at her own mother's birthday and at times her husband felt insulted in his own home. Mr and Mrs Kelly hid their feelings from Petra, and her own delight with Bastian meant she simply could not see it from their point of view. She was also disappointed when she failed to persuade her parents to return to Germany after John Kelly finally retired in 1987 (he would lose part of his pension). The last time the Kellys saw Petra face to face was at the end of 1991, and when I asked if they felt Bastian had become between them and their daughter, they answered simply and sadly – 'yes'.

By contrast, Omi's devotion to her granddaughter remained unclouded and she became a stalwart fan of Bastian. She knew just how much support Petra needed and was abidingly grateful that he had taken over these arduous duties. She wrote him thankful dedications on his birthday; 'What you are doing for Petra is wonderful, if you were not around she could not live any more.' Marianne Kelly recalls that Omi lent Bastian money on more than one occasion. Petra, who idealized family life, was bitter about her parent's reaction and would often speak and write of Omi as 'the only real family I have'.

BASTIAN'S DILEMMAS

Piecing together all the evidence under the wider lens made possible by time and distance suggests that Christmas 1990 was a pivotal moment for anyone trying to understand how Petra Kelly lost her life. That Christmas, Petra was in Berlin dancing with Palden Tawo, while Gert Bastian was with his wife and family in Munich struggling with an assortment of internal demons.

Bastian's first dilemma was indeed a difficult one. With great effort because of Petra's fear of being left alone, he had managed to keep his two worlds in separate compartments, both literally and psychologically: Petra, excitement and redemption in Bonn; Lotte, his family and honour in Munich. But now things were going badly wrong. Until Petra's affair with Tawo, Bastian had believed in his promise to Lotte, that he would return to her and they would grow old together. He would, in the end, do the honourable thing. From the first time he had been unfaithful to her (gossip has it that this was when she was expecting their first child) he had managed to construct an idiosyncratic idea of honour around the notion that as long as he did the right thing in the end, what happened before would be forgiven, and throughout their married life Lotte had given him no reason to doubt this happy ending. Perhaps the same sort of logic had persuaded Bastian that through Petra he could also achieve redemption for wartime sins; in the end if he did the right thing, then the past would no longer be held against him.

For Bastian everything began to unravel during Petra's affair with Tawo. Now she was out of the Bundestag and there was a risk she might leave him altogether, it dawned on Bastian that he could no more live without Petra, than Petra could live without her shrines to Gracie. The inescapable consequence of this revelation hit Bastian that Christmas. If he could not manage without Petra, then how could he keep faith with his promise to Lotte? He was being forced to chose between redemption for his sins and the peculiar sense of honour he had constructed around his wife.

It is also possible to see a second dilemma intruding into Bastian's misery. From the moment the Berlin wall was breached, the opening of the millions of files kept by the STASI, the East German secret police, became inevitable. Despite a certain hysteria surrounding the files, the desire to know the truth had overwhelmed the temptation to lock them up and let bygones be bygones. Vera Wollenberger, who discovered that her husband of eleven years was a STASI agent, confirms that however painful it may be, it is easier to live with truth than with suspicion.

Bastian himself always denied that the STASI had ever tried to contact him. But, like the way he brushed off any possibility he had known about Nazi atrocities during the war, these denials are a trifle glib. Officially, it is improbable the STASI would have been allowed to overlook a NATO general openly expressing doubts about Western European security policy. The claims by Günter Bohnsack that Bastian's speeches had been drafted by the KGB and given to the STASI to hand over may be tainted by lack of documentary evidence – and by the fact that Bohnsack was once head of a STASI department which specialized in *dis*information. However, it remains highly likely that Bastian – perhaps naively, but certainly knowingly enough to want to keep it secret – received briefings from, or exchanged information of some sort with, the STASI at some time, maybe even before he finally resigned his commission. By 1990, Bastian was certain that the slightest whiff of such a past connection would mean not only that his life with Petra would be over but also every scrap of honour from his principled stand in 1980 would be wiped out. Any residual doubts or, more accurately, any hopes he nurtured on this score were erased in July 1992, when Petra interviewed Dirk Schneider, the former Die Grünen MP exposed as a STASI agent. Her disgust focused, not on any distortion he may have brought to the party's defence policy, but on Schneider's sustained betrayal of the trust and confidence of his colleagues.

It would be wrong to imply that Bastian examined his situation in the clinical way it has been laid out here. On the contrary, his misery stemmed from the muddle of his emotions and his apparent inability to work out any strategy which would avoid what seemed like inevitable defeat on all fronts. Petra was trying to escape, his family were fed up with him, and the risk of shrieking tabloid headlines accusing him of being a spy increased daily. Bastian's brooding gloom over that Christmas forced him to contemplate the worst. What would he do if he could not stop his neatly ordered world from collapsing around him?

The idea of suicide was not alien to him; it was part of the culture of honour which pervaded military organizations, and the very fact that he had kept his guns – one particularly suitable for suicide – proved his lingering attachment to that culture. But could he do it?

By the time Bastian rejoined Petra at Swinemünderstrasse in the New Year of 1991 he had little more than a foggy idea for a holding operation. As with the rest of his life, Bastian would largely leave the initiative to others and let destiny decide his fate. The affair with Tawo was as good as over, he knew that, and he was confident he could once more convince Petra of his need for her; it would not take much to reinforce her dependency on him. Then he would simply wait to see what happened. Nonetheless his mental journey to the end of the road that Christmas did prompt him to make one or two provisions should he have to take this particular route out of his dilemma. What Bastian dreaded most of all was that Petra's disappointment in him, her disgust, would live on after his death. Just to think about her discussing it in a public interview made him wince. If Petra survived him there would be no hope of even the tiniest scrap of his honour being left intact.

If he had to kill himself, Petra must die with him. Then at least there would be a hope that Lotte, with her stolid loyalty and years of practice, might be able to salvage something. He would do what he could to help her and to try to make up to her at least for having to spend her old age alone. He would redouble, through Petra, his efforts to be seen as the champion of the high moral ground, and he would try to augment the widow's pension on which Lotte would have to exist.

The chance came to achieve the latter sooner than he imagined when in the spring of 1991, Petra gifted a substantial part of her savings – DM150,000 – to Gert Bastian. No one knows why she did this. Was it a spontaneous gesture on her part or did Bastian manoeuvre to achieve it? That it was destined for his family is not in doubt; after his death they knew where to retrieve the relevant papers from the little study in Swinemünderstrasse. [13]

FLYING THROUGH THE ROCK

In the course of 1991, Petra and Gert Bastian did work extremely closely together. The ring-binders in which they kept copies of all their texts hold a large number of articles and essays, often authored by them both, about the Gulf War and the rise of neo-Nazi activity in the newly-united Germany. They also began to edit a series of contributions to a book about Guernica together. [14] The articles were gloomy, outlining the problems but proposing no solutions, and so they proved difficult to get published. In one of their joint essays written in February, they wrote dispiritedly about how the military crackdown in the Baltic States and the war in the Gulf had shattered the promise of the East European revolutions.[15] 'The disastrous situation will of course not change fundamentally until the overwhelming majority of Germans are resolved no longer to tolerate the new disgrace but to relegate the aggressive mode to the obscurity from which it emerged,' Bastian wrote in October.[16] The following month Petra ended a very long speech in California about all that was wrong in Germany and Europe with a simple call for more civil disobedience, more civil courage and an 'upright stance' in Germany.[17] 'It is such a struggle to even get a letter printed these days,' Bastian complained.

When I met Petra in February 1991 at a debate at the Oxford Union she seemed to be fine. As we whispered to each other during the debate and then talked afterwards at her hotel, Petra was certainly disappointed about the way European politics had gone in general and by the performance of Die Grünen in particular, but she had lost none of her combativeness:

> We need policies of eco-justice, and we need to realize the spiritual dimensions of our life, of our interconnected planet Earth, of each other! We cannot have a feast on global resources while the world's poor struggle to survive on inhospitable lands. It is as simple as that. It is the rich who are making the world poorer. Environment and poverty are one crisis, not two.[18]

There was no shortage of invitations to speak. In March, Petra travelled with Gert Bastian to Dharamsala in India and Davos in Switzerland to attend the third and fourth International Conferences on Tibet (and to see Nima). In San Francisco in early April they launched a third book on Tibet in the presence of the Dalai Lama. After the painful rejection by her party at its Neumünster conference at the end of April, Petra spoke in Hawaii on a New Challenge for the International Peace Movement: The New World Order of President Bush ('I am rather pessimistic, I admit, but I have not yet given up!')[19] Both Petra and Bastian gave speeches about German nationalism in Austria.[20] In September, they were invited to attend the Morelia Symposium in Mexico hosted by the Grupo de los Cien (Group of 100). Petra was very excited by this meeting, which she felt might herald a new international green alliance.[21] 'A unique exchange has taken place,' the final declaration said. 'For the first time environmentalists, scientists, representatives from the native tribes of North and South America, political activists and writers from twenty countries have spent a week in Mexico discussing the state of the world as we approach the end of the millennium.' The conclusion of all participants that the planet was in grave danger was unsurprising, but everyone found the chemistry of coming together most inspiring.

In Mexico, Petra met Vladimir Chernousenko, a fifty-year-old Ukrainian nuclear physicist, one of the supervisors of the team instructed by the Russian authorities to 'liquidate the consequences' of the reactor fire at the nuclear power plant in Chernobyl. In 1990, Chernousenko had left the Ukraine to get treatment for problems related to his exposure to radiation, and to devote the few years he believed he had left to exposing the incompetence and corruption of the authorities during the aftermath of the accident.[22] At Morelia, his story of penury and courage in the face of attempts to silence him while struggling with ailing health went directly to Petra's heart. With the Tibet campaign well and truly launched, she had a vacancy for a good cause and Chernousenko was to become the last one she would champion. During the final months of her life, Petra provided him with a great deal of money, and worked hard to obtain wider recognition and financial support for him. She lobbied universities in America for lectureships, the Right Livelihood Award Committee for the Alternative Nobel Prize, and all her international contacts from the anti-nuclear movement to support a research fellowship at the Institute for Applied Ecology at Freiburg.

In November, Petra went to Heidelburg to open a day-clinic which had been funded through the Grace Kelly Foundation, and began to prepare in earnest for the series of environment programmes, *Fünf vor Zwolf* (Five minutes to Twelve) she was to present for the television channel, SAT 1. From the start, this partnership was destined to be an unhappy one. SAT 1 wanted a lively, popular moderator for their programme, and Petra, who had never been moderate about anything in her life, wanted a platform for her causes. Furthermore, the causes she knew most about did not sit easily within the programme's definition of environment. Petra's role as moderator required her to read her text – a text the programme editor felt comfortable with – at a reasonable speed from an autocue. The result was a wooden Petra, all life and spontaneity edited out of her face; even her expressive hands were kept out of sight. Within weeks, serious arguments were taking place over her inability to appear vivacious while speaking slowly from an autocue and the grim approach she took to her topics. Ratings for the programme were tumbling and SAT 1 lawyers were clucking about some of her assertions.

Then, on 21st March 1992, as he arrived in Munich, partly to address a meeting at Lucas Aerospace with Petra, and also to join his family for his birthday celebrations, Gert Bastian was run over by a taxi. He received a compound fracture of the knee and shin of his left leg. He and Petra had driven from Halle, where they had been guests the previous evening at the 65th birthday celebrations of Hans-Dietrich Genscher, Germany's former foreign minister. On the way they stopped in Nürnburg to visit Omi who was in the middle of tests prior to a cataract operation. The visit was longer than anticipated (Omi was feeling neglected and wanted more time with them), so by the time they arrived at the Eden Wolf Hotel near Munich's central station it was nearly 10p.m. Petra asked Bastian to go over to the station to buy some fruit before he left for his family. Bastian agreed, although he was weary after the long drive, and, as always, feeling nervous and unsettled by the closeness of his two worlds. Tired and distracted, he ran into the road and the taxi.

The hotel alerted an ambulance which took him to the hospital but refused to take Petra; she must follow another way. Panic-stricken at the idea of coping alone, Petra phoned Erika Heinz to ask her to come quickly. Erika could not come at once but arranged for one of her cousins, an architect who lived in Munich, to help Petra until Erika herself could get there. At the clinic, Petra found Bastian very shocked by the accident, and though it is usual to operate quickly on such fractures, in this case it was not possible. Since he had suffered a blood clot in his leg a few years ago and was prone to mild angina, Bastian took pills which reduced the ability of his blood to form clots. Until his blood was returned to normal, an operation was out of the question. He lay in his bed with Petra sitting on one side and his wife Lotte on the other.

Many years of living with her husband's infidelity had given Charlotte Bastian the ability to remain calm and dignified on such occasions. Besides her concern for him, she even felt a little sorry for Petra, who felt so responsible for the accident. Later, Frau Bastian would say that by this time she knew her husband would break his promise to one day come home for good. During the last Christmas holidays he had been even more distracted and miserable than usual, so much so that his son Till had written him a letter listing his father's failings and the family's disappointment in him. Much of the time

Bastian had stayed in his room where he kept a sort of shrine to Petra with photographs and newspaper cuttings. Even all the little notes she had written on envelopes, paper napkins and 'post-its' he had kept and carefully classified year by year in large envelopes.

Bastian's two worlds clashed noisily when his daughter Eva arrived at his hospital bedside. Unlike her mother, she was not concerned about dignity, and had for many years nurtured a pure hatred towards the woman who had commandeered her father. Now her worry and love for both her parents made her explode at Petra. The doctors steered everyone out of the room.

On 26th March, his sixty-ninth birthday, Gert Bastian went into the operating theatre for a six hour operation during which a stainless steel metal pin, plate and a lot of screws were used to reconstruct his shattered knee. After he came round from the anaesthetic it was Petra who stayed at his side, and when he moved to the Büler Höhe, a luxurious rehabilitation hospital in the heart of the Black Forest, Petra moved in with him.

Between Bastian's accident and his operation, Petra had already established an office in his room at the clinic. Within two days faxes and letters were sent all over the world to inform friends of Gert's accident and to give them an address for cards, flowers and gifts. At his insistence Petra attended the Lucas Aerospace meeting, and as Bastian recovered, she began to prepare what would be her last programme for SAT 1. This had to be taped in Munich; to leave his side would be impossible. Shortly afterwards the company fired her, which Petra countered by claiming the producers were trying to censor her and that they were in breach of their contract. Later in June, while he and Petra were staying at Petra's favourite hotel, the Lederer in Bad Weissee (where she often spent Christmas with Omi), Bastian sent a letter to friends in Germany and abroad asking them to lobby the editor and director of SAT 1 to apologize to and reinstate Petra. They didn't do either, but after an unpleasant wrangle agreed to pay her salary for the whole series.

When Erika Heinz arrived in Munich, she and Petra moved into an apartment hotel, the Arabella. In the mornings they went shopping and it was during one trip that Petra bought the black leisure suit decorated with pink roses which she was wearing when she died. As always, said Erika Heinz, Petra gravitated towards bookshops, and they spent hours browsing for books for each other or for friends. For Bastian, Petra bought a pile of crime novels. 'It's what he likes to read best,' she told her friend. The afternoons and evenings they spent with Bastian, working.

The accident and operation took a great deal out of Gert Bastian physically, and for the first time in his life he looked as well as felt his age. Erika Heinz recalls celebrating her birthay on 18th May with Petra and Bastian at the Bühler Höhe convalescent hospital – and Bastian grumbled jokingly about being wheeled around by two women. Petra had decided to check in with him. Several times in the past, she had been sent to the Bühler Höhe to recuperate, but because she never stayed for the full number of days prescribed by her doctor and would sign herself out when she felt better ('I got so bored') she had two weeks 'credit' with the hospital. This seemed like a good time to use it up.

As it was so isolated there were few visitors to the convalescent hospital. Vladimir Chernousenko came. Petra was having difficulty in finding support for him, not everyone was as convinced by him as she was. A Swedish television company came to interview her. Erika Heinz also visited regularly and she and Petra would take long walks in the woods while Bastian played cards with one of the hospital staff. Heinz remembers several, sometimes heated, arguments between Petra and Bastian over the future, their money worries, and an application Bündnis 90/Die Grünen was organizing for all green MPs past and present to obtain access to files held on them by the STASI. Bastian didn't want to bother, while Petra was extremely curious to find out what was in them.

While convalescing, Bastian wrote some articles, one on the Bundeswehr for *Die Andere*, another on Sarajevo for *BUNTE*.[23] He also started to rally support for Petra's nomination for the 'Sakharov' Award, which Cora Weiss of the Samuel Rubin Foundation – a New York based peace organization – was to co-ordinate. The award, made to outstanding international activists by the Gleitsman Foundation, carried with it a US$100,000 honorarium – this would help to alleviate Petra's financial difficulties. Told that she stood a very good chance, Petra began to talk about her plan to use the money to open an office to work on human rights, particularly in eastern Europe.

By mid-July Petra and Bastian were back in Swinemünderstrasse,

Bastian on crutches but walking well and improving rapidly. A proposal from US publishers, Parallax Press, to translate Petra's book *Mit dem Herzen denken* was changing into a plan to publish a new collection of Petra's speeches. Faxes were exchanged as the editors proposed different ways to do this. Parallax editor Arnold Kotler made an arrangement to meet Petra in Berlin. She would bring more texts, and he would arrange for her to hear Thich Nhat Hanh speak at the European Buddhist Union Congress; 'I'll be sure two tickets are kept for you.' A former Buddhist monk himself, Kotler hoped Petra's interest in Buddhism would bring her inner peace.

As summer progressed, the book on Guernica was finished, and by the time they went to Nürnburg to spend the last fortnight of August with Omi while she recovered from her cataract operation, both Petra and Bastian looked much better. As far as he was concerned, keeping up with Petra had proved to be good physiotherapy (he was able to walk quite well with the help of only a stick) and the weeks of enforced rest had done Petra a power of good. On 21st August Bastian went to Munich to visit his wife for what would be the last time.

Lukas Beckmann met Petra and Bastian at the photocopier late one night in the Bundestag at the beginning of September. He had not seen Bastian since the accident. Beckmann thought he looked weak and exhausted and said so. 'I feel it,' Bastian responded with a smile, and Petra added (not, Beckmann pointed out, for the first time) that she feared she was destroying Bastian's life: 'Yet I can't live without him. If Gert died I wouldn't want to go on living without him.' They talked for quite a while about the future of Petra and how she was not sure what to do next. Petra said she had met Ludger Volmer, one of the speakers of the party executive, and he had offered her third place on the list for the next elections for the European parliament, due in summer 1994. She had laughed at the irony of Volmer having the power to offer her a place, and said she hesitated because she wondered whether she should take her chance with the Bundestag elections, due several months after the Europeans. There was more power in the Bundestag, and she had had an offer from a local party in Bavaria. 'What do you think I should do?' she asked Beckmann. 'It's up to you,' he replied. 'Only if that's what you want, you must go *now* to Bavaria and prepare it. Whatever you decide to do, decide early, that's all.'

Four days after their talk in the Bundestag, Lukas invited Petra and Bastian to dinner and a meeting, along with Gerd Poppe, Reinhard Weisshuhn, Milan Horaček, Frieder Wolf, Heinz Suhr and Elisabeth Weber. The Greens had put in their applications to the STASI files like everyone else but there were hundreds of thousands to be processed. Was there any way to speed things up for the past and present Green parliamentarians? The group was keen to do so before a seminar they planned to hold on the relations between the Greens and the East German citizens' movements during the 1980s. The meeting, Beckmann recalled, 'was just like the old days, when we planned our campaigns – our preparations for Alexanderplatz, the demonstration in Ankara, the occupation of the embassy in Pretoria, or the demonstration at the SPD party congress in Munich in 1982 (where Petra and Lukas Beckmann had unrolled a huge banner and been unceremoniously ejected).'[24] Everyone laughed a lot that evening and the next meeting was only delayed until 2nd December because Petra's diary was so full.

On 12th September Petra and Bastian set off in his Volkswagen Golf car for Salzburg and the World Uranium Hearing. Petra was on the board of advisors for the hearing but not, in this instance, invited to speak. The purpose of the meeting was to provide a forum for indigenous peoples from every continent to testify to the destruction of their land, their livelihoods, their cultures and their health as a result of uranium mining, or the testing or storage of nuclear materials.

Freda Meissner Blau was chairing a session when Petra and Bastian arrived, and she remembers feeling uncomfortable that they had no formal role; but both seemed fine and were warmly welcomed by many friends. Bastian appeared to have almost completely recovered from his accident; he had driven from Bonn and moved up and down stairs with no difficulty. If he still used a stick at times, he did so discreetly and no one was aware of it. Petra seemed more still, Meissner Blau thought, not so overexcited, although peace activist Robert Jungk (a former laureate) became slightly exasperated with Petra for badgering him to intervene on behalf of Vladimir Chernousenko with the Alternative Nobel Prize committee. Talking to Gert Bastian afterwards, Meissner Blau found him depressed at how difficult it was to find a platform. 'I feel like a salesman, going from paper to paper, just to get a letter through,' he complained. There were also money problems they said. Petra needed DM2000 a month for her mortgage, and there was Omi and Nima to support too. It was still possible for her to go back to Brussels, Petra said; she only had a few months to complete before she was eligible for a pension and had been offered a post in the Agriculture Commission – 'But, oh! anything would be better than that!' Meissner Blau did not pay much attention to these moans, as she knew Petra and Bastian were not staying in the accommodation provided by the conference, but in a luxury hotel. Things could not be as bad as all that. As far as she could see the relationship between the two was unchanged; they were together all the time and gave every sign of pleasure in each other's company.

The day after the Salzburg conference ended, the Second Global Radiation Victims' Conference started in Berlin on 21st September. Most of the participants were the same. Neither conference was cheerful, and some had found them harrowing. Christine von Weizsäcker, a biologist who edited a book of profiles about women environmentalists (including one by Lew Kopelew on Petra),[25] remembers being ill herself for over a week after she returned home, and Monika Griefahn, SPD minister of the environment in Lower Saxony, board member of Greenpeace International and not known for her faint heart, recalls having to leave the meeting room at times. Griefahn had found Gert Bastian to be his usual calm self, although he was fretting about some article which a newspaper would not publish. Otherwise he was somewhere in the background while she and Petra talked. Since the UN Conference on Environment and Development, Petra was worried that 'things were falling apart'. She was certainly politically depressed – post-Rio almost everyone was – but Petra did not appear emotionally depressed at all. On the contrary, despite the grim topic of the meetings, the last impression Griefahn had of Petra was of her energy and her plans for the future; she was trying to decide about a lectureship in the United States and whether to stand for the European Parliament. On 24th September, Petra did a short television interview (it was not broadcast) and afterwards, unbeknown to her, the camera was left on as she chatted animatedly with the interviewer. This, the final film taken of Petra Kelly, shows her looking well, lively and cheerful.

Publisher Arnold Kotler and Buddhist teacher and writer Stephen Batchelor were the last people to spend any length of time with Petra and Bastian. Both were in Berlin to attend the meeting of the European Buddhist Union. Kotler had a longstanding arrangement to meet Petra on the evening of Saturday 26th September to discuss the book of her speeches. Batchelor was writing a book on Buddhism and European culture which he planned to finish symbolically with an account of the Buddhist Union meeting and the story of Dalai Lama's visit to East Berlin, so he was anxious to hear Petra's version of what had happened. Kotler invited him to join them in the open-air restaurant of the Hotel Boulevard where Petra and Bastian were staying.[26]

Batchelor had met neither Petra nor Bastian before. He had heard a lot about Petra and was looking forward to meeting her, but he knew nothing about Bastian at all. With his book in mind he took notes throughout the evening:

Petra ordered tortellini, Arnie a salad and Gert potato broth. Petra discoursed incessantly on her current passions, with Gert injecting brief supportive comments in his softly caring voice. She told us of a film they had seen that afternoon on the effects of radiation of the children of Chernobyl; she predicted that the extreme-right would win seats in the Bundestag at the next election; she admired the sweet mournful voice of Sister Phong [who had sung at the Buddhist meeting]; she bemoaned the fact that the principles of green politics seemed incompatible with the holding of power. Her eyes were like animated emeralds, glittering from the dark brown pools around them.[27]

Despite his fear that he might not get a word in to ask about the Dalai Lama, Batchelor found that evening spent listening to Petra to be exciting and stimulating: 'On any topic raised, she could discourse passionately and informatively.' Bastian he found to be never less than affectionate and supportive: 'When he got a word in edgeways, it was to endorse what she was saying.' Later that night Batchelor told his tape-recorder: 'She's a very intense, passionate, obsessed woman. Her husband/her friend/her partner is a very sweet elderly man. They are both very committed and inspiring.' At the end of the evening when, arm-in-arm, Bastian and Petra accompanied Kotler and Batchelor to the U-Bahn (underground train), Bastian's concern for Petra as they crossed the road was particularly noticeable.

Even after repeatedly rerunning their memories of conversations with Bastian and Petra under the magnifying glass of hindsight, neither Kotler, Batchelor nor any friends who had been at the meetings in Salzburg and Berlin can recall the slightest indication that there was anything amiss with either of them, or in the relationship between them. When they heard the news of the deaths, Kotler and Batchelor issued a statement recounting their evening with Petra and Gert: 'The relation between them seemed caring, relaxed and intimate. Since the entire tenor of their presence was overwhelmingly forward looking, courageous and life-affirming we cannot believe . . .' . . . cannot believe that a few days later the very sweet elderly man would kill Petra Kelly. Yet he did. Why?

In the year this book has been in preparation, I have found not one supporter of the theory that there was a suicide arrangement between the two. No one who knew Petra Kelly found her to be anything but positive and full of hope. Even when her *angst* struck, it was never associated with the sort of despair which turns into a yearning for oblivion. Petra, said Dr Mott, deserved top marks for will. And indeed the power of Petra's will was so massive and so in favour of life, that despite the handicap of her chronic anxiety, she worked, travelled, wrote, spoke and managed to exude hope and inspiration all over the world – to a schedule that few others would be strong enough to sustain. Without Petra's will, it is doubtful if Die Grünen (for all its troubles still the world's best-known and most exciting Green Party) would have been forged from the array of political egos which were surging around at the time. Only someone who was very different and much bigger than them all could have generated enough extra heat to weld everyone together.

So strongly did Petra emanate a love of life, that 'if she were to call me now on the phone, or ring at the door,' said Erika Heinz, 'I would not be surprised.' Gerd Poppe, who sits in the very place Petra occupied on the foreign affairs committee in the Bundestag, feels her presence as he comes across traces of her work – old motions, parliamentary questions, speeches. 'Much is still as topical as it was in her day and the need for action is just as great.' Her efforts in the Bundestag live on, he feels, and still bear fruit in the fact that cross-party motions on human rights are now possible and a new working group on Tibet has been set up.

Among the central pieces of evidence against Petra willingly surrendering her own life is the absence of any farewell message. In the Bundestag chamber, outside on the street, Petra would unfurl a banner, expose a new T-shirt, set up a petition on at least a weekly basis. One Bundestag security guard speaks with affectionate nostalgia of the times he had to escort her from the chamber. 'She doesn't do protests,' someone once commented, 'Petra herself *is* a protest.' Petra would not knowingly fail to make the most out of her final act of defiance.

I am certain that when Petra went to bed in, presumably, the early hours of 1st October, she fully anticipated rising the following afternoon to contact Richard Hendrick about the interview series and tackle what would certainly be yet another huge pile of mail waiting for her at her box number in the nearby Tannenbusch post office. That she was worried is not in doubt – about money, about how the future would be as Gert Bastian got older. He was nearly seventy, and his accident had forced her to contemplate life without him, either because he died or because he returned to Lotte. She, Petra, would be incapable of coping with an infirm Bastian on her own. And, of course, there was Omi and the distant Nima – also dependent on her. Her distance from her parents made her feel she could not ask them for help.

All this she had discussed endlessly with Erika Heinz, during their long walks in the Black Forest. She loved Bastian, was aware of, and worried about, her dependence on him ('I'm ruining his life, yet I cannot live without him'), but she also had lots of plans for dealing with her worries. Hopes for winning the Sakharov Prize were high, there was the television interview series, most probably a seat in the European Parliament (less convenient, but more suitable perhaps than the Bundestag), and maybe a couple of lecture series in the United States to tide her over. She had invitations from the University of California and from Hawaii and there was even talk of a return to American University. If she could earn enough money to run a proper office, then a lot of the pressure would be off both her and Bastian. As far as the Grace Kelly Foundation was concerned things were going well. While in Berlin she had visited a project she had been involved in: the bringing together of all the children's units into one centre, and in Münster a *Familienkinderhaus* – a sort of mini *Kinderplanet* –

was in the planning phase.

However, one worry niggling at her as she went to sleep was that, beyond his shock at the accident, she sensed that Bastian was unhappy. Even after the post–Tawo reconciliation, he remained preoccupied. When she quizzed him, Bastian blamed his disquiet on the rise of the neo-Nazis and his irritation over how difficult it was to get his opinion published. Petra said she would, of course, do all she could to help with this. He was right, it must be their number one campaigning priority, but still she feared his disquiet was over her, that he was thinking of leaving her. However much he tried to reassure her, she wondered sadly if he was really yearning to leave the fray of Bonn and go back to Lotte. The last thing Petra did before going to bed was prepare two faxes to newspaper editors, one in Australia and one in the United States, asking for space for 'a commentary about the present situation in Germany written by my *closest* political and personal ally and friend, Gert Bastian'.

While he had been in Salzburg and Berlin, Gert Bastian had had no difficulty in sustaining his role as Petra's closest political and personal ally. As long as he was near Petra he was fine. To be on the arm of this wonderful woman – in public – was, after all, his favourite role. No one, not even Petra or Lotte, had the slightest suspicion of the deeper reasons for his agitation.

When he got up on 1st October, only a few hours after Petra had come to bed, Bastian had never felt more aware of his age. He dreaded the piles of mail which were waiting. But first a letter to Lotte. His worlds had been restored to their proper place, although both were much changed by the last two years. Lotte remained unswervingly the same, but his children were furious with him and that hurt very much. The money-making potential of Petra's projects suggested that even his Bonn world might sort itself out, if only all this work could be transferred from the house to a properly staffed office again. He was a bit concerned that most of Petra's projects – the interviews, the US lectureships, the European parliament – were not German projects based in Germany. It was not entirely clear where he – Major General Gert Bastian (rtd), increasingly elderly and on a short-string to Munich – would fit in. But time, as usual, would sort everything out. Immediately or perhaps after a delay of some hours, he put another piece of paper into the typewriter. Erika. He must, as he and Petra agreed in the car coming home yesterday, write to his lawyer about Erika.

A sneeze, a noise – something – interrupted him in the middle of the word *müssen*. Let us assume it was a sneeze. He went downstairs to look for some tissues and decided to make another cup of coffee. While waiting for the water to boil, he sifted through the faxes that Petra had torn off the machine the night before. He had gone straight to bed, exhausted by the long day, the drive and his incipient cold. The Lötters had been in while they were away to send the most urgent messages on to them, so it was not too bad. He found one from Lukas Beckmann asking Bastian to call back as soon as he could. He guessed what it was about. Around noon Bastian called Beckmann. It was as he feared. Very soon his STASI file would be opened.

In their final report, the Public Prosecutor's Office pointed out that 'the files held by the State Security Service of the former German Democratic Republic about the two politicians have been examined and evaluated and contain nothing which could be relevant to the deaths of Petra Kelly and Gert Bastian.' The Public Prosecutor's interpretation of what was relevant might not, of course, be the same as Bastian's. To officialdom, a contact made in the 1970s might hardly suffice as a motive for murder in 1992, while to Bastian, it would be more than enough to destroy his world with Petra and, beyond that, his own honour. Furthermore, even if there was nothing in this particular file, and even if it was true that STASI chief Erich Mielke had ordered the destruction of foreign agent files, the STASI was known to use an extensive cross-referencing system to check the 'consistency' of the information they obtained. It was only a matter of time.

After he put down the phone, Bastian began to think. It could be that it was now, rather than earlier, when he returned to his study and put a second sheet of paper in his typewriter – moving automatically as his brain tried to think through the sequence of events which he feared might now unfold. What could he possibly do? Perhaps by the time he reached the word *müssen* his trained military brain had reviewed all the options and come to rest on the only possible strategy for escaping this final, intolerable shame. If he was dead, then only his family would have the right to obtain access to his file. Lotte, he felt confident, would absorb, forgive, and keep secret any sin it might contain, just as she had done so often in the past. The salvation of his honour he could entrust to her.

Over the last two years, Bastian had often contemplated death, both as a theoretical solution to his dilemmas and (since his encounter with the Munich taxi) as a practical reality. He had even played the scene over and over again, experimenting in his mind with different scripts. Now, he went into Gracie's room and rummaged between the jumpers and scarves until he found his Derringer. Once the gun was in his hand he felt quite calm. Finally, he was in control of his own destiny. The fog of worry and confusion cleared from his mind as he moved smoothly through the most often rehearsed script, where he shoots Petra in her sleep, then himself lying beside her. They are discovered in an embrace, Lotte saves his honour, and he is remembered affectionately as the man who literally gave his life for the wonderful but very difficult Petra Kelly. A happy ending. Gert Bastian went into the bedroom, put the gun to the left temple of the peacefully sleeping Petra Kelly and pulled the trigger.

Notes

1   Including a monthly column for a Munich paper, *Munchner Abendtzeitung* which she wrote from October 1984 until April 1986, and regular contributions to the Australian magazine *Simply Living*.
2   Three months before Fischer was sworn in, a demonstrator, Günter Saré had been killed during an encounter between police water cannons and an antifascist demonstration in Frankfurt – the capital of Hesse.
3   Diana Johnstone, 'Blues for the Greens: is the party obsolete?' *In These Times* (13-19 January 1988).
4   Die Grünen press release No 860/87.
5   Book: Paige and Gilliatt (eds.) (1992) p. 155.
6   Interview: Sabena Norton (February 1989).
7   Extracts from this interview were published in *The Guardian* (7 December 1990).
8   Rede von Antje Vollmer auf der Bundespressekonferenz zum Wahlergebnis, 4 December 1990.
9   Essay: (14 December 1990).
10   See Glossary.
11   Book: Paige and Gilliatt (eds.) (1992) p. 158.
12   Bastian (1983).
13   Marianne Kelly was so upset by this that she sought through the courts to overrule the gift, but failed.
14   Book: with Gert Bastian (eds.) (1992).

15 Petra Kelly and Gert Bastian, 'A Dream Fades', mimeo (February, 1991).
16 Gert Bastian, 'Prepared to living in disgrace?' mimeo (October 1991).
17 Speech: Stanford CA (7 November 1991).
18 Speech: Oxford (18 February 1991).
19 Book: Paige and Gilliatt (eds.) (1992), p. 85.
20 Speech: Neuberg an der Mütz, Austria (26 June 1991).
21 Speech: (2 September 1991).
22 Chernousenko (New York, 1991).
23 Published in English as: 'Army without a function wheels to the Right', in *Broadside Weekly*, Australia (10 June 1992).
24 Beckman and Kopelew (eds.) (1993).
25 Lew Kopelew, 'Ein grosses Herz' in Christine von Weizsäcker and Elisabeth Bücking (eds.) *Mit Wissen, Widerstand und Witz: Frauen für die Umwelt*, (Herder Verlag, Freiburg, 1992).
26 Batchelor (1994).
27 Stephen Batchelor, 'A Convenient Fiction', in *Resurgence*, no.156 (January/February 1993).

POSTSCRIPT

When I began this book at the beginning of 1993, I imagined it would end with a succinct, but profound, summing up of Petra's legacy to green politics. But very quickly I abandoned this idea. I have left her story to speak for itself. So full and passionate was Petra's life and the shock at the manner of her death still so tangible, it would, I felt, take more *récul* than is possible in one year to synthesize it all. However, with my original purpose in mind, I did ask many people what they perceived to be most important about Petra. Many of the responses are to be found somewhere in the book, but for the end I have retained one, from Elisabeth Weber, for many years a staff member with the Green parliamentary group, and added to it a story recounted to me by Lukas Beckmann. Neither may appear to be the most obvious way of summing up Petra's legacy to green politics, but, as time passes, I suspect they may prove to be the most important.

Elisabeth Weber shared Petra's commitment to an *Ostpolitik* which insisted that respect of human rights be the yardstick against which all governments (without exception) must be measured. 'Petra was so clear about this, I could go to her with any policy problem, and she would think for a moment and then say how it should be. Today, with European politics more complicated than ever, I would give anything to have her here, so I can still measure my own thoughts against her certainty.'

Lukas Beckmann's story is of a farmer who waylaid him at a cattle auction nearly a year after Petra died. He had not, the farmer said, been the slightest bit interested in politics until he first saw Petra on television.   After that, he had followed events with interest. She had touched him deeply he said: 'She was such a *glaubwürdig* (believable) person, emotional and honest, so unlike all them others, I'm sorry she's gone.'

About halfway through writing this book, at the point where her relationship with Die Grünen reached rock bottom, I wondered if Petra might not have made a mistake by getting involved in politics in the first place. Her love of literature, art and music, as well as her political courage, brought her the friendship and admiration of cultural giants like Joseph Beuys and Heinrich Böll. Perhaps she might have found less pain if she had released her passion at the wicked world as Böll did, and let her words and emotions cascade into books and poems rather than the dispiritingly destructive maw of politics. But I soon realized this was nonsense. Petra could never have stayed off the political battlefield. It was here, in the heart of public life with all the wrongs to be righted and the causes to be championed that she was stimulated to soar ever higher. During the phase of pushing, shoving, dragging – *forcing* – green issues onto the political agenda in the 1980s, Petra had been the undisputed star.   Reagan's US Ambassador to Bonn, Arthur Burns, would dismiss all his aides in order to talk to Petra alone. Her frankness was valuable to him, and he wanted to honour it with the same frankness from his side.

Some time ago, when I found myself in a randomly selected Delhi taxi, the driver, keen to display his command of English, wanted to know about my job. 'Green politics,' I replied, bracing myself for long explanations. He instantly swivelled in his seat, eyes alarmingly off the busy road; 'Are you Petra Kelly?' From ambassadors to taxi drivers, the range of her influence was quite stupendous.

But could she, I asked, make the transition to the next phase of green politics, where the challenge was less to draw attention to the problems, more to work out *how* they might be solved? The general view in response to this question was, yes, Petra was as important to the future as the past. For all her huffing about power, she knew perfectly well from her time at EcoSoc and in the Bundestag (not to mention her own personal compromises) that future deals would need to be struck. The road to a green Germany, a green Europe and a green world would be a long and rocky one, but, as she frequently said herself, 'If there is to be a future, then it will be a green one!' Petra might never have come to delight in the details of organization and policy, but the ease with which the East European revolutions had been rerouted from even contemplating any 'Third Way' had made it clear to her that the 'Green Way' would have to be given a great deal more substance if it was to have any chance at all. With the worst of the hard-left out of the way, a *rapprochment* of the *Realos* and Petra would not have been out of the question. She needed them to fill in the gaps in her political skills, and they needed her to provide a lodestone of principle so they did not lose themselves in the dangerous seas of political pragmatism. In the spring before he died Heinrich Böll had urged Lukas Beckmann to make Petra take care of herself. 'Give her my greetings, tell her not to work so much, in the future we will need her.'

But could Petra have recovered from her sometimes crippling *angst* and her debilitating dependence? This was a much more difficult question. And in a sense, an irrelevant one. For between Petra's emotional recovery and her possible return to independence was Bastian and the weighty encumbrance of his needs. She might, with professional help, have been able to reclaim enough self-confidence to dispense with some of the external props she had come to depend on, but while she was tied to Bastian emotionally, I don't think she would ever have been able to fly high and fast again. He was intellectually and spiritually incapable of accompanying her, and not happy for her to fly without him.

In the end, such speculations are empty. Petra has already flown, as Jonathan Livingston Seagull did, through the rock and into the world of limitless possibilities. Bastian, I fear, never learnt how to fly high and fast enough to be able to follow her. Like Jonathan, Petra will live on to inspire others. I miss her greatly.

In her book *Mit dem Herzen denken* (Thinking with the Heart), Petra quoted Anne Frank. It is appropriate that I leave the last words to her.

Oh no, I would not like to have lived in vain, as most people do. I would like to be of use, or bring joy, to the people around me, even if they do not know me. I would like to carry on living, even after my death.

POST-POSTSCRIPT

In May 1993, the Sakharov Prize was awarded jointly to Nelson
Mandela and Wei Jingsheng (the imprisoned Chinese pro-democracy
leader). Posthumous awards (no honorarium) were made to Helen
Joseph (anti-apartheid campaigner) and Petra Karin Kelly.

BIBLIOGRAPHY

PETRA KELLY: BOOKS
(CHRONOLOGICAL)

with John F. Carroll, (eds), *A Nuclear Ireland?* (Irish Transport and General Worker's Union, Dublin, 1978).

with Jo Leinen, (eds), *Ökopax - die neue Kraft* [Eco-peace - The New Force] (Olle & Wolter, Berlin, 1982).

with Manfred Coppik, (eds), *Wohin denn Wir?: Texte aus der Bewegung* [Where Are We Going? Texts from the Movement] (Oberbaumverlag, Berlin, 1982).

(ed.) *Laßt uns die Kraniche suchen* [Let Us Look for the Cranes] Werkhaus, Munich, 1983).

Um Hoffnung Kämpfen [Fighting for Hope] collection of speeches and essays (Lamuv Verlag, Bornheim-Merten, 1983) published in English as *Fighting for Hope* (Chatto & Windus, London, 1984).

Hiroshima (Lamuv Verlag, Bornheim-Merten, 1986).

Viel Liebe gegen Schmerzen: Krebs bei Kindern [Love can Conquer Sorrow: Cancer in Children] (Rowohlt Verlag, Reinbeck bei Bamburg, 1986).

with Gert Bastian, (eds), *Tibet - ein vergewaltigtes Land* [Tibet - A Violated Country] (Rohwalt Verlag, Reinbeck bei Hamburg, 1988).

Mit dem Herzen denken [Thinking with the heart], collection of speeches and essays, also in Japanese and Spanish (C. H. Beck Verlag, Munich, 1990).

with Gert Bastian and Klemens Ludwig, (eds), *Tibet klagt an* [Tibet Accuses] (Peter Hammer Verlag, Wuppertal, 1990).

with Gert Bastian and Pat Aiello, (eds), *The Anguish of Tibet* (Parallax Press, Berkeley, 1991).

with Gert Bastian, (eds), *Guernica und die Deutschen* (Sammlung Luchterhand, Hamberg, 1992).

Glenn Paige and Sarah Gilliatt, (eds), *Petra Kelly: Nonviolence Speaks to Power* collection of speeches and essays (Centre for Global Nonviolence, Hawaii, 1992).

Arnold Kotler, (ed), *Thinking Green! Essays on Environmentalism, Feminism, and Nonviolence* edited collection of speeches and essays (Parallax Press, Berkeley, forthcoming).

PETRA KELLY: CHAPTERS AND ARTICLES (SELECTED, MOSTLY ENGLISH, CHRONOLOGICAL)

'Educational and vocational training study of the 9 member states in the European community', background document for Economic and Social Committee, CES 266/70 (1973).

'Mister New Europe', in *Vista* magazine of the UN Associations (April 1973).

'Women to the barricades', in *Staff Courier*, journal of the European Commission, no.252 (17 April 1973).

'Cancer data bank', in *Agenor* (Brussels), no.45-6 (October 1974).

'The economic and social situation of the woman in the European community' Background Working Document of the Section for Social Questions, Economic and Social Committee, CES, 156 (1975).

'A woman's questions and concerns in regard to the Tindemans Report and the European institutions', in *The Bulletin*, no.1 (1976).

'A European conquest', in *European Community* (April/May 1976).

'Women and the European Community', in *The Courrier*, no.48 (March/April 1978).

'Energiepolitische Ziele für 1990 und Programme der Mitgliedstaaten [Energy policy objectives for 1990 and programmes of member states]: Technical appendix', mimeo, SEC (79) 27, (9 January 1979).

H. Steffen (in collaboration with P. K. Kelly), 'Particular aspects of the treatment and rehabilitation of chronic/cancer-ill children and adolescents with their families', Commission of the European Communities, EUR 6795 (1980).

'Women and the future' in *Undercurrents*, no.55/56 (September 1982).

Petra Kelly, 'Open letter to Willy Brandt' (Die Grünen, Bonn, 5 November 1982).

'Preface', in proceedings of Tribunal Against First Strike and Mass Destruction Weapons in East and West (Nürenburg Tribunal), (Die Grünen, Bonn, 1983).

'A chance to stop', in *Resurgence*, no.96 (January/February 1983).

'Foreword', in Jonathon Porritt, *Seeing Green* (Basil Blackwell, Oxford, 1984)

'Life on earth', in Satish Kumar, (ed.), *The Schumacher Lectures* (Blond & Briggs, London, 1984).

'Women and the future', in Cambridge Women's Peace Collective, *My Country is the Whole World: An Anthology of Women's Work on Peace and War* (Pandora, London, 1984).

'Why Ireland must stay neutral', in *New Hibernia*, no.13 (June 1985).

'Petra Kelly', in Philip L. Berman, (ed.), *The Courage of Conviction* (Dodd, Mead & Company, New York, 1985).

'New forms of power: the green feminist view', in Thomas Perry and James Foulks, (eds), *End the Arms Race: Fund Human Needs* (Gordon Soules Books, West Vancouver, 1986).

'Afterword', in Gail Chester and Andrew Rigby, (eds), *Articles of Peace: Celebrating*

Fifty Years of Peace News (Prism Press, San Leandro, 1986).

'The green movement', in Tom Woodhouse, (ed.), *People and Planet: Alternative Nobel Prize Speeches* (Green Books, Bideford, Devon, 1987).

'Neutrality - a strategy for peace: the neutrals and the EC', in *The New Federalist* (May/June 1988).

'Introduction: The roots of conflict' in Frank Barnaby, (ed.), *The Gaia Peace Atlas* (Pan Books, London, 1988).

'Towards a green Europe and a green world', in Felix Dodds, (ed.), *Into the 21st Century* (Green Print, London, 1988).

'Do the impossible', in John Elkington, Tom Burke and Julia Hailes, (eds), *Green Pages* (Routledge, 1988).

'Women and Ecology', in Daniela Gioseffi, (ed.), *Women on War: Essential Voices for the Nuclear Age* (Simon & Schuster, New York, 1988).

'Gandhi, disarmament and development', *The Other Side* (Delhi) (January 1989).

'Green disarmament and human rights', in *The Other Side* (Delhi) (July, 1989).

'Linking arms, dear Sisters, brings hope', in Judith Plant, (ed.), *Healing the Wounds: The Promise of Ecofeminism* (New Society, Santa Cruz, 1989).

'The train of German unification is running away 'in *Tribune* (Australia), no.2618 (28 February 1990).

'The need for eco-justice', in *Fletcher Forum of World Affairs* (Medford, MA) 14, no.2 (Summer 1990).

'The greening of Germany', in John Button, (ed.), *The Best of Resurgence: A Selection From the First Twenty-Five Years* (Green Books, Bideford, 1991).

'We must feminize power', in Sara Parkin, (ed.), *Green Light on Europe* (Heretic, London, 1991).

'Women and global green politics', in *Women of Power*, issue 20 (Spring 1991).

'Reunification and the German Greens', in *Capitalism Nature & Socialism*, vol. 2, issue 7 (June 1991).

'Why not here? Prospects for Green politics in America', *Greenpeace* (Jul/Aug 1991).

with Gert Bastian, 'The anguish of Tibet', in *Resurgence*, no.147 (July/August 1991).

Petra Kelly, 'Homes warmed by Irish laughter', in *Élan* (30 August - 1 September 1991).

'Austria's human rights initiative: reason for hope?', edited German version in *Bündnis 2000*, no.196 (September 1991).

'The new world order', in *Resurgence*, no.148 (Sept/Oct 1991).

'Germans in a murky landscape' *Index on Censorship*, vol.20 no.10 (1 November 1991).

'Beyond the Greens', *MS Magazine* (November/December 1991).

'Ethnic Voice', in *Resurgence*, no.149 (November/December 1991).

'Globalization of the green movement: prospects within a world system in transition', in Katerine and Majid Tehranian, (eds.), *Restructuring for World Peace* (Hampton Press, Cresskill NJ, 1992).

'No.Title', in David Friend and Editors of Life, *More Reflections on the Meaning of Life* (Little & Brown, Boston, 1992).

'The United States must heal itself', *New York Newsday* (22 October 1992).

'Joseph Beuys - "Beuys war immer schon fort, wenn die anderen kamen!" ', in

Joseph Beuys, Petra Kelly, *"Diese Nacht, in die die Menschen . . ."* (FIU Verlag, 1993). Texts from the 1982 Bavarian campaign plus extracts from the 'Paralleles Denken' symposium during the Joseph Beuys retrospective exhibition *Natur, Materie, Form,* Düsseldorf (18 January 1992).

PETRA KELLY: BUNDESTAG (MAJOR SPEECHES)

KEY

Aktuelle Stunde	Topical Debate
ÄndAntr	Amendment to a motion
Antr	Motion
Aussprache ohne Vorlage	Emergency Motion
GesEntw	Proposal for legislation
GrAnfr	Major question (reply in parliament)
RegErkl	Government statement (always by Chancellor)
Unterrichtung	Point of Information

1983

4 May — RegErkl *Government Programme*
Maiden speech (on Peace, Human Rights and European Policy) 'As opposed to you, Mr Kohl, we hold peace and human rights to be indivisible.'

15 June — RegErkl *Result of the NATO Conference 6-10 June* 'We don't want to be the backyard of America.'

22 June — RegErkl *European Council meeting in Stuttgart* 'The people of Europe are human beings, not just 270 million consumers.'

16 September — RegErkl *Outcome of the CSCE Conference in Madrid and the status of disarmament and arms control efforts* (addresses remarks to Dr Manfred Wörner, Secretary General of NATO) 'The question is actually, would you rather be dead or a mass murderer, Mr Wörner?'

13 October — GrAnfr *Poison gas: storage, danger - legal basis* 'The government is violating international law in maintaining secrecy about its transport and storage.'

11 November — GesEntw *To carry out consultative referendum on stationing new atomic middle-range weapons (Pershing II, Cruise Missiles) in the German Republic* 'We demand a basic right to a say in matters of war and peace . . . every citizen has the right to freedom from fear.'

22 November — RegErkl *The double-track decision of NATO and the position of the Geneva INF negotiations* 'The Americans say they are not willing to sacrifice Chicago for Hamburg. Well, we are not willing to sacrifice Hamburg for Chicago.'

1984

28 March
RegErkl *Progress of the EEC Summit in Brussels*
'Europe is being used by the multinational corporations to become an economic superpower, exactly what we don't want.'

28 June
RegErkl *Result of the Economic Summit in London and the EEC Summit in Fontainebleau*
'After a pan-European sports team and an EEC national anthem, what else are you all planning for Europe - an all-Europe nuclear capability?'

4 October
Aktuelle Stunde *Civil disobedience during the Autumn [troop] manoeuvres*
'The arms race and the destruction of the environment are, in both military blocs, in a symbiotic relationship.'

8 November
Antr *Treaty on the limiting of the military use of space*
'Our country will not be judged by its ability to send spy satellites into space, but by whether we can guarantee sufficient personal care for children with cancer or disabled people.'

28 November
GesEntw *Federal budget Plan for 1985*
'Considering the government's DM260 billion budget, it would be a modest gesture of humanity to approve this DM6 million for the 1,700 children who develop cancer each year.'

7 December
RegErkl *Report on the talks of the heads of state and foreign ministers in Washington and the results of the European Council in Dublin*
'The tastelessness of established politics is constantly increasing.'

1985

18 April
GrAnfr *Provision for children with cancer in German Republic*
'On the 13 October 1982 Chancellor Kohl said we must all contribute to our country becoming more pro-children. Tonight we can concretely begin by passing this bill.'

26 June
Aktuelle Stunde *Geneva Conference to review the non-proliferation treaty 27 August - 20 September*
'Since 1974 the Federal Republic has pursued a nuclear policy which has encouraged nuclear proliferation and it does atomic business with countries which did not sign the treaty.'

27 June
Antr *European policy*
'We believe that European identity doesn't have anything to do with weapons agencies . . . we are for a western and eastern Europe where people are loyal to each other, rather than to the military and economic blocs.'

3 October
GrAnfr *Prevention and treatment of cancer in adults*
'Cancer is the tribute to and the result of an industrialization, a consequence of economic growth which has failed and still fails to consider the quality of the environment.'

8 November
RegErkl *EUREKA (European High-technology Research Programme)*
'The concept of economic and social solidarity, the vision of a

civil and socially just Europe of Regions has been replaced by the plan for an exploitative technological and military European superpower.'

28 November   GesEntw *Federal budget plan for 1986*
'It is shameful the way the BDR (Federal Republic) can finance military hardware, but no psychosocial therapy for its own ailing children.'

5 December   RegKrkl *European Council meeting 2-3 December in Luxemburg*
'What is being sold to us as a new European identity is . . . in reality a division of labour between America and Europe.'

1986

5 June   GrAnfr *Atomic weapons limitation treaty and nuclear effort of the German Federal Republic*
'If Germany does not aim to be a nuclear nation, why does it have huge reserves of plutonium . . . and seek more joint nuclear power projects with France?'

1987

8 October   Aktuelle Stunde *Position of the Federal Government on the human rights violations in Tibet*
'Are we [members of the Bundestag] indifferent to the suffering, the degradation, or [do] we choose to ignore it to preserve our oh-so-good economic relations with the Peoples Republic of China?'

1988

3 February   Aktuelle Stunde *Concerning the current events in East Berlin and the DDR*
'This is not the time for the usual Bundestag ritual over human rights violations in East Germany . . . there is a chance for change in East Germany.'

4 February   RegErkl *25th Anniversary of the treaty on German-French cooperation and the result of the official visit of the Chancellor to the CSSR*
'When the Chancellor describes the Germans and the French today as brothers, he really should say brothers-in-arms. That would more closely approach reality.'

14 April   GesEntw *Bill concerning the verification claused in articles Xi, Xii and Xiii of the INF agreement*
'We support the good intentions of the bill . . . but it collides with some facts . . . [future use of plutonium in warheads] . . . The hopes of humanity . . . have been disappointed.'

5 May   Antr *Establishing an international conference centre for Peace and Reconciliation in Guernica, Basque Country*
'Those who are prepared to participate in a DM100,000

	monument to the American Navy ought not be so timid in Guernica, where it is a matter of German guilt.'
10 May	Continuation of debate of 5 May.

1989

15 June	Aussprache ohne Vorlage (tabled by all parties) *Events in the Peoples Republic of China (massacre in Tienanmen Square)* 'I am voting for this bill although it contains no express acknowledgement of the impressive and consistent non-violence which characterized the student protest . . . never before have hope and admiration been struck down so brutally with the victims.'
22 June	Antr *Death sentences in the Peoples Republic of China* 'All our resolutions are impotent without the economic sanctions to back them up. How can we begin to practise solidarity if we continue to appeal only morally?'

1990

25 January	Acktuelle Stunde *Prevention of the renewed coup attempt by the Khmer Rouge in Cambodia* 'Once again, West German weapons exports are a factor . . . a Khmer commander has called the German anti-tank 'Armbrust' weapon the most important he possesses.'
15 March	Antr *Support for a peace plan for Cambodia* continuation of debate of 25 January.
5 October	GesEntw *Law for the Treaty of 12 September 1990 (Two-Plus-Four) about the final settlement concerning Germany.* (explaining why she will abstain) 'I find the clause concerning Germany's refusal to produce and possess nuclear weapons only half true.'
30 October	Antr *Political developments contributing to resolving the population problem in the Third World* (explaining why she will vote against resuming economic relations with China, broken off after the unanimous resolutions of 15 and 23 June 1989) '[The resolutions] were the only possible answer to the inhumanity of the old men of the largest communist party in the world, who, in a bloody massacre, used tanks to run over and machine guns to shoot down their young who demanded democracy.'
31 October	Unterrichtung *Report of the Federal Government on Human Rights for the 11th legislative period* Final speech (on human rights around the world) 'Amnesty international reports that 90 countries have recived military training and equipment from the Federal Republic. Since 1960 there has hardly been any act of genocide committed

against a usually defenceless minority in which there haven't been German guns firing or in which the officers, policemen or secret agents who arrested, tortured or murdered were not trained by Germans.'

PETRA KELLY: SPEECHES
(ENGLISH, CHRONOLOGICAL)

'Speech of policy', American University public speaking assignment (no date, c.1969).

'A new man's new world symphony', summation address at the symposium on the future role of the liberal arts tradition, Council on Academic Reform, American University, Washington DC (1 November 1969).

'Are we invulnerable to justice?' ITGWU Women's Conference, Dublin (9 March, 1975).

'Europe . . . it is a little mainland off the south-east coast of Northern Ireland . . .', University of Coleraine, Northern Ireland (7 May 1975).

'Women in Europe', Irish Trade Union Congress Anti-Discrimination Seminar, Galway (19 October 1975).

'Are we perpetual minors?' Irish Widows' Association Conference, Dublin (14 February 1976).

'Untitled', 31st Atomic Disaster Anniversary World Conference (Against A and H Bombs), Kyoto (1-2 August 1976).

'Women are the source of all labour in that they are the producers of all labourers', Right to Work Conference, Liberty Hall, Dublin (8 March 1977).

'Ecology, non-violence and feminism', Australian Movement Against Uranium Mining Rally, Sydney (July 1977).

'Comments', Labour Issues Forum, Sydney (6 August 1977).

'Untitled', Hiroshima Day Rally, Sydney (6 August 1977).

'Equal opportunity and the freedom of choice', Careers for Women 1977 Conference, Dublin (19 November 1977).

'Untitled', Anti-Windscale demonstration, London (29 April 1978).

'What Progress? EEC Directives relating to equality for women - A cause for discontent!' Irish Trades Union Congress Women's Advisory Committee Annual Seminar, Bray, County Wicklow (5-7 May 1978).

'Towards a decentralized, non-nuclear, non-violent European Community', Irish Trade and General Workers Union Nuclear Energy Symposium, Dublin (12-14 May 1978).

'My kind of feminism - a moral passion of revolt against a nuclearized, militarized, Europe', Women's Political Association, Dublin (December 1978).

'Women and the future', World Congress on Alternatives and Environment, Vienna (no.date, 1979).

'Untitled', Unification meeting of the British anti-nuclear and anti-military movements, London (24 November 1979).

'Untitled', Harrisburg Rally, London (March 1980).

'Euroschima, Mon Futur', Tokyo and Hiroshima (July-August 1981).

'Euroshima ????', Campaign for Nuclear Disarmament Rally, London (24 October 1981), published in *Peace News* (13 November 1981).

'No Euroshima', Peace Sunday Rally, Pasedena (6 June 1982).

'My vision of a non-violent, ecological and non-exploitative republic', Alternative Nobel Prize acceptance speech, Stockholm (9 December 1982).

'Who are the Greens?' (late 1982).

'First strike and weapons of mass destruction in East and West', Inaugural Address for Green Tribunal, Nürnberg (18 February 1983).

'Untitled', American University, Washington DC (21 September 1983).

'We Must Disobey!' Philadelphia (6 October 1983).

'We shall overcome and we speak out for life on earth', E. F. Schumacher Memorial Lecture, Bristol, (5 November 1983).

'Untitled', Festival of Hope: Griffiss Plowshares Group Benefit, New York (28 April 1984).

'Women must link arms and have a vision', Australia and New Zealand Association for Advancement of Science 1984 Congress: Symposium on Women and Political Practice (15 May 1984).

'What is troubling us in Europe about Australia', ANZAAS 1984 Congress: Symposium on Nuclear Weapons, Canberra (16 May 1984).

'Untitled', Conference on Socialism and Freedom, Cavtat, Yugoslavia (8 October 1984).

'International relations without violence', Berkeley University Symposium on the Arms Race, Berkeley (24 October 1984).

'Women and power', COMHLAMH (Third World Volunteers), Dublin (20 November 1984).

'Women and health - holistic health - holistic peace: healing self and society!' Women's Political Association, Dublin (24 November 1984).

'Both sides build much faster than they talk', Forum on First Strike Weapons, New York University (18 January 1985).

'Violence ends where love begins', Youth Symposium of the International School of the United Nations, New York (1 March 1985).

'Women and ecology', European Green Congress, Dover (24 March 1985).

'Defending values', European Nuclear Disarmament Convention, Amsterdam (5 July 1985).

'Namibia - the first genocide in the history of the Germans!' Die Grünen Public Hearing: The Federal Republic of Germany and Namibia: Present state of relations and perspectives for independence, Bonn (16 September 1985).

'Non-violent resistance and new forms of power', Young President's Organization Conference, San Diego (25 October 1985).

'Media hostility to women's achievement', Women and Media Conference, Athens (21 November 1985).

'The grand coalition for a military Europe: from the European Union to a European atomic power', Conference on the Spanish referendum on NATO membership, Madrid (8/9 March 1986).

'New forms of power: a green feminist view!' Vancouver Centennial, Vancouver (26 April 1986).

'Civil nuclear energy is neither safe nor essential', Oxford Union, Oxford (20 June 1986).

'Europe and the US', European Nuclear Disarmament Convention, Coventry (16 July 1987).

'Disarmament or arms control: choices beyond the INF-Zero option', SANE Public Hearing, Washington DC (21 July 1987).

'Towards a green Europe! Towards a green world! Do the impossible!' International Green Congress, Stockholm (30 August 1987).

'The debate about fascism in the Federal Republic: a political perspective', Goethe Institute Symposium, Los Angeles (25 September 1987).

'The foreign and security policy of the Federal Republic in the East/West context', Trilateral Commission, Munich (24 October 1987).

'Finland's route - an alternative future!' Vihreä Liitto (Green League), Helsinki (16 November 1987).

'We cannot have both - children and the bomb', Statement before local court of Simmern, Germany (25 January 1988). Trial following 21 November 1986 sit-in at Hasselbach.

'No women in the army, rather men out', Die Grünen Women's Forum (7 March 1988).

'Feminism and the power of non-violence', Annual Corliss Lamont Lectureship, Amherst, Massachusetts (10 March 1988).

'Green disarmament and human rights', Annual Corliss Lamont Lectureship, Amherst, Massachusetts (11 March 1988).

'Peacemakers create a difference: signs of hope amid the crises', American University School of International Service, Washington DC (21 March 1988).

'Tibet - a violated country', welcoming speech for the Dalai Lama at launch of *Tibet - ein vergewaltigtes Land*, Stuttgart (16 June 1988).

'Too many people committed to the state, too few committed to their fellow citizens', Federal Congress on Paths Leading to Social Defence, Minden, Germany (17 June 1988).

'Neutrality - a strategy for peace: the neutrals and the EEC', END Convention, Lund (2 July 1988).

'Iceland: ecology and peace', (not given due to illness) General Congress of Youth Organization of Progressive Party, Langarvatn, Iceland (2-4 September 1988).

' "The Problem is not the Atom Bomb, but the Heart of the People" - Albert Einstein', Annual Gandhi Lecture, (not given due to illness) London (2 October 1988).

'Think globally - act locally! The need for alliances at the grass roots level!' Australian Conservation Foundation National Congress: The next 200 years, Sydney (7 October 1988).

'Untitled', European Green Congress, Florence (1 November 1988).

'Towards a nuclear-weapon-free and non-violent world', Peace Conference, New Delhi (14 November 1988).

'We must remain a force for radical, non-violent change, instead of becoming "junior partner" in government at any price!' Fifth Congress of the European Greens, Paris (9 April 1989).

'No end to the violation of human rights of the Kurds!' International Conference on Human Rights in Kurdistan, Bremen (14 April 1989).

'Hiroshima is everywhere!' Annual Hiroshima Commemoration, Dublin (6 August 1989).

'The Earth is one but the world is not!' Ecopolitics Conference, Adelaide (21 September 1989).

'If there is a future - it will be green!' Ninth International Physicians for the Prevention of Nuclear War World Congress, Hiroshima (9 October 1989),

'Welcome speech for the Dalai Lama', Bonn (8 December 1989).

'This house believes that the West must contain economic growth and personal liberty to save the planet', Oxford Union-Observer Mace Debating Competition, Oxford (22 February 1990).

Concluding speech, International Tibet Support Group Conference, Dharamsala (10 March 1990).

'Why haven't disarmament movements taken social defence seriously? Why should they?' Conference on non-violent struggle and social defence, School of Peace Studies, Bradford (4 April 1990).

'We need sites of non-violent encounter!' East Hessen Peace Initiative Easter March, Point Alpha on East-West German border near Rasdorf (15 April 1990).

'Chernobyl - the forgotten catastrophe or the catastrophe of forgetting', Hanau Group for Environmental Protection Rally, Hanau (26 April 1990).

'Untitled', Women's Foreign Policy Council Forum: Women in the New Europe, New York City (6 June 1990).

'Untitled', Comments at International Convention on Asian Peace, Tokyo (25 May 1990).

'Remarks concerning the dramatic changes in Eastern Europe, the reunification of Germany and the impact of the Green Party! For feminization of power!' National Organisation of Women Congress, San Francisco (30 June 1990).

'Reweaving the world', Women of the Year Luncheon, London (15 October 1990).

'Poisoned food and world hunger: The poor are feeding the rich . . .', World Food Day Seminar, Dublin (16 October 1990).

'The green revolution: politics as if the earth mattered', Healing the Planet Symposium, Santa Monica (27 October 1990).

'What troubles me about the present unification process? Thoughts of a Green MP in the Bundestag', Goethe Institute "What is to become of Germany?" Conference, Beverly Hills (11 November 1990).

'A green view of German reunification and Europe's future', American University School of International Service Alumni Dinner, Washington DC (19 November 1990).

'The western Governments are ignoring the Environmental Catastrophe of the Third World', Oxford Union Debate, Oxford (18 February 1991).

'Globalization of the green movement: prospects within a world system in transition', University of Hawaii Institute for Peace, Hawaii (2 June 1991).

'National/rational states and the German state of affairs', Neuberger Gespräche, Neuberg an der Mütz, Austria (26 June 1991).

'Politics and ecology', The Morelia Symposium: Approaching the year 2000, Morelia, Mexico (2 September 1991).

'Untitled', address to President Salinas of Mexico, Mexico City (6 September 1991).

'Global economies, local ethnicities: European politics, economics and culture in 1991', Goethe Institute/Stanford University Conference on Culture and Crisis of the National, Stanford, California (7 November 1991).

'For a just and healthy planet', International Women's Day Rally, New York (8 March 1992).

PETRA KELLY: INTERVIEWS
(SELECTED, ENGLISH, CHRONOLOGICAL)

The Proceedings of Meet the Press, vol. 83 (Kelly Press Inc. Washington DC, 10 July 1983).

Ed Hedemann, 'Petra Kelly and the Green Party - An interview', in *War Resisters League News*, (Part 1 Sept/Oct: Part 2 Nov/Dec 1983).

'Conversations with Charlene Spretnak', quoted in Fritjof Capra and Charlene Spretnak, *Green Politics*, (E. P. Dutton, New York, 1984).

Merle Hoffman, 'The greening of the world', *On the Issues* (USA), Vol. IX (1988).

Rob Burns, 'Interview with Petra Kelly', in *Marxism Today*, (February 1989).

Ann Forfreedom, 'Inspirational women of our time', interview with Petra Kelly in *The Wise Woman* (USA), vol. II, no.2 (1990-1991).

Sabena Norton, 'The trials of Petra Kelly', *Living Marxism* (February 1989).

Samantha Trenoweth, 'If there is a future it will be green', in *Simply Living*, Australia (Spring 1991).

Eric Williams, unpublished interview, (March 1992).

PETRA KELLY: ESSAYS
(SELECTED, ENGLISH, CHRONOLOGICAL)

'For one brief shining moment . . . The religious views of William James and their application in the 20th century,' mimeo (9 January 1968).

'Scientific thought and Roman Catholicism, or God's not dead, theologians have been!' paper for Science and Civilisation Course, American University (13 May 1968).

'The Far-reaching Influence of The Dogmatic Constitution on Divine Revelation on the Ecumenical Dialogue, paper for Contemporary Religious Discussion Course, American University (no date, post November 1968).

'The penetration of American foreign policy by the politician general since 1947' mimeo (7 December 1968).

'The Judas embrace: 21 August 1968 and what happened to pan-slavism and world communism?', mimeo (January 1969).

'The West German worker and the West German student,' mimeo (1969).

'The Federal Union of European Nationalities (FUEN) or separatists unite!' submission to the Conference on the Atlantic Community Ethnic Minorities Seminar, Georgetown University, Washington DC, mimeo (February 1973).

'Women's lib - does it come out of Bruxelles? (hardly)', mimeo (July 1973).

'The migrant worker experience in Europe', report on Annual Human Rights Lecture (given by John Berger, chaired by Sicco Mansholt) (10 December 1973).

'An open letter to all within the European Communities: The Faustian pact with nuclear power plants! or Technicians become our new gods!' mimeo (23 March 1975).

'The Third World - from a woman's point of view', mimeo (1976).

'Travelling with the paper cranes - in a crusade of hope', a personal view of the 31st Atomic Bombing Disaster Anniversary World Conference against A and H Bombs in Japan, mimeo (1-9 August 1976).

'Civilian and military uses of nuclear energy - Siamese twins', mimeo, (no date, c. 1977).

'Keep the Uranium in the ground', report on Movement Against Uranium in Australia, mimeo (July/August 1977).

'The anti-nuclear movement in Europe - a survey', mimeo, (March 1978).

'Youth unemployment as a problem of the European Community: what the Economic and Social Committee is doing about it', Heinz Schwarzkopf Stiftung, Junges Europa, Hamburg, mimeo (19 April 1978).

'The position of the Green Party and the German peace movement as regards the NATO decision of 12 December 1979', mimeo (July 1982).

'Das erste Jahr im Bundestag!' [The first year in the Bundestag!] Report to Die Grünen im Bundestag (3 March 1984).

'Likely trends in green politics in Europe in the 1990s', mimeo (10 August 1987).

'What is the matter with the peace movement and the greens?', mimeo (July 1988).

'Turning Europe green!' mimeo (1 December 1989).

'Our silence is killing Tibet', [German version in *Die Zeit*] (10 August 1990).

'The plight of children', letter to UN World Summit for Children, mimeo (28 September 1990).

'Reflections at the beginning of October 1990', mimeo (4 October 1990).

"The future of the West German Green Party and its agenda for the Future!' mimeo (14 December 1990).

with Gert Bastian, 'A dream fades', mimeo (February 1991).

with Gert Bastian, 'The German government shares part of the responsibility for the illegal arms exports to Iraq and must resign!' mimeo (German version dated 10 March 1991).

with Gert Bastian 'Bowing before the junta: black days in August for East and West', mimeo (August 1991).

'Another candle being lit: The Morelia Conference in Mexico' (September 1991).

with Gert Bastian, 'The Earth Summit - another global disappointment? (A common future connot emerge from economic and ecological apartheid!)' mimeo (March 1992).

OTHER REFERENCES

John Ardagh, *Germany and the Germans* (Penguin, London, 1991).

Richard Bach, *Jonathan Livingston Seagull* (Pan Books, 1973).

Generale für Frieden und Abrüstung and Gert Bastian, (eds.) *Generale gegen Nachrüstung* (Hoffmann und Campe, Hamburg, 1983).

Gert Bastian, 'General Bastian zur Lage, in *Neue Politik*, 25 Jahrgang/11 (15 February 1980).

Gert Bastian and Alfred Mechtersheimer, *Offiziere gegen Atomkriegsgefahr,* (Pahl-Rugenstein, Cologne, 1981).

Gert Bastian, 'Why a nuclear war in Europe becomes conceivable', mimeo (July 1981).

Gert Bastian, 'Nuclear deterrence - the way to disaster' mimeo (undated c.1982/3).

Gert Bastian, *Frieden schaffen! Gedanken zur Sicherheitspolitik* (Create peace! Thoughts of the politics of security) (Kindler Verlag, Munich, 1983).

Gert Bastian, letters to Die Grünen parliamentary group (9 January and 9 February 1984).

Gert Bastian, 'Geneva - disproof of the peace movement?' mimeo (March 1985).

Gert Bastian, personal statement in connection with proceedings at Bitburg District Court on 14 October 1985 relating to my participation in a symbolic blockade of the American air base at Bitburg on 3 September 1983, mimeo (October 1985).

Gert Bastian, letter to local groups involved in violent actions (November 1986).

Gert Bastian, statement on behalf of Generals for Peace and Disarmament concerning the reservation expressed by the government of the Federal Republic of Germany on the Pershing missiles (10 August 1987).

Gert Bastian, letter to Herr Lothar Rühl, State Secretary in the Federal Ministry of Defence, Bonn (10th June 1988).

Gert Bastian, 'Untitled', speech at Annual Hiroshima Commemoration, Dublin (6th August 1989).

Gert Bastian, 'Are Germans Cowardly?' mimeo (February 1991).

Gert Bastian, 'Should German soldiers be deployed worldwide under the UN flag?' mimeo (March 1991). (German version published in *Bündnis 2000*, no.14 (14th June 1991) and *Ohne Rüstang leben*, Information 57 (no date), edited version published in *Panther*, no.6 (June 1991).

Gert Bastian, 'Germany - a postnational state?' (speech at Neuberger Gespräche 1991, Neuberg an der Mürz, Austria (27 June 1991).

Gert Bastian, 'The misuse of energy by the military', Statement at the Morelia Conference, Mexico City (3 September 1991).

Gert Bastian, 'In search of a raison d'etre: German Military Forces', *The Nonviolent Activist* (USA), vol. 8, no.6 (September 1991).

Gert Bastian, 'Prepared to live in disgrace?' mimeo (October 1991).

Gert Bastian, 'Army without a function wheels to the Right', in *Broadside Weekly*, Australia (10 June 1992).

Gert Bastian, 'Der Lack ist Ab!' (The Varnish is off), Die Zeit (10th September 1992).

Stephen Batchelor, 'A Convenient Fiction' in *Resurgence*, no.156 (January/February 1993).

Stephen Batchelor, *The Awakening of the West: The Encounter of Buddhism and European Culture* (Thorsons, London, 1994).

Lukas Beckmann and Lew Kopelew, (eds), *Gedenken Heißt erinnern*, (Lamuv, Göttingen, 1993).

Paul Berkowitz et al. 'Trip Report: Tibetan Refugee Settlements, India, Nepal', submitted to US Congress (3rd March 1989).

John M. Blum et al. (eds), *The National Experience* (Harcourt, Brace & World, New York, 1968).

Vladimir Chernousenko, *Chernobyl: Insight from the Inside* (Springer-Verlag, New York, 1991).

Gordon Craig, *The Germans* (Penguin, London, 1991).

Daily Press, Newport News VA, (25th June 1967).

Mr von der Decken, Rapporteur, 'Working Document for the Council Directive Laying down basic standards for the health protection of workers and the general public against the dangers of microwave radiation,' mimeo, Economic and Social Committee, 1390/(1980).

'HHH phones girl in dorm; Students join VP on TV', *The Eagle* (22nd October 1968).

Candidates for the American University Student Senate, *The Eagle* (23rd April 1969).

Earthwatch Oregon (June/July 1979).

Eboli and Piga, rapporteurs, *'Health and Environmental Hazards arising from the Use of Asbestos,'* Economic and Social Committee, Document: ENVI/37, CES 230/79 (22nd February 1979).

Economic and Social Committee, 'OPINION: Social Questions on the Education in the European Community', Economic and Social Committee, Dossier 71/SOC, fin 367/ (1975).

The Economist (10th July 1982).

E. Gene Frankland and Donald Schoonmaker, Between Protest and Power: *The Green Party in Germany* (Westview Press, Boulder, 1992).

Die Grünen, press releases, party programmes (various dates).

Guardian (6 October, 30 November 1982, 7 December 1990).

Konrad György, *Antipolitik* (Duhrkamp, Frankfurt, 1985).

Hampton VA local paper (no date, 1966).

Hansard (Lords) (30 October 1984).

Vaclav Havel, *Summer Meditations* (Faber and Faber, London, 1991).

Franz Helling, *Neues Deutschland* (15 November 1990).

Mark Hertzgaard, 'Who Killed Petra Kelly?' in *Vanity Fair*, vol.56, no.1 (January 1993).

Walter Heynhowski, Gerhard Scheumann and Gerhard Kade, *Die Generale*, book (Verlag der Nation, Berlin, 1986); and film (English version distributed by ETV Films Ltd, London, 1986).

Isabel Hilton, 'Who Killed Petra Kelly', *The Independent*, (24 October 1992).

Werner Hülsberg, *The West German Greens* (Verso, London, 1988).

Irish Times (28 April 1987).

Diana Johnstone, 'Blues for the Greens: Is the Party Obsolete?' *In These Times* (13th-19 January 1988).

Official Journal of the European Communities, no. C 275/6 (18 October 1982).

Petra Kelly, letters and post cards to Dr Mott (various dates, commence 1968).

Petra Kelly, 'Speech of Policy', for American University Public Speaking Assignment, mimeo (no date c.1968).

Petra Kelly, papers for seminars she held on world politics, School of International Service, mimeo (1969/1970).

Petra Kelly, 'Global Development', Paper submitted to 24th Annual National

Student Leadership Institute course for exceptional students and world leaders (14-20 June 1969).

Petra Kelly, 'The answer my friend is in the hearts of men', 24th Annual National Student Leadership Seminar, New York (June 1969).

Petra Kelly, 'Outline of a comparative study of the development of the political strategy within various private European organisations which have since 1945 attempted to promote European unity', Europa Institute of the University of Amsterdam, mimeo (no date c. 1970).

Petra Kelly, letter to Hubert H. Humphrey (8 February 1970).

Petra Kelly, 'We have been making a kind of "Europe" but where are the Europeans?', memo to all concerned leaders within the European Federal Movements and in like-minded interested groups and organisations (13 March 1972).

Petra Kelly, 'International Woman's Year 1975', information note (10 July 1974).

Petra Kelly, 'Possible themes to be considered by the Social Affairs and Environmental Sections of the Economic and Social Committee', information note (12 November 1976).

Petra Kelly and Roland Vogt, 'Ökologie und Frieden', in FORUM E, no. 1/2 (1977).

Petra Kelly, 'Medizinische Indikation', in FORUM E, 1/2/3 (1978).

Petra Kelly, Candidature for list for 1980 elections to the Bundestag, (14th March 1980).

Petra Kelly, press statements (various dates, 1983-1990).

Petra Kelly, personal letter to Die Grünen (14 February 1984).

Petra Kelly and Gert Bastian, open letter to signatories of the Krefeld Appeal of 16 November 1980 (19th February 1984).

Petra Kelly, report on trip to Barcelona and Madrid, (November 1984).

Petra Kelly, 'Eine verhinderte Rede: Rot-grünes Bündnis 1987 - Hoffnung oder das Ende der Grünen?' mimeo (18th December 1984).

Petra Kelly, 'Die mögliche Bedeutung Rosa Luxemburgs für Politische Kultur', Speech at the German-Italian Culture Festival: Rosa Luxemburg/Antonio Gramsci, Hamburg (1st September 1985).

Petra Kelly, 'Entspannung von unten! Auf der Demonstration anläßlich des Reagan/Gorbatschow Gipfeltreffens, Geneva (16th November 1985).

Petra Kelly with Gurt Bastian, 'Open letter to the Prime Minister of Finland', (19 July 1988).

Petra Kelly, personal statement on the legal action against Penthouse in Berlin on 13 December 1988 (14 December, 1988).

Petra Kelly, 'An meine Omi - eine öffentliche Liebeserklärung' (To my Granny - a public declaration of love), in Werner Filmer u. Heribert Schwan, (eds), Meine Mutter: Ein deutsches Lesebuch (Econ. Düsseldorf, 1989).

Petra Kelly, Letter to Rajiv Gandhi, Prime Minister of India (August 1989).

Petra Kelly, Bewerbung für das Amt einer Sprecherin im Bundesvorstand (10 April 1991).

Petra Kelly, 'Grunde für neue Hoffnung', in Bündnis 2000, no. 19 (6 August 1991).

Petra Kelly, letter to Cora Weiss (6 September 1992).

Eva Kolinsky, (ed), The Greens in West Germany (Berg, Oxford, 1989).

Lew Kopelew, 'Ein grosses Herz' in Christine von Weizsäcker and Elisabeth Bücking, (eds), *Mit Wissen, Widerstand und Witz: Frauen für die Umwelt* (Herder Verlag, Freiburg, 1992).

Heinz Kuby, 'Priorities,' mimeo (undated, circa May 1972).

Dalai Lama, 'Address to members of the European Parliament', Strasbourg (15 June 1988).

John Lambert, 'Mansholt - Man of Vision', *Irish Times* (3 October 1972).

Letters of recommendation from Professor Said, Dr Mott, Hubert H. Humphrey and Professor Trowbridge (UNA of the USA) (March/April 1970).

Anne Morrow Lindbergh, *Gift from the Sea* (Chatto and Windus, 1955; new edition, 1992).

Sicco Mansholt, *La Crise* (Editions Stock, Paris, 1974).

Sicco Mansholt, 'Les remedes a la crise sont connus mais les Occidenteau sont sourdes', *CJN* 153 (November 1974).

Thomas Merton, *Conjectures of a Guilty Bystander* (Doubleday Press, Garden City, NY, 1966).

'The Case of Vladimir Mijanović, Miodrag Milić, Dragomir Olujić, Gordoan Jovanović, Pavlusko Imstrović, and Milan Nicolić - prosecuted for exercising their constitutional right to assemble and for an alleged delict of opinion, mimeo (August 1984).

Minneapolis Tribune (7th November 1968).

Minutes of the Seminar Leaders Meeting, School of International Studies, mimeo (2nd February 1969).

'Petra und die Bösen Schwestern', *Mannheimer Morgen* (7 April 1984).

Dr Albert Mott, introduction to Petra Kelly speech at School of International Service Alumni Dinner, taperecording (19 November 1990).

New Solidarity (18 June 1982).

'Untitled', in Japanese language edition of *Newsweek Magazine*, 4th Anniversary Issue (January 1990).

Sara Parkin, *Green Parties: An International Guide* (Heretic, London, 1989).

Sara Parkin, *Green Light on Europe* (Heretic, London, 1990).

Sara Parkin, 'Outsider with a green passion', in *The Times* (21 October 1992).

Young People from German Democratic Republic, letter to government of the GDR on the occasion of the International Youth Year (January 1985).

'Das Ziel: Der Kinderplanet' (The goal: the Children's Planet), Die Grace P. Kelly Vereinigung zur Unterstützung der Krebsforschung für Kinder e.V. (1986).

Ferdinand Protzman 'Politics or Passion: The Killing of Petra Kelly' in *Lear Magazine* (February 1993).

Joseph Rovan, 'La raisons geographiques de la poissance des "Les Verts" en RFA', in *Revue de Géographie et de Géopolitique* (January/March 1983) pp.48-55.

Abdul A. Said, Introduction to World Politics (course contents), School of International Studies, mimeo (Spring 1970).

Antoine de Saint-Exupery, *The Little Prince* (Pan Books, London, 1974).

Alice Schwarzer, *Eine tödliche Liebe* (A deathly love) (Kiepenheuer & Witsch, Cologne, 1993).

Jeremy Seabrook, *Pioneers of Change: Experiments in Creating a Humane Society* (Zed Books, London, 1993).

Gene Sharp, *The politics of Nonviolent Action: 1. Power and Struggle; 2. Methods of Non-Violent Direct Action; 3. The Dynamics of Non-violent Direct Action* (Extending Horizon Books, Boston MA 1973).

Monika Sperr, *Petra Karin Kelly: Politikerin aus Betroffenheit* (C Bertelsmann Verlag, Munich, 1983).

Sprechregister Deutscher Bundestag - Bundesrat 10 (Wahlperiode 1983-1987) and 11 (Wahlperiode 1987-1990).

Charlene Spretnak and Fritjof Capra, *Green Politics* (E. P. Dutton, New York, 1984).

'Der alte Mann und das Mädchen' (The old man and the maiden), in *Der Spiegel*, no. 44 (26 October 1992).

Stenographischer Bericht des Bundestages ('Hansard' of German Federal Parliament) 1983-1990.

Norman Stone, *Hitler* (Hodder and Stoughton, Sevenoaks, 1980).

'Men at the Top Listen to Petra Kelly', *Stars and Stripes*, (14 May 1968).

'Pope Grants Wish', *Stars and Stripes*, (2 August 1968).

Sunday Times (3 October 1982).

'Dank für Bastians Mut', (open letter from Greens to the Die Grünen parliamentary group in Bonn), *Taz*, (14 February 1984).

Hearings before the subcommittee on European Affairs of the Committee on Foreign Relations, United States Senate, S. Hrg. 99-400, Pt 2 (US Government, Washington DC, 12/13 September 1985).

US News and World Report (1 November 1982).

Henry David Thoreau, *Walden and Civil Disobedience* (Penguin, London, 1983). First published 1849 and 1854.

The Times (16 September 1980).

Hans-Jachim Veen and Jürgen Hoffmann, *Die Grünen: zu Beginn der neunziger Jahre* (Die Grünen: from the beginning to the nineties) (Bouvier, Bonn, 1992).

Antje, Vollmer, Rede auf der Bundespressekonferenz zum Wahlergebnis (4 December 1990).

Washington Post (30 March 1969).

Ulrike C. Wasmuht, *Friedensbewegung der 80er Jahre* (Focus-Verlag, Geissen, 1987).

Alan Watson, *The Germans: who are they now?* (Methuen, London, 1992).

Carlo Weber, 'The Birth Control Controversy', *The New Republic*, vol. 159, no. 21 (23 November 1968).

INDEX